27198

KT-130-987

MUSIC SERIES

Sound and Silence

THE RESOURCES OF MUSIC SERIES

General Editors: WILFRID MELLERS AND JOHN PAYNTER

Sound and Silence

Classroom Projects in Creative Music

JOHN PAYNTER
AND
PETER ASTON

CAMBRIDGE · AT THE UNIVERSITY PRESS · 1970

Published by the Syndics of the Cambridge University Press
Bentley House, 200 Euston Road, London, NW1 2DB
American Branch: 32 East 57th Street, New York, N.Y.10022

© Cambridge University Press 1970

Library of Congress Catalogue Card Number: 75-85735

ISBNS: 521 07511 4 hard covers
        521 09597 2 paper

First published 1970
Reprinted 1973

First printed in Great Britain by
Spottiswoode, Ballantyne & Co. Ltd, London and Colchester
Reprinted in Malta by St Paul's Press Ltd

Through music today it is possible to be aware of reality in a very important way.
LUCIANO BERIO

Contents

CONTENTS

List of Illustrations

Foreword

This book may be described as the primer in a series which has grown out of the Music and Education courses run by the Music Department of the University of York. It's a primer because it asks fundamental questions and doesn't attempt to short-circuit the answers to them by an appeal to history. It's not concerned with what (say) Byrd's music was, or Bach's, or Mozart's, or Beethoven's: but with what music is inherently, here and now, both in its nature and its functions. Of course, any students who have lived through the book (it's not a book merely to read, but to act out) will have acquired an enhanced understanding of any music, including the European classics: because those students will have felt what it's like to create through sound, and will have experienced the growth of harmonic consciousness within their own senses. On some such first-hand cognition any re-cognition of the past that is meaningful must depend. But if the book is experience rather than education, it certainly 'leads out'; and it tells us what we can also learn from living— that the experiences most worth having are those that are at once a difficulty and a delight.

WILFRID MELLERS

Preface

We have to acknowledge our debt to so many friends: colleagues, students and children. To mention everyone by name would be impossible. Nevertheless, we should like to mention:

the children of Class 5 (1963–4) at the Florence Melly Infant School, Liverpool; the pupils of The Jessie Younghusband C.P. School, Chichester, especially Form 4 (1965–6) and Class 8 (1967—8); members of the top class (1966–7) at Burnt Yates Endowed School, Ripley, Yorkshire; the third-year juniors of Farsley Farfield C.P. School, Pudsey, Yorkshire (1966–7); pupils of Park Boys' County Secondary School, Dudley (1960–3) and Moseley Grammar School, Birmingham (1963–4); members of the York Children's Theatre Workshop (1966–7); and numerous students of Anstey College of Physical Education, Sutton Coldfield; The C. F. Mott College of Education, Prescot, Liverpool; Bishop Otter College, Chichester and the Department of Music in the University of York. Where individual works of music, art or poetry appear in the book they are acknowledged by name.

To all the headteachers and teachers who have so generously collaborated with us we express our gratitude; especially to Mrs E. Barton, Mr Philip Cooper, Mr P. Highley, Miss Margaret Horsley, Mrs S. Jones, Miss E. F. Knowlson, Mr Gordon Murray, Miss G. Talbot and Mr J. M. Woodruff.

We have also received much help and encouragement from Mr I. P. Salisbury, H.M.I., Mr John Coe, West Riding County Council Inspector, and Miss M. Spence, Music Adviser to the West Riding Education Authority.

Of other friends and colleagues we should like to thank especially David Henshaw, Patricia Johnson, Robert Sherlaw Johnson, Margaret Langdon, Jeff Lowe, Sheila McCririck, Michael Morgan, Richard Orton, Anthony Pither and Paddy Rothwell for their help and inspiration.

We thank Mrs Paula Abel for her patience and interest in preparing the final typescript, and we acknowledge gratefully the care and skill exercised by John Stevens in taking so many of the photographs.

For invaluable constructive criticism throughout the preparation of this book we are indebted to the Cambridge University Press.

Finally, we should like to place on record our deep gratitude to Professor Wilfrid Mellers. This book would never have been written had it not been for his interest, encouragement and guidance.

Department of Music, University of York   J.P.
August 1968   P.A.

Acknowledgements

For permission to use copyright material, both literary and musical, acknowledgement is made to the following:

for an extract from an interview with Luciano Berio which appeared in Number 6 of *Circuit Magazine* to the editor and publishers of *Circuit Magazine*; for an extract from *Silence* by John Cage to Wesleyan University Press and Calder and Boyars Limited; for a passage from *Except the Lord* by Joyce Cary to Michael Joseph Ltd and Harper and Row, New York; for an extract from *The Interpretation of the Music of the XVII and XVIII Centuries* by Arnold Dolmetsch to Novello and Co., Ltd; for *Heartless Beauty* from *The Peach Blossom Forest and other Chinese Legends* to the authors, Robert Gittings and Jo Manton; for rhymes from *The Oxford Nursery Rhyme Book* by Iona and Peter Opie to Oxford University Press; for an extract from *The Evolution of the Art of Music* by C. Hubert H. Parry to Routledge and Kegan Paul Ltd; for passages from the articles 'Learning from the Present' by John Paynter and 'A Creative Approach to Harmony in the Classroom' by Peter Aston to the editor, *Music in Education* and Novello and Co., Ltd; for *Spell of Creation* from *Collected Poems of Kathleen Raine* to Miss Kathleen Raine and Hamish Hamilton Ltd; for extracts from *The Nature of Music* by Hermann Scherchen to Dobson Books Ltd; for a passage from *The Oxford Companion to Music* by Percy A. Scholes to Oxford University Press; for an extract from *Stabat Mater* by Pergolesi, edited for schools by Charles Kennedy Scott to Oxford University Press; for an extract from *Petrouchka* by Igor Stravinsky to Boosey and Hawkes Ltd; for *Sair Fyeld, Hinny* from *Voices* edited by Geoffrey Summerfield to Penguin Books Ltd; for passages from *A History of Melody* by Bence Szabolsci to Barrie Books Ltd, Corvina Press, Budapest and St Martin's Press Inc., New York; for *Joy in the Gates of Jerusalem, Hey, ho, nobody at home*, and *Derry ding ding Dasson* (all by Ravenscroft from *Pammelia and other Rounds and Catches* edited by Peter Warlock) to Oxford University Press.

Introduction

Music in a liberal education

Alan, aged six, moves stealthily across the classroom. He is the Wolf creeping out of the deep, dark forest. As he creeps he makes music: a pattern of mysterious taps and scraping sounds which tell us that the Wolf and the forest are sinister and fearful. No-one has instructed him: Alan chose the drum himself and decided for himself how the Wolf's music should go. As he creeps slowly across the room, he is lost in the world of his imagination, intensified by the music he is making.

A group of children in their early teens are on a camping holiday. They have just returned from an exhausting hike and are sitting with steaming mugs of cocoa around the glow of a camp fire. Someone is strumming a guitar. The others are singing. They know the song well because it's been sung at previous camp fires for as long as anyone can remember. As we listen we realise that not everyone is singing the tune. Now and again the music breaks into parts, the harmony enriching the melodic line. None of the children has heard of a dominant seventh or a perfect cadence and most of them cannot read music: yet they are responding to the harmonic implications of the melody by improvising other parts around it.

Two students at a College of Education are playing music which they have painstakingly evolved for piano and drums: the lid of the piano is removed and Leslie gently strokes the strings inside with the flat of her hand. Catherine's drums reply, softly and sensitively. The music builds. It is coherent. They know now exactly where it should go. As they play, the piece becomes Theatre; their sensitivity to the sounds is reflected in their movements. Before this morning neither of them had ever thought of creating music. They chose to do this, decided on the sounds they wanted to explore, and have worked these sounds over and over until they have become the right sounds, the only possible sounds through which to say what has to be said. By this time tomorrow their piece will be refined and carefully notated in a system of their own inventing. They will have thoroughly explored their own music and met on the way with the music of Cowell and Stockhausen. They will not have been *taught* anything: can we say how much music they will have learned?

Why do we teach music anyway? How do we fit it into the pattern of education today? Certainly, school music now is a great deal more lively than it has ever been before, and the last few years have seen an enormous increase in the number of young players and singers taking part in school concerts and performing in youth orchestras and choirs. But while all this has been happening concepts of education have been changing, and it is not always easy to see where music fits in or what its rôle should be.

It might help us to find answers to these questions if we begin by looking at the essential differences between general and specialist forms of education. Apart from those of us who are concerned solely with certain clearly-defined skills such as the techniques of playing musical instruments, the work of most teachers in schools is essentially a contribution to the *general* education of children. Even if a teacher finds himself working in a school as 'the music specialist' or 'the science specialist' he must not let this cause him to forget his first duty: the education of the whole person. He makes a contribution to this 'total education' through the medium of his own subject. Moreover, he must not gear his work only to the abilities of the gifted few, but should find ways of using his specialist knowledge to serve the education of *all* the pupils in his classes.

Education does not begin with specialist boxes filled with facts to be memorised. It should be child-centred and start from the needs of the individual. As teachers we must try to see our subject, not as collections of highly-developed disciplines, but rather as areas of experience which embody some of the most fundamental human reactions to life. We can't teach history all by itself: it's concerned with people, their way of life, their reactions to their times and their relationship to us and our own times. Once we start looking at people we must consider not only how they live but *where* they live. Geography is inextricably linked with history and begins on our doorstep with a close look at our own immediate environment and what this means to us and those who have lived here before. Investigating our environment brings us face to face with the wonder and excitement of discovery. This is the mainspring of any work in the sciences and mathematics. When we look closely at nature and are filled with wonder by its intricacies, we are often moved and must find a way of expressing our feelings: it is from here that the arts spring, as do all aspects of language and the need to communicate ideas and emotions. The value of anything we learn in school lies in the extent to which it helps us respond to the world around us. Our 'special subject' cannot live if left in a box by itself, a set of disciplines and techniques unrelated to anything else. It is part of the wide field of human experience and needs to be understood in that context first.

Because all our knowledge comes from experience of living, its many areas are related and interdependent. If we begin by erecting barriers between them we shall be in danger of hiding from our pupils the essential relevance of our subjects. The liberal education we all wish for our children implies a breadth of understanding and experience that will be possible only when we make conscious efforts to remove the boundaries between 'subjects'. This applies to the more advanced work of the Secondary School as much as it does to the work of the Primary School. Areas of knowledge are often so closely related that they can be seen simply as various ways of saying the same thing; 'materials' through which we may communicate experience. Education should make us alive to what is happening around us and aware of our potential as human beings.

We who are writing this book are practising teachers and musicians who are concerned with general rather than specialist education. We believe that young people deserve a truly liberal education, alive with the excitement of discovery. This excitement is a first step: the details, disciplines and skills will follow. Without a sense of adventure true education is impossible.

What contribution can music make? It can give immense pleasure to the listener and to the performer. This side of it should certainly not be neglected. However, it is as a *creative* art that music is beginning to play an increasingly important rôle in education. Like all the arts, music springs from a profound response to life itself. It is language, and, as a vehicle for expression, it is available in some degree to everyone. If a child is to grow in awareness of himself and his world, he will need to be articulate. The very processes of becoming articulate deepen our perception. Perhaps we should place slightly more emphasis on creative music in schools than we have been doing. Music is a rich means of expression and we must not deny our children the chance to use it.

Society has always produced artists, poets, and musicians. They train our eyes and ears. Rarely do we look at things as closely or as intensely as artists do. They see the beauty in nature and their intuition and skills define it in terms we can understand. Sometimes this definition is in the form of an abstract elaboration of nature's patterns or an occurrence in human life. At other times it is more clearly a record of something seen in reality. But the artist does more than make a record: he projects feelings into his materials—paint, wood, stone, words, movement, sound or whatever—until the materials become like the reality

3

of his imagination. Through his work we feel what he feels, we see with his eyes and hear with his ears. Henry Moore shows us new ways of looking at the human figure. Through his work we begin to appreciate forms we had never before noticed, though they were always there in nature. The recent interest in the music of India may owe something to the Beatles who were able to relate the sounds of Indian music to what they wanted to say through a song like *Within You Without You* on their 'Sergeant Pepper' disc. On another level Picasso, in his *Guernica*, painted during the Spanish Civil War, draws our attention to the suffering of ordinary people in time of war. The picture is at once a powerful comment and a terrible warning. Similarly the composer is able not only to make us aware of new qualities of sound but through his use of his material to say something to us about the great issues of existence. So Benjamin Britten, in his *War Requiem*, sees a relationship between the ancient text of the Requiem Mass and certain poems by Wilfred Owen—a relationship no-one had seen previously—and with his skill as a musician he presents this relationship to us in the setting of penetrating music. Nearly half a century earlier, Wilfred Owen had summed up his own task as a poet when he wrote, 'My subject is War, and the pity of War. The Poetry is in the pity. All that a poet can do is to warn'.

Artists of all kinds function as visionaries and commentators: their job is not simply to entertain us. We rely upon them to help us come to terms with life and its problems. The art that is *most* relevant to us is that of our own time. We need the professional artist but at the same time we must also cultivate the artist within ourselves, for each one of us has something of that child-like innocence which is the characteristic of the artistic mind, which draws fresh inspiration from familiar things and expresses feelings in words, action, visual symbols or music. We must not stifle this innocent eye or ear; our understanding of the professional artists' work may depend considerably on our ability to participate, even a little, in their activities.

When, in school, we involve children in the creative use of language or the materials of visual art, we are encouraging them to think like poets and artists. The majority of subjects taught in school today begin with children's natural interests, and knowledge is acquired as much through feelings as from information. In this context the arts in education take on a new importance. They are accepted as ways of saying what we feel. We all have the capacity to perceive, reflect and express. We all have the capacity to create.

The materials of music are as available for creative exploration as the materials of any other art. However, this seems to be an area of activity where music has not kept pace with other school subjects. When the Plowden Committee reported on Primary School education in England,* they said they had found the planning of music as a creative subject lagging behind work in language and the visual arts and crafts. One wonders why. What is it about music, or about us as music teachers, that makes us ignore the opportunities others have taken?

If any one aspect of education today is characteristic of the whole, it is probably the change of emphasis from children being instructed to children being placed in situations where they can learn for themselves. Teachers of English, drama and the visual arts have found the new ideas stimulating. They have used them as springboards for a great deal of exciting work. Music, on the other hand, has tended to go its own way and remains largely unaffected by recent moves in education. More often than not, school music has concentrated on the skills of perform-ance. Even much so-called 'creative music' is really only an extension of directed ensemble performance. Of course these skills are important. Performance is an essential musical activity; but it is not the whole of music.

It is now some time since Marion Richardson and Herbert Read showed how art in education should start with what the *individual* has to say. They saw education taking place through art without in any way destroying the values of specialist art education. In school, necessary techniques can be developed through the self-directed exploration of materials. Similar attitudes can be found in creative drama, which has flourished under the inspiration of Peter Slade and others. Here again, real experience is taken as a starting point, and bodily movement, gest-ure, and language are the materials for experiment and expression. We have grown used to work of this kind over the past twenty years. More recently new attitudes to the creative use of written language have come into the schools, heralded by the work of Sybil Marshall, Margaret Langdon and David Holbrook, all of whom have encouraged children to write about things they feel deeply. As David Holbrook says in *Children's Writing*, '... the process depends upon "whole experience ..."', the writer is 'working on his inner world ...'. It's not surprising that when the Plowden Committee came to look at this aspect of education they found the amount and quality of children's writing 'perhaps the most dramatic of all revolutions in English teaching. Its essence is that much of it is personal ... and the writers are communicating something which has really engaged their minds and their imaginations'.

* *Children and their Primary Schools* (H.M.S.O.).

In art, drama, dance and creative writing children are using a variety of materials as language for the expression, not of second-hand experience, but of things that are close to them and real to them. What is more, the language they use is a living language; that is, it embodies in essence many of the techniques and attitudes of contemporary art and literature. On the walls of our Primary School classrooms we can see paintings which reflect the experiments of painters like Jackson Pollock, Paul Klee and Ben Nicholson. Children who have experimented in this way would certainly be the better equipped to approach the work of contemporary artists. Giving examples of the creative writing of children in a variety of Secondary Schools, David Holbrook suggests literature the children would appreciate, having come to terms in words with similar experiences. His suggestions include work by Joyce, Lawrence, Hemingway, and Eliot. The boys and girls we teach rarely seem to find difficulty with the language of contemporary art. Young people today have an outlook which chimes in with the liberalism of the twentieth-century artist; they too, are prepared to follow many paths and search in many directions. Fortunately there are teachers to help them in their search and to encourage them in their exploration. These teachers themselves draw considerable inspiration from the living art of the present while being aware of its roots in the past.

Music can be approached in the same way. The techniques used by composers in the twentieth century are comparable with the techniques used by their contemporaries in other arts. Here again we find the same diversity of style. A musician's imagination is stirred by many things: the technological achievements of science; post-renaissance philosophies and traditions which make us what we are; a desire to reject the world as it is and begin again from primitive roots. The musical techniques of our time are relevant to our situation because they grow from it. They must, therefore, have a place in the work we plan for our classes in schools. Music is as much an aspect of language as any other means of creative expression; but if it is to matter, those who use it must be alive to the music of their own time as well as the music of the past.

Too often we are encouraged to regard music as a *leisure* activity, as though its only function is to entertain. This may have led us to emphasise *re*-creative rather than creative activities in school music; and although creative work in language, drama and the visual arts has quickly found general acceptance, creative work in *music* has often been challenged as being of doubtful value in itself, having little bearing on conventional musical education. The critics argue that to devote time to such work is to deny the more musical child the essential academic

6

teaching he needs for G.C.E. and other public examinations and for the acquisition of performing skills. However, the first step must be the understanding of the medium and its potential. We can only discover this through creative experiment.

What is creative music? First of all, it is a way of saying things which are personal to the individual. It also implies the freedom to explore chosen materials. As far as possible this work should not be controlled by a teacher. *His* rôle is to set off trains of thought and help the pupil develop his own critical powers and perceptions. The processes of composition in any art are selection and rejection, evaluating and confirming the material at each stage. It is essentially an experimental situation.

This book sets out to provide suggestions for creative experiment in music. It is arranged in the form of a series of projects based largely on the principles which underlie the various directions twentieth-century music has taken, as far as these principles seem relevant to the materials being used. For example, in the earlier projects the nature of the material is very often related to the techniques of primitive music. While these are the techniques which children (who are also at a primitive stage of development) explore naturally in their own music, they are also crucial to the musical language of many twentieth-century composers. Throughout the book, the aim is to help the pupil define his musical material and explore its possibilities. He must first decide what *kind* of sounds to use. It might be simply the sound of cymbals or strings; it might be voices or piano. These are the composer's raw materials just as paint, clay, wood or stone are the materials of the visual artist. Musical material can also be the *organisation* of sounds and silences into rhythmic, melodic and harmonic patterns. The materials of any art form impose their own limitations. There are things which clay cannot do; equally, we must face the limitations which an instrument or method of sound organisation presents. We must learn how to discover what the materials can do.

This cannot be learned from a text-book. It is knowledge which can only be gained by practical experience. There is much more value in ten minutes spent doodling at the keyboard than in ten weeks reproducing rigid and unimaginative exercises.

It is important that, in schools, we provide sound-sources of great variety, and these should be available for investigation by groups and by individuals. Musical instruments of good quality are essential. Too often we stint on items like this and hamstring the child's musical imagination before he even begins. Good instruments offer a wide range of expressive possibilities. Once these have been experienced, other sound-sources might be explored, for all sound is a potential source of music. We must not look on the exploration of instruments in this way as a 'play' activity suitable only for the reception class of the Infant School. Stravinsky's words, 'fingers are great inspirers', remind us of the composer's need for first-hand contact with the sound he is going to use. All his life he may, to some extent, feel the need to go to his materials as a prelude to the act of composition. Many of us can remember the excitement of discovering, at a very early age, how certain chords our fingers found at the keyboard were satisfying while others sounded ugly. This is something which every child should be allowed to discover for himself. We can begin to explore music creatively at any age; for the first and last 'rule' in making music is the ear. It is our only guide in evaluating the sounds which express things we want to say. The *true* 'rudiments' of music are to be found in an exploration of its materials— sound and silence.

Introduction to the projects

This book does not set out to lay down a course: neither is it a series of lesson notes. The projects which follow are suggestions for lines of work. They represent ways of thinking about creative music-making, and we see them only as gateways. From any one of these, teachers may devise for themselves courses of work through which a great deal of music could be taught. In this sense, the projects we offer are not complete in themselves: we hope teachers will evolve others like them.

In another sense, however, the projects as given in this book could be used in isolation. A teacher may rightly feel that what matters more than following an idea through for a whole term or half a term, is a broad view of what is happening in music. He could give his pupils this by working at a variety of projects. Apart from the considerations given below, there is no particular order in which the projects should be tackled. Naturally, we have had to consider the order in which we should print them and, to a certain extent, the earlier projects are less complicated than the later ones. Even so, we hope teachers will feel able to dip into the book here and there, taking whatever is suitable to their own situations, adapting it and using it in the ways best suited to their pupils.

The first twenty-four projects are primarily instrumental and relate to trends in twentieth-century music. They deal with a variety of topics. The examples in these projects are taken from a wide range. They include group pieces and individual compositions by children in Primary and Secondary Schools as well as work by students at Colleges of Education and University. Projects 25–36, on the other hand, can be seen as a unit. They are primarily concerned with vocal music and the making of melody and harmony. We believe that an exploration of harmony is not something which should be confined to the specialist music course. All children have a latent harmonic instinct which has no bearing on their general academic abilities. The time to begin to develop this harmonic awareness is during the last years of the Primary School, when it should arise naturally from practical work involving the whole class and be closely related to other creative activities. Most of the examples of children's work in Projects 25–36 are by classes of Secondary children between the ages of eleven and fifteen. With the exception of two compositions by G.C.E. pupils, all the pieces are group compositions made by non-specialist classes of widely ranging academic ability. Some are by really able children, and there are a handful by dance students at a College of Education, but the majority were made by unstreamed classes in a non-selective Secondary School. In each case, the composition was the outcome of an assignment, or series of graded assignments, in which a specific harmonic principle had been discovered through practical experiments. Some of the preliminary work in these projects will need to be done under the teacher's guidance, but wherever possible the discovery of a new harmonic principle and its creative application should arise from group improvisation which, where necessary, can be directed by individual children. Like the earlier projects, numbers 25–36 are not intended as a course, and are not complete in themselves. They may be used as an approach to, or in conjunction with, a more formal academic study of harmony; or they may be simply an extension of the creative experiments suggested in the earlier projects. In either case, we hope that the teacher will regard them as a way of exploring various aspects of harmonic technique and will evolve other projects on the same lines.

Our only recommendations about the order of using the projects are:

(1) Projects 2–24 and Project 36 may be easier to approach if Project 1 has first been followed through (although Projects 4, 5, 8 or 11 would also make good starting points);

(2) Projects 25–36 are conceived as a progression. They will be more easily approached if some of the earlier projects have been followed through, and in any case Project 27 should be used as an introduction to those that follow. These all tend to be 'class' projects as opposed to 'small-group' or 'individual' projects.

The age range for which the projects might be suitable is deliberately wide. We have used some of these ideas with children of eight years and found the same principles acceptable for work with students of eighteen to twenty. In creative work, fundamental attitudes tend to be the same for young and old alike: the difference in approach and results lies in the degree of experience and background each person brings to the work. Some of the projects, however, are clearly more suited to sixteen- to eighteen-year-olds and to student level than they are to the Primary School. This is not to say that they should be entirely ignored by the Primary School teacher. Each project contains graded assignments:

in the more 'advanced' projects the simplest of these assignments might well be adapted for younger children. We have tried not to assume musical knowledge in the pupils. Although in some cases an acquaintance with notation may help, it is by no means essential.

All the projects are laid out in the same pattern: most have four sections, and these are labelled in the text A B C D.

A introduces the project. It outlines the principles behind whatever technique is to be discussed; it suggests the kind of background material we think will be needed by the pupils. This could form the basis of a short introductory talk before the class embark on the creative work itself.

B is the creative work in the form of an assignment or a series of graded assignments for a class, small groups, or individuals according to the nature of the material and techniques. In most of the projects the style we use in this section indicates the kind of things we might say to a class or a group. It is not meant to be used as a 'script' for a lesson. The language in which assignments are presented will obviously depend a lot on the age-group and background of the pupils. We offer here merely one possible approach without a particular age-group in mind. In some cases this B material is 'spelled-out' in a way not normally necessary with an average class. Judgement must be exercised by the teacher to know just how much information to give. For example, in Project 17 it would be better for the pupils to find out for themselves what happens when tape-speeds are altered.

C contains examples of other people's working of one or more of the assignments. These are included only for the guidance of teachers so that they may have some idea of what results to expect. In addition to the written descriptions of music a record is available on which some of the work described can be heard. We do not envisage this being played to pupils. It is merely offered as a guide to teachers.

D is material for follow-up work.* Creative work cannot be all 'giving'; there must be time for pupils to take something in. Periods of refreshment and 'putting back' are essential because no-one can go on giving out endlessly and to order. This is the time to listen to recordings and to study other people's music.

There is another point: when we allow our pupils the kind of freedom in music that we allow them in other creative work, not surprisingly we find obvious parallels between the music they make and the music of professional composers, especially twentieth-century composers. We

* In some projects, where it would not be relevant, this fourth section is omitted.

see this happening in art and in poetry: should we be surprised when it happens in music? All art, at any level, is the product of its own times. With this in mind it is important to help children to realise that the music they make is part of the mainstream of human creative endeavour. When they have worked their own way through an assignment and have faced the problems and decisions of composers, it can be encouraging to know that other composers think and work as they do and produce music which exploits similar sounds and combinations of sounds; but the creative experiment must come first. If we put the listening and the study before the assignment it may be taken simply as a model. Placed after the experiment (*'here is another composer making music like yours'*) it is confirmation and enrichment. It will be more easily understood because the assignment has given some insight through experience. This is the essence of 'musical appreciation'.

A discography is provided at the end of the book. Most of the music mentioned in the D sections of the projects has been recorded. Some of the numbers given are now deleted from the catalogue. We include these because no other recordings have replaced them and we hope teachers may still find them available in some way (record collections in public libraries, private collections held by friends and colleagues, and so on). Occasionally we suggest as follow-up material music which has not yet been recorded. We hope teachers will encourage their pupils to hear live performances wherever this is possible, but in Britain the BBC's Third Network broadcasts each week a high percentage of twentieth-century music and every effort should be made to use this excellent service.

The principal 'method' behind the creative activities in this book is what is normally termed 'empirical composition'. This means going directly to our materials—the various instruments or musical ideas—and experimenting with them by improvisation until we have fashioned a piece of music. The process is one of selection and rejection, evaluating as we go along and confirming the details mentally (that is, without necessarily writing them down) until we can remember what happens clearly so that the piece can be performed with reasonable accuracy. It is an experimental, trial-and-error process. Folk music is based on a similar process and most 'composed' music also has its origins in this way of working. A composer works on an idea either in actual instrumental improvisation or else in a kind of mental improvisation in the abstract. Either way the music has to evolve and the composer needs time to explore his materials. Even though he may have developed the ability to do this in his head, at some time in his life he will almost certainly have spent long periods doodling on an instrument. We can't expect our pupils to create music if we do not give them this opportunity to work at first-hand with the materials of music.

While the techniques of empirical composition are primarily improvisation and evaluation, there must first be a reason for making the music: we must have something to say. This is the point of the first section, A, in each project: it suggests a line of thought, sometimes concerned directly with purely musical materials, at other times taking a starting point in the natural world or in an experience of some other art. We must begin by discussing this starting point: there can be no creative work without plenty of adventuresome conversation between teacher and class. Then a beginning can be made by deciding on the *kinds of sounds* to be used. This is a decision that may be made in the abstract but is much more likely to be made by some kind of experiment with actual sound-sources. In some cases this first experimentation may be in itself a full-scale improvisation of a piece of music; in others the musical continuity will be built up gradually. This could be done by an individual or by a small group.

On occasions we suggest work for large groups and even whole classes. In Projects 27–35 it is usually necessary for the whole class to work on the earlier parts of the assignment together; but in most of the other projects it is often best to begin with work in small groups. Five people to a group is a good number: it offers a pool of useful ideas, and with five pairs of of hands it is possible to play several instruments at once. Of course this won't apply in every case, but as a general rule some experiment in a small group is a helpful way of beginning. Once they have experienced the process, pupils may be ready to work in smaller groups, in pairs, or even individually.

The teacher's function is, of course, to help his pupils evaluate what they are doing with the sounds. How can he judge what is happening? In the first place, only by direct knowledge of the techniques involved and the music of composers who have used similar approaches. He will need to have done this kind of thing for himself and he must listen to a great deal of music. There is no short cut. If you want to help children use the language of art and appreciate pictures, you must do it yourself first. You must paint; you must visit art galleries or look at reproductions; you must *take part* in art, not simply read about it. Only then will you be able to introduce your pupils to the thinking of artists by way of an exploration of some of their techniques. The same is true of music. Secondly, if the children's activities are truly creative there will be no one 'right' answer. The only judgements worth making will be those we want the children to make for themselves in the processes of composition:

does this piece hang together? Does it 'read as a whole'? Does it say what I want it to say? Is there anything in it which should be rejected because it destroys the wholeness of the music? This is a crucial point: the *wholeness* of the music. We should aim at a coherence of expression. The teacher helps those making the music to refine their materials and leads them towards this coherence. He can guide beginners away from the temptation to be constantly inventing new material and show them how a piece can be unified by *working* a very small amount of musical material.

At the same time there must be variety. This does not necessarily mean new material but more probably a varied treatment of existing material. By a balance of unity and variety composers make their music 'go on'; but the overall wholeness of a piece must always be kept in mind.

When a piece is complete you may want to preserve it in some way. Tape-recording is an obvious answer. The more usual way, of course, is to write the music down. Notation is a continually evolving thing. True, there are accepted conventions, but even these vary slightly in meaning from one period to another. The following example* from Couperin's second book of *Pièces de Clavecin* together with the composer's own note shows something of the degree of freedom accepted in the seventeenth and eighteenth centuries:

'Although the values of the Treble do not seem to fit with those of the Bass, it is customary to write thus.'

In recent years composers have been finding the traditional notation inadequate: they are evolving new systems, many of which use graphic symbols. Notation is not music. The sound comes first. If children want to write their music down that may be the moment to teach some of the conventions; but guard against the danger of killing the music's spontaneity. It might be better to let them invent their own notation or to adapt the conventions in some way. Much of what children create music-

* Quoted by Arnold Dolmetsch, *The Interpretation of the Music of the XVII and XVIII Centuries* (Novello, 1946), p. 68.

ally, like a lot of music by contemporary composers, will need its own notation anyway: the complexities will be too great for the traditional system.

The amount of time given to any one project will depend on the circumstances in which it is started. One project could take no longer than a half-hour lesson. On the other hand, a project like number 17 on *musique concrète* and electronic music could provide a Secondary School class with at least a term's work. If you have no more than a single lesson, a simple plan would be to spend about five minutes introducing the topic; then allot assignments to groups or individuals who work at the assignments for about fifteen minutes; then hear the results of one group's work, and conclude by playing a recording of music suggested in the follow-up section, D, with relevant comment. All this is better than nothing, but fifteen minutes is really too short a time for thorough exploration of the material. The results might well be disheartening because few children find it possible to make any worthwhile music in a quarter-of-an-hour. It is advisable to try to devote at least four lesson periods to a project. We offer the following suggestions for organisation.

In the first lesson the project is introduced and work is begun on one of the assignments, perhaps by one small group under the guidance of the teacher, the rest of the class watching and joining in discussion on the music's progress. Don't take too long over this: five or ten minutes should be plenty. The small group is then sent off to complete the piece while assignments are allotted to other sections of the class. Group-work continues in various places. The next music lesson is devoted entirely to work in small groups on the assignments, the teacher visiting each group in turn and assisting them by discussing the problems of the music and helping them to see what might be done with the material they have invented. The third lesson is a 'reporting-back' session when the groups meet together, again as a class, and play their music to each other. This is an opportunity for the teacher to comment on the success of this or that working-out of the assignment and perhaps to begin drawing parallels between the children's music and the music of other composers. The fourth lesson is given to follow-up work in which some of the music made by the groups can be matched by recordings of other music and, if appropriate, scores can be studied.

The biggest problem for creative work in music is the noise it makes and the number of work spaces needed. If you have divided your class into six or seven groups of five, as likely as not it will be impossible in the average school to find separate areas where the groups can go to work at assignments simultaneously. Of course, some of the projects are designed for work in the school hall and certainly up to the age of about twelve, children can often work at this kind of thing in groups around a hall without distracting one another. It will not be possible in every case, however, and the following are suggestions for getting round this difficulty.

Plan I

Music lesson 1 : during a music lesson devoted mainly to work other than creative experiment, introduce a creative project, possibly with some demonstration. Arrange groups and allot assignments, instruments, etc.; then arrange a time-table of lunch hours and breaks when each group can work at its assignment unsupervised (although the teacher might be there to set them off and look in once or twice to advise on progress).

Music lesson 2 : groups report back and play their pieces to each other. They could notate their music or tape-record the pieces. This might be followed by discussion using material from Section D of the project, after which the next assignment (same project) or a new project would be introduced. Arrange groups and proceed as before.

Plan II

Music lesson 1 : introduce project. Select one group and work with them at an assignment for part of the lesson to demonstrate the processes involved. The rest of the class joins in discussion on the progress of the music. Commission another group to carry out the same or a similar assignment during the week, working at lunch-times or breaks.

Music lesson 2 : the commissioned group reports back and plays its music. Discuss and follow-up with the whole class (some material from Section D). Work briefly at another assignment of the same project with a 'demonstration' group, and then commission two groups to complete music for the following week.

These suggestions could apply to short-term or long-term working on projects. It is most probable that teachers will find enough material in one project for several weeks' work. In any case, we hope, as we have already said, that teachers will take our suggestions merely as starting points and evolve additional material and further assignments of their own. One thing is certain: this work is not the sort of thing to be done on odd occasions, once or twice a term. Children need time to get them into this way of thinking about music. The first attempts are bound to be fairly unsophisticated. We must not be disappointed: time and experience will be needed for the work to become established.

1　*King and Queen* by Henry Moore

2   Sunset

Ideally, some aspect of creative experiment should be included each week so that the pupils have a chance to develop their powers of empirical composition and the insight they gain can penetrate into their periods of listening to music.

A number of the projects would gain considerably from some kind of team-teaching, especially where they are used in Secondary Schools. Music suffers from isolation in the curriculum: it has for so long been regarded as a highly specialised subject. In fact it needs the other arts as much as they need it. If a team of teachers (art, movement, drama, English, music) work together with a class on one project, each will enrich the others. A variety of work could be going on at any one time: some music, some art, some writing, and so on. In practice it will probably be easier to work through stage by stage. It may be impossible to get the whole staff team together at the same time, though it is important that as many of the team as possible take part in the various stages of the project.

Let us suppose we have decided to explore with a class the idea of VASTNESS. A project like this might take at least half a term. We should begin, the team and pupils together, by talking about space and vastness. If possible we'd try to have some first-hand experience: going out on to a hill-top or a moor if we lived in the country; to the top of a church-tower to survey the landscape; to the beach to look at the vastness of the sea. If we lived in a town we might look at and talk about the canopy of sky above the roofs of a city, or the vast stretching-out of tall factory chimneys.

Back in the classroom we could begin to use art materials to express vastness. There might be more discussion and we should look together at pictures like the one on page 17. Henry Moore's King and Queen survey the vast landscape laid out in front of them. They were made to fit into this landscape—open moorland at Shawside in Dumfriesshire in Scotland. Even in a photograph we can appreciate the majesty of these figures. They seem to draw greatness out of their surroundings and in doing this they say something to us about the high moorlands. The hills are so strong; they seem to have been there for all time. The King and Queen are like the hills and through them we feel not only the strength and the breadth of the landscape but also its great age and power.

We would notice how the sculptor has used his materials to convey this sense of vastness and grandeur. We could move on from there to consider a writer's use of language to tell us about similar feelings, as, for example, Joyce Cary does in his novel, *Except the Lord*:

The last white head of mist had now disappeared—we stood on the topmost island of a scattered archipelago. The morning was all around us, clear and cold. Only a few very high clouds, small and thin, like the frosty breathing of some genius of the moors, floated through the immense sky opening now before us at speed, gathering to split the universe apart.

A passage like that could stimulate more 'adventuresome conversation' between teacher and class, which in turn could move easily into creative writing. Some may have experienced a sunrise like the one Joyce Cary describes. Most of us have seen a magnificent sunset and perhaps imagined the evening sky to be a vast, endless ocean and the clouds small, golden islands. There's always the sky above us to give us a feeling of vastness and, whatever our surroundings, we can all let our imagination take us into outer space or to land on a planet.

In the project, art work and writing could go on simultaneously. Pupils who have already done something with paint might like to return to art materials and try working in three dimensions. They could make figures which suggest immensity, strength or great age, and consider where these figures might ideally be set. Would they look out across hills or face an ocean, perhaps from the top of a cliff? ('*Choose suitable materials and make a piece of sculpture to stand on the sea-shore*'.) In this context we'd certainly need to look at some of the sculpture of Barbara Hepworth.

When our subject has been thoroughly explored in the more familiar materials of art and language, a very short step will carry us into music. If we make music about vastness, space, oceans or mountains, what kind of sounds should we choose? A large cymbal may be useful (*cymbal is struck or rolled with a soft stick*). Or we could try stroking the lower strings inside the piano while the sustaining pedal is held down. Does this sound suggest great space? We mustn't forget the silences: they are part of the music and we shall need to listen carefully to judge exactly the right length of silence between sounds. How should we begin our piece? Perhaps with a roll on the cymbal (*cymbal rolled with soft stick*), letting the sound die into silence? Then a slow stroking of the piano strings, remembering to keep the pedal down. That sounds like great depths or vast space. How should we go on? Should we have these sounds again or should we have new sounds? If we go back to pictures of sculpture and look at one like this of *Trio* by Austin Wright, we can see that the sculptor makes his three figures 'all of a piece' by using the same material throughout and by using similar *ideas* for each figure. He doesn't make one of them in one way and then think up another way of making a figure for the second, and yet another way for the third. They are parts of a whole

3 *Trio* (plaster for bronze) by Austin Wright

and he wants us to feel this trio as a whole: three huge and spacious figures belonging together.

Music is like that. If you start off too many new ideas you end up with something which won't sound like one piece at all but like what it is—bits, all tacked together. The sculptor keeps to his one material and his one way of working it. We should do the same. Let's limit ourselves to the material we've got so far: the cymbal, the piano strings—and silence. We may need to repeat some of the things we do with the sounds; that will also help to make the music hang together.

So we might begin: a quiet cymbal roll ... and we let it die. Then again ... and again we let it die. Once more, but this time making the sound grow a little ... Now we introduce the piano-strings idea ...

This is the point at which to take stock of what we've done. It isn't difficult music to remember, so we can play it again. If it seems satisfactory, we could continue to improvise and evaluate in this way; or we could work out an overall plan to make our ideas go on. This might be something very simple, such as beginning as we have done already but very quietly. The sounds could then grow gradually bigger and broader to a climax point, and then slowly calm down again.

Once we have made a piece like this, several more groups could make similar pieces of their own. They can take inspiration from their own paintings and writing. The words might even be read against the background of some of the music. A group must decide on the sounds they will use and how they will put their music together. The ideas are tried out and gradually built up into a whole piece, remembering the bits that are successful and rejecting the things that don't fit. They go on like this until they are satisfied that the music hangs together, has a definite beginning and a definite end, and really says in sounds and silences what its makers want to say about vastness or grandeur. These pieces can be tape-recorded and later heard and discussed alongside music by a professional composer who has been inspired by the same idea. In this instance we might choose the third section of *Et Expecto Resurrectionem Mortuorum* by Messiaen. We should notice how the composer uses silence; how the silences become part of the music. There are three 'sound-ideas': the first a jumping, jagged pattern played by the woodwind; the second a series of beautiful, solemn bell sounds which seem to echo down long valleys; and the third a group of powerful brass sounds out of which grows an immensely long roll on a huge gong. One by one the sounds are allowed to die into silence; and the vast silences become the material which welds the piece together. It's almost as though the sounds were there so that we should hear the silences.

It is in ways like this, developed over several lesson periods, that we would aim to give children and young people a genuine experience of what music is really about; to help them feel its expressive power and enable them to use it to say something. The projects in this book do not constitute a 'method' of teaching music. This must be avoided at all costs. We hope our suggestions adequately represent our attitude to the place of music in education. We hope teachers will try to release the natural creativity in those they teach, whatever the age and the ability of the pupils. Creative experiment is only one small part of music in education: but we believe it is a very important part and one that should not be neglected.

Project 1
What does music say?

A

Let us begin with Messiaen: the third section of *Et Expecto Resurrectionem Mortuorum*. Woodwinds jump, growl and shriek. Silence. Eight solemn bell strokes echo and die. Again silence. Suddenly the brasses blare, and out of the trombones' awesome processional grows a steady roar ... the big gongs, the tam-tam beaten in a long and powerful resonance, shattering and echoing across mountains and along valleys. This is music of the high hills, music for vast spaces: 'The hour is coming when the dead shall hear the voice of the Son of God'. We can feel the awe and the majesty, the High Alps and the great churches. The instrumental sounds are vast, the silences are deep. The words of St John are alive in the music, and through these sounds Messiaen reveals himself and his vision.

This is what music is about. Music is language. Through it we can express the things we feel and perceive. All the time we are reacting to the world around us, to the minute by minute business of living. For most of the time these reactions of ours are hardly worth remarking upon, but there are times when we feel a little stronger about something. We may feel excited, or elated, depressed, fed up or very sad. We may even feel happy and a little sad both at the same time. Or again, our feelings may be bound up with a deep and absorbing interest which grows in us as a result of something we have seen or read.

Any one of these reactions may be strong enough for us to want to say something about our feelings or about whatever has caught our imagination. Naturally most of us would be content with the spoken word on such occasions. Some of us might want to go further and, if we were very moved, write down our thoughts in prose or in poetry. Language has many aspects and many media of expression for thoughts and ideas. Words may be the most obvious way, but they are not always sufficient. Sometimes we say we are 'speechless with indignation': we feel so indignant, there are no words to express what we feel. We may have to resort to some action of annoyance. There are other situations which can leave us wishing for ways to say things where we don't have to rely on words. The words run out and we must look for another medium.

We might use paint and canvas. We might use clay. We might use bodily movement. These would help us to say things in ways words cannot. When we had finished organising our materials we should have a permanent *visible* record of what we wanted to say, a reminder, perhaps, of some exciting moment. And, more important, it will go beyond mere recording and say something *in itself*. The materials themselves may indeed embody the original excitement we want to preserve: the excitement, that is, of discovery. In this instance, when we have found out about them and have moulded them into a satisfying whole, we shall have said what we wanted to say—about the materials.

Artists often find excitement in the very processes of exploring their materials. A picture does not necessarily have to represent anything: it can be satisfying as an organisation of colour and form for its own sake, as is the painting on page 26.

A picture can be 'about' paint. Music can be 'about' sound. The materials of music are sounds and silences. They can be explored like any other materials—words, paint, clay, wire, metal, polystyrene— and they can be used as language when we have something to say. What we have to say may be concerned with something in life around us, some feeling about something seen or heard or imagined. It may even be an extension of something said previously in another art form: musicians are often inspired by literature. On the other hand the something we have to say may well be 'about' the materials themselves, sounds and silences —perhaps some particular sounds, or sounds made on a particular instrument. They may be sounds of certain pitch chosen from a recognised scale and ordered to form a melody; but music doesn't have to be melodic. The sounds we choose to control and order may be any sounds. The music lies in us and our control and ordering of the materials, for music is the organisation of sounds and silences for some expressive purpose.

How shall we know whether it is music or just noise? In the first place noise just happens: it's around us all the time and we don't control it. Music, on the other hand, is the result of a *planned* use of the materials, even though this planning may be largely intuitive, at least to begin with. The process may be one of trial and error—so it is for anyone trying to say something: hunting for the right words, selecting carefully the right materials or colours. We should give the finished piece a sense of wholeness, of belonging together, and to this end we must reject anything which in any way destroys the wholeness. This part of the task will

Painting by Sheila McGirr

be easier if we impose some limitations on ourselves before we start. For example, we might make music designed to reveal the sounds we have discovered and liked in *one* instrument. Technique is what we can do with the materials, so we might begin by *discovering* our techniques with a simple instrument, say a cymbal.

B

(i)   Any cymbal will do of course, but the better the instrument the greater the range of sounds. For this piece a cymbal at least 15″ in diameter, suspended or on a stand would be best. It can be struck with a soft-headed stick. Even with a technique as simple as this you will be able to find a lot of different sounds: strike the cymbal a number of times in quick succession or in slow and solemn beats; strike it once very hard and listen to the sound dying away; let the stick fall gently and glance off the cymbal producing the faintest hum; play a roll with two soft sticks, one on either side, gradually getting louder; strike it hard and immediately dampen the sound by grabbing the cymbal with your fingers; strike it at the rim or on the dome at the centre—this will produce two quite distinct qualities. Moving on from there, try using sticks of different kinds—wood, metal, rubber—or wire brushes. Play on the cymbal with your fingers. Some very interesting sounds can be obtained by playing on the edge of a cymbal with a cello bow: you must press fairly hard and it's best if the bow direction is upward. Another unusual sound is produced if you drag a rubber chime-bar beater across a cymbal.

Experiment with these different effects and see if you can find others. Learn to control the sounds you produce. You are building up not only a repertoire of cymbal sounds but also your technique with these sounds.

(ii)   When you have found a wide repertoire of sounds and you can control them sufficiently well to use any of them at will, start using them to make a piece of music. It will be a piece 'about' the cymbal sounds. The first sound you make is very important: that is like the first mark made with brush and paint on a new canvas. Once it is there things will never be the same again. What happens next will depend on your reactions to that first sound. You may, of course, have a design in mind. This could be something quite simple such as a gradual increase in loudness and then a dying away. If your design is for the music to start very quietly you will have to find the quietest sound in your repertoire—which is this? On the other hand, your plan may be to reveal the wide variety of sounds you have found in this one cymbal. How will you begin? How will you go on? Although you will know the various sounds you want to incorporate in your piece, you must be ready to take advantage of the ways in which the situation changes as one sound follows another in your improvising. Sounds are 'related' to other sounds on either side of them. Every new sound changes the total picture in some way. If we're sensitive to these changes they will tell us where to go next. In other words, the progress of the music is going to depend on our ability to hold the total picture in mind and weigh up the effect of each sound in relation to the other sounds.

You will have to go back many times over each section, making certain of its shape and refining it by rejecting anything which sounds out of place, while confirming the things which sound right. Remember, it is your piece of music so nobody else can really tell you how it should go. You must aim at an overall *wholeness* in the music; but this doesn't mean it must all be the same. This would be too dull. Music needs repetition and unity, but it also needs variety. It is by carefully balancing variety with unifying repetitions that composers make their music 'go on'.

The trial-and-error process you have been using (what we call empirical composition; that is, where we are guided in what we do by the results of experiment and observation only) has been used for a long time. A great deal of the world's music has always been made like that. Composers have discovered the sounds and combinations of sounds which they like, sounds which say what they want to say, and they have refined them, remembering the finished versions of their worked-over improvisations. Much of this music has been handed down to us orally and never written down. Notation is not necessary while the memory serves. Do not confuse notation with music. At its simplest, notation is merely a device for assisting the memory. In its more complex forms it can become something else— a means of composition. But you must first acquire a feeling for creating music and this comes before the need of notation.

When you are satisfied with the shape and content of your Cymbal Music, you can tape-record the whole piece. At the same time keep it in your memory. A week later, perhaps, you might try 'handing it on' to someone else. Play it to them several times during a music lesson: the others in the class can judge how accurately they can reproduce it. Listen to their performance a few days later. Note any small differences in their version when compared with the original tape-recording of your own. If the person you have handed the piece on to were to hand it on to another, and he in turn to another, it would be interesting to notice the differences in performance. Each performer has his own personal

5   Playing a cymbal with a violin bow

way of using musical material, and when the material is transmitted
orally it is often subject to changes—we might regard them as refinements—although the core of the music remains unchanged. This is
what happens in folk music the world over.

(iii)   Enlarge the scope of your cymbal technique by experimenting
with several cymbals of different sizes, some suspended and others
'clash' cymbals held in the hands. Make a piece for one player on all
the cymbals using one kind of stick only.

(iv)   Make another piece for one player but use a variety of sticks so that you can have many different effects. In making the music don't forget the value of silences, both for dramatic effect and also to help relax the tension of the music when you need to. Although you will be using a lot of different effects, be careful not to lose sight of the unity of the piece.

(v)   Working as a group of about four players, create a group composition for cymbals. It is not necessary for all four to play all the time. There may, of course, be some places where you will want the maximum sound from all four players at once, but try also to make use of the *differences* between one cymbal sound and another. Remember that each new sound changes the total picture; we have to try to keep in mind where the music is 'going to' as we improvise. Each player must listen to the sounds other players make and he must react to them with his own sounds. Go over the music in sections until you have it just as you want it. Then put the whole thing together as one piece.

C

Music for Cymbals (band 1 of the accompanying disc): this piece was the result of a group improvisation by four players. The improvisation was weighed up carefully section by section until the shape and direction of the whole piece was agreed on and 'fixed'. The group had four cymbals of different pitches which they played with a variety of sticks and with bows. Two of the cymbals were suspended, two were hand-held. The plan of the piece is simple: there is a gradual increase in volume and activity, followed by a gradual decrease with a consequent relaxing of the tension.

The music begins with two gentle bowed notes on one of the suspended cymbals. The bow produces soft, high harmonics which are allowed to die almost to nothing before we hear a few very soft taps with the wire brush on one of the hand-held cymbals. After a silence this section is repeated, slightly louder. In this repetition greater force is used on the bow and the note produced is allowed longer to vibrate before we hear the brushed cymbal. After a pause the cymbal is bowed again, this time even more strongly and the bow stroke ends with the heel of the bow striking the under edge of the cymbal. A hand-cymbal is then struck with the wire brush in a series of fast strokes, increasing all the time in volume and speed. At the climax of this crescendo the other suspended cymbal (which has a deep note) is struck once with a soft stick. As this note dies away, the fourth player draws a wooden stick around the edge

Music for Cymbals

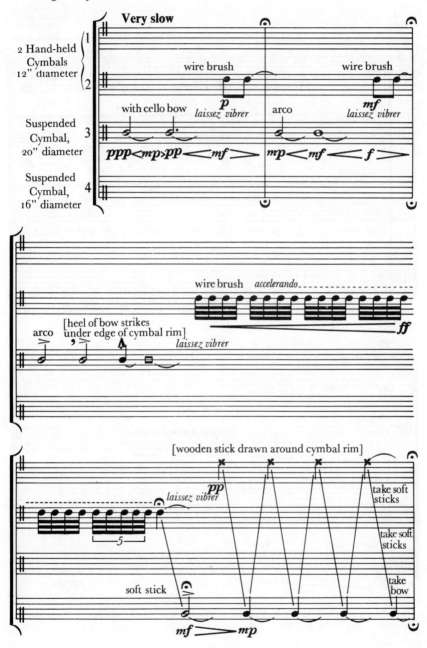

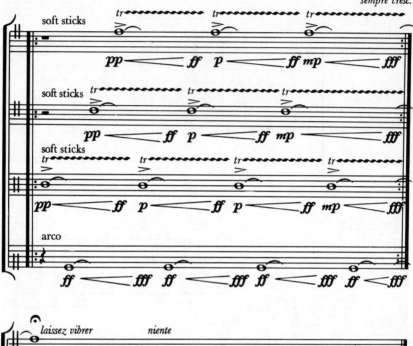

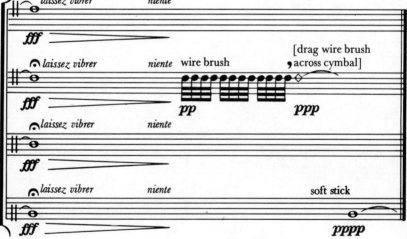

of another cymbal several times. These sounds are punctuated by single strokes with a soft stick on the low-sounding cymbal. After another pause, this cymbal is bowed very loudly while at the same time the other suspended cymbal is rolled with soft sticks in a crescendo from very quiet to very loud. The two other players join in and three cymbals are rolled in a series of crescendi ad lib., the sound of one piling on top of another. The low-sounding suspended cymbal is played very loudly with a bow throughout this passage. The activity stops and the huge 'wave' of vibrations is allowed to die through several seconds and is then followed by a quiet but urgent little pattern of repeated short notes played on one cymbal with the wire brush. The pattern ends with the player drawing the brush very gently over the surface of the cymbal, and this leads to the final sound, played almost inaudibly with a soft stick on the second suspended cymbal.

The sounds and the periods of stillness are controlled to a remarkable degree considering that the piece is not written down. (The example given above was notated from the recording and is given here merely for reference.) What we are hearing is a worked-over and remembered improvisation. The content has been refined through careful evaluation and the result is effective music.

D

Some of the more unusual cymbal effects, including the cymbal played with a bow, can be heard in the *Concerto for Orchestra* by Roberto Gerhard.

The bowed cymbal is also used in Schönberg's *Five Pieces for Orchestra Op. 16*: in the final bars of the fourth piece (pocket score, Peters Edition no. 3376a, p. 45) is the instruction, 'Tremolo auf einem Beckenteller mit einem Violoncellbogen' [tremolo on the cymbal with a cello bow].

Bartók's orchestral music provides a number of examples of different cymbal effects. The following are in the *Violin Concerto No. 2* (score, Boosey and Hawkes, 1946):

Cymbal struck 'with blade of a penknife on the edge' (p. 85; fig. 126). This is in a quiet, slow section of the last movement. The cymbal is exposed and therefore easily heard at this point. The only other instruments playing are the triangle (*pp*), the harp (*pp*) and the solo violin (*p*);

A quiet roll 'to be played with the thin end of a side drum stick on the dome of the cymbal', followed immediately by a single note 'to be played with the thicker end of a side drum stick at the rim of the cymbal (*f*)' (p. 109; fig. 386);

'Two cymbals trilled together'; in the final five bars of the first movement (p. 53; fig. 383). The cymbals are rolled together in a gentle crescendo while the solo violin trills on a low note.

In Bartók's *Dance Suite* there is an interesting direction to the cymbal player to 'strike with the hand' [*colla mano*]. This is at fig. 31 in the third movement (pocket score, Boosey and Hawkes; p. 43).

Results of work on the assignments in Section B might be followed-up by listening to the second movement ('Largo') from the *Toccata for Percussion* (1947) by Carlos Chávez. In this movement he exploits the metallic instruments (bells, cymbals, chimes, gongs) and the xylophone. Although this is a more extensive palette than we have been using, the total effect of the movement will probably make a useful comparison. Note the composer's use of silences and the way in which he balances one sonority against another. In particular, notice the cymbal sounds.

Stockhausen's *Zyklus for Percussion* (Universal Edition) will also be of interest. This is a virtuoso work for one player. It uses a large number of percussion instruments and a very wide range of effects. If we consider the cymbal effects alone there is quite a variety: there are two suspended cymbals with the instruction to 'vary the striking point continually'; a hi-hat cymbal which can be struck with a stick while it is closed, or struck with a stick while it is open, or struck at the centre (on the dome) while open; and, of course, there are indications for different sticks, hard and soft. (For a fuller description, see Project 16.)

Listen also to Messiaen's use of great varieties of percussion sounds in *Et Expecto Resurrectionem Mortuorum* and *Couleurs de la Cité Celeste*.

Project 2
The music within us

A
Where did music begin?

Nature's capacity to create, nourish and simulate is the starting-point for all music; rhythm informs the beat of the heart, the thrumming downpour of rain and the thud of horses' hooves; melody is evoked in the mind by a bird-call or the howl of a jackal; form can be produced quite casually through repetition or memory. The first music was born independently of man, yet it was man who created genuine music from natural sounds. Man was most strongly influenced by the natural sounds he experienced directly, through his own physical senses, or which he could produce himself: above all, he had his own voice, which, though it was incapable of refined articulation, served to communicate his emotions—a sound which was partly howling and whining, and partly already singing and speech. In fact the two elements of music, pitch and rhythm, were both carried in the human body as natural, cosmic phenomena.*

So music probably began when man became conscious of the expressive possibilities that were available to him in the sounds he could make with his voice and in the natural rhythms and pulses of living. At a much later stage men began to use instruments for music; a kind of extension of their 'bodily' music. These instruments would have been anything that was to hand: drums and rhythm sticks of resonant woods, horns and shells.

In our own time a number of composers are looking back to that distant past for inspiration. Perhaps this is because of a dissatisfaction with society as it is today and, by association, dissatisfaction with music as it has evolved since the renaissance. One way and another, a familiarity with so-called 'primitive' music is crucial to our understanding of so much twentieth-century music from Debussy to Cage. There is a lot to be said for 'going back to scratch' when you are searching for a new musical language. Let's begin again where music itself began. The true resources of music are within each one of us and they are part of the business of living. We must not belittle music by thinking of it all as

* Bence Szabolsci, *A History of Melody* (Barrie and Rockliff, 1965), p. 1.

35

entertainment. Essentially it is a language—a means of expression. In primitive communities there is a uniformity of life which over-rides all personal characteristics. Everyone's actions are understood, and the art of a primitive community is never esoteric because it too is something everyone can take part in. It grows out of the life of the whole tribe. We are not primitives and, therefore, we can't expect to be able to feel and respond as primitives. Nevertheless, it may help us to come closer to the essential nature of music if we momentarily shrug off some of our sophisticated post-renaissance concepts of music. So let's make music, using as our materials the most fundamental resources we have: the silence around us and the noises we can hear in the silence.

B

(i)   Working in groups of about three or four, create a piece of music as you did in Project 1 but this time using primitive resources rather than highly-developed musical instruments.

Music begins in silence. In the silence we can hear our own *regular* breathing. Ancient peoples thought of breath as the very stuff of life itself: 'Then the Lord God formed man of dust from the ground, and breathed into his nostrils the breath of life ...' (Gen. 2.7.) Here, then, is an elemental sound from within us, and it can become material for music. The thud of our heart-beat is also musical material.

Take the pulse beat of one member of the group as a basic pulse for the music. Count it out. Now indicate it in any way you choose but *not*, for the moment, on a musical instrument. Join this to the elemental breath sound. Breathe in and out heavily in time with the pulse beat. Continue this for a short time placing weight on the outgoing breath. Before long a pattern will begin to take shape. Allow the breath sound gradually to take on some more definite vocal quality, such as a vowel sound *Ah*, *Oo* or *Oh*. The syllable you choose might also begin to take on a note—probably low in pitch. When you have explored the possibilities of these sounds linked to the basic pulse rhythm, consider how you can incorporate other natural sounds—wood, stone, etc.—added to or against the basic pulse. Now build up a musical continuity using all these sounds.

(ii)   Create a second piece using the same groupings and the same sound material. This time let each member of the group take his own pulse as his basic 'beat'. Can the individual members of the group hold their beat against the other sounds? Does this produce any noticeably wide differences of beat? Find some way of marking the individual beats absolutely steadily. Can you fix the rates with a metronome? You will probably need to tape-record any music you make like this before you can fully appreciate the cross-rhythms which may occur.

As you control your sounds and improvise the music, try to be aware of what you are doing with the sounds: let them 'go somewhere', that is, give the piece a sense of shape. The group should decide beforehand what limitations to impose on the way they use the available sounds.

C

An interpretation of Assignment (i): there were three in the group and they began by looking for simple natural sounds. They chose as their musical material the rustling of twigs and leaves and the song of birds. The music they made begins very quietly with the gentlest rustling of the twigs. The natural world stirs to life, the sound grows. Gradually we are aware of the sound of breathing rising above the rustling and increasing in strength. Bird song, stylised in a whistled motto, appears over the other sounds, which by now are quite strong. Suddenly all is silent. Then the breath sounds only begin again. This time the three timbres are clear-cut and counterpoint against one another. The speed begins to increase, the sounds grow even stronger and are clearly moving towards a climax. When it comes it is unexpected and shattering. The climax is a piercing scream. It is the *humanity* of the voice which disturbs us. We have heard noises in the silence grow into musical patterns but remain either sounds of the inanimate world or at most the merest beginnings of life. The breath sounds have struggled to take vocal 'shape' and the scream seems to contain the whole spectrum of one human voice. It shatters us, not only with its sudden fortissimo, but also by the very personal nature of real vocal tone. Growing out of the dust, the voice becomes Humanity with all its fears and consciousness in the midst of a mysterious natural world.

D

A much fuller exploration of this topic will be found in Wilfrid Mellers' *The Resources of Music* (Cambridge University Press). The first section provides assignments on the lines of those given above but in much greater detail. They lead towards a performance of 'Nature Song', the first movement of *Life Cycle*. Examine the score of 'Nature Song'. If possible work at the music and perform it. The material is flexible and there are many opportunities in this song for the performers to 're-create' the music. In his notes Wilfrid Mellers lists recordings of primitive music and music by twentieth-century composers whose work has been influenced by these primitive musical resources. These recordings can be used as a follow-up to creative work based on primitive musical resources or on the work of modern composers (see Projects 3 and 15 in this book).

Project 3
Music and mystery

A

Among primitive peoples inflection of spoken words and melody are closely connected. Transferred to instruments—'speaking tools', as they were known—we have the drum-language of African tribes. In the earliest music, speaking and singing were in fact the same thing. If the voice was raised in emphasis it turned into chanting and singing. There is, even today, evidence of this kind of thing among Australian aboriginals. When excited, they have been known to pour out torrents of words which form themselves into set rhythms and regular patterns, giving an effect of chanting. Whenever people are excited, elated or terrified they may express what they feel in a frenzy of words which turn quickly into similarly frenzied music. Solemn and mysterious moments produce the monotonous repetitions of the dirge and the incantation.

In primitive societies words, music and dance are never far from one another and all expression of this kind is linked with the day to day life of the community. Art and music are very closely related to living. The feelings and thoughts they express are concerned with the hunt, with formulated rituals of life and religion, with fears and fancies and delights. Primitive arts are vital because they spring directly from the perception of things close to people. Only in relatively recent times have we come to think of music as something to be listened to or as something able to exist by itself. Earlier civilisations as well as primitive peoples would have found music meaningless apart from words and action. So in this project we shall make use of words, old words with a flavour of mystery and ritual about them.

First we shall try to enlarge our musical resources. We'll continue to use the primitive 'corporeal' resources we used in Project 2 (i.e. rhythms derived from pulse beat and sounds derived from breathing) but we can add one or two large cymbals and gongs if they are available, and also a hand drum or two (Indian drums or bongos). These are all highly-developed musical instruments, of course, but musical instruments are only able to exist at all because of an elemental factor as basic as our breathing or pulse beat. This is the phenomenon of the harmonic series and we shall use this also to enrich our resources for music.

A single sound produced on a musical instrument is not a *pure* note. In fact, this apparently single note is accompanied by other notes which we call 'overtones' or 'harmonics'. If you strike the lowest C on the piano it will give a full-bodied sound because you are also hearing the harmonics which sound with the fundamental note. You may not be conscious of hearing these overtones but you'd miss them if they were not there. The harmonics give any sound its particular characteristics. If you take the note C as a fundamental, then the most prominent harmonics that sound with it would be those shown here:

Of course they are all heard *with* the fundamental like this:

If four people can stand at one keyboard and *hold down without sounding* the notes numbered 2–16 in the example above, while a fifth person strikes the fundamental once sharply, it will be possible to hear the strings vibrate in sympathy with the harmonics which are *present in the fundamental*. This harmonic series is part of nature: a pattern as regular as the rise and fall of tides.

We can use these sounds in making our next piece of music. Of course, any note has its harmonics. For the moment we'll restrict ourselves to the notes of the harmonic series which has C as its fundamental; that is, those given in the example above.

B

Choose at least six *different* notes from the harmonic series on the fundamental note C: hold them as a sustained (or very slowly repeated) chord throughout the piece. Play these notes very quietly on any instrument(s) which will give the pitches required, or sing the notes (to *Ah* or as a quiet hum). If you wish to sustain the chord without a break, wind instruments or stringed instruments will be essential, unless you use voices or piano recorded on a tape-loop (see Project 17). If the chord is repeated slowly like a heart-beat, it could be played by several players on one piano. One person should keep the two pedals depressed all the time.

Using the harmonic series chord as a background (very quietly indeed) add breathing sounds and low-pitched sighs, moans or not too definite *Ahs* and *Oos*. Some quiet sounds on cymbals or gongs might be added at a slow pulse beat. A gong struck and lowered slowly into a trough of water while it is still vibrating will produce a mysterious sound which you might want to use here. Let all these sounds move to a very slow pulse.

Keep this background moving with a gentle regularity and then introduce a few voices chanting these words on a very low note:

This ae nighte, this ae nighte,
— *Every nighte and alle,*
Fire and fleet and candle-lighte,
    And Christe receive thy saule.

When thou from hence away art past,
— *Every nighte and alle,*
To Whinny-muir thou com'st at last;
    And Christe receive thy saule.

From Whinny-muir when thou may'st pass,
— *Every nighte and alle,*
To Brig o' Dread thou com'st at last;
    And Christe receive thy saule.

From Brig o' Dread when thou may'st pass,
— *Every nighte and alle,*
To Purgatory fire thou com'st at last;
    And Christe receive thy saule.

If ever thou gavest meat or drink,
— *Every nighte and alle,*
The fire sall never make thee shrink;
    And Christe receive thy saule.

If meat or drink thou ne'er gav'st nane,
— *Every nighte and alle,*
The fire will burn thee to the bare bane;
    And Christe receive thy saule.

> This ae nighte, this ae nighte,
> — *Every nighte and alle,*
> Fire and fleet and candle-lighte,
> *And Christe receive thy saule.*

These anonymous fifteenth-century verses are from *The Lyke-Wake Dirge.** A watch is being kept over a dead body at night and the words of the dirge tell of the soul's progress to Purgatory. The mystery which surrounds the soul's journey is the mystery of life itself. The sounds of the words convey Man's fear of the unknown and his hope for what lies beyond this life.

All the sounds we have found, including the words, are raw materials for the music. We've hinted at a way of organising these materials. Explore this organisation for yourselves and make your piece of music grow out of it to express the mystery which is in the words.

C

A version of the assignment can be heard on the accompanying disc (band 2). As it follows closely the suggestions given above, further description and comment will be superfluous.

Although, as it stands, this assignment is probably more suited to Secondary School level, the idea of mystery, and the power of music to convey mystery, is something that might well be explored with younger children. Choose words appropriate to the age-range; for example, the rhyme *This is the key of the kingdom* or Herrick's poem *The Bell-Man* (both are in Walter de la Mare's anthology *Come Hither*).

D

Once again, comparison should be made with the first and last sections of *Life Cycle* by Wilfrid Mellers (and see the assignments in Project 2 of this book if they have not already been worked).

Although the musical material does not compare directly with the material suggested in this project, Britten's setting of the *Lyke-Wake Dirge* (in the *Serenade for Tenor, Horn and Strings*) may be useful as an example of a composer's use of these words in a piece which conveys all the mystery and fear with great power. A 'folk' version of the *Dirge* is sung by The Young Tradition on the first of their long-playing records.

---

* For the complete dirge, see Walter de la Mare, *Come Hither* (Constable, 1960), p. 248 and the explanatory note on p. 641.

Project 4
Music and words

A

Words are an obvious way of expressing ourselves or communicating with other people; but they also do something for *us*. Writing words down helps to clarify our thinking. Poetry is a refining of thoughts. By concentrating on one tiny aspect of our life or our surroundings, the act of writing poetry can help us to see more clearly. Music, of course, can have the same power. Finding the right sounds and building them up into a whole piece of music increases our own awareness of whatever our music is about. This could be something close to us which now, through our own writing and our own music, we see properly for the first time.

Most of us take our surroundings for granted so much that when we do start looking closely at quite familiar things, we find we have any number of things worth talking about right on our doorstep. We may go no further than simply describing what we see quite factually. In the excitement of really seeing for the first time this could be enough— many a poet does little more and by the concentration of his words conveys the excitement of discovery. An experience like that can lead us to talk with other people about similar things we've seen, their differences and their likenesses. Occasionally quite a simple thing seen closely for the first time or in some unusual light, magnified, reflected or viewed upside down, will spark off trains of *imaginative* thought which develop into fantasy. If we try to write about it, before long our thoughts may well refine into something approaching the poetic.

B

Working in groups of about four or five, go and look at REFLECTIONS. Note down all the reflections you can find—mirrors, puddles, polished wood surfaces, polished metals. Try to remember others you have seen at different times—distorting mirrors at a funfair; your own face reflected in the window of a railway carriage as a train goes through a tunnel. Do any of these reflections make you think of people or situations, or does any kind of story begin to form in your mind? Discuss these ideas in

your groups. Now write a piece of poetry or prose about REFLECTIONS. You can either pool all the ideas within a group and make a composite piece, or each member of a group could make his own piece. Don't clutter it up with unnecessary detail. Use only the best ideas; select carefully and keep in mind the *intention*—to write a piece about REFLECTIONS which conveys thoughts and feelings and some sense of the "mirrorness' of reflections.

When you are satisfied that you have a piece of writing that says all that you feel about reflections, and which hangs together well, read the piece (or pieces) aloud. Now imagine you are to present this as part of a programme on radio. You're just a voice coming from a loud-speaker. Can you help your audience to *feel* the effect of reflection by using music? What kind of music will you make? You will need to create only the general effect of reflection or glassiness. Don't try to translate your words line by line into sounds: the results will be too jumbled, too disjointed, and will simply end up like sound effects. Sound effects can only imitate details (like a train bowling along or horses galloping). Music can take us beyond what we see, intensifying things by making us *feel* as well. In your presentation the words you have written will take care of the details. The music you make can be more or less the same kind of music all the time, creating the atmosphere in which we hear the words. If your first ideas in sound are not too complicated, you might do different things with them at points where the words speak of different kinds of reflection. But try to make your musical sounds hang together so that when we hear them at different places in the poem—changed, perhaps, in some simple way: made louder, made quieter, stretched out or made shorter, allowed to go on vibrating, stopped off short, turned backwards; in order to highlight the words—we shall nevertheless realise by the way the sounds are put together that they are basically the same sounds you began with.

What kind of sounds will you choose? Glassy sounds? How can you suggest reflections? Explore the musical instruments available. See how many different sounds you can get from each, then choose the sounds most likely to be useful in the Reflection Music (or Mirror Music). Everybody in the group can contribute some sounds and ideas for using them. Try a number of sounds together. Build them into a continuous pattern, perhaps repeating some sections so that we can get used to them and enjoy them again. Repetition will also help to hold the music together so that it doesn't wander aimlessly. Remember that the final version must 'illuminate' the words.

When you have found appropriate sounds and built them into some

45

kind of shape, play the music while one member of the group reads the poem. It should be read without a break while the music is played quietly in the background. Now experiment with this combination: try various ways of combining words and music so that together they speak tellingly to us (or our imaginary radio audience) about reflections. You might, for example, let the music begin and, after a few moments, when the atmosphere is created for the words, the reader could start, placing his words carefully into the music's 'setting' as a stone is placed in the setting of a ring. Then again, perhaps the music should not continue throughout the poem but would appear only at the beginning and at the end, growing out of the final lines as a postlude which leaves us with the *feeling* of glass or mirrors. If there are four or five separate poems from your group, you could play the music (it need be only a short piece in this case), read the first poem, repeat the music exactly, read the second poem, and so on, the music linking this series of poems which are all on the same subject. Are there other ways of combining the words and music?

Whatever organisation you adopt, your music should *present* the words. When you have rehearsed your final version a few times, taperecord it and judge for yourselves the success of the presentation. Have you managed with words and music to penetrate the idea of REFLECTION which you set out to investigate and comment upon?

C

Mirrors
Trains in tunnels
Buses in the dark
Water in puddles
Looking out of the kitchen window
When it's black outside.
Wheel hubs: queer distortions
When fat people get fatter and
Thin people disappear.
Fairground mirrors when I can be
As tall as I like, and where
Even ordinary people look
Grotesque. You can
Turn yourself upside down if you look
In the bowl of a spoon, or
See yourself reflected a thousand times
At once if you have just
Two mirrors.
How convenient to observe
Without staring, to gaze thoughtlessly

Out of the window of the tube train, but really
You're watching him
Furtively
Gobbling
Sweets.

JANE PHILLIPS

The music was for piano (the strings struck with felt xylophone-beaters and plucked with the fingers), glockenspiel, xylophone and metallophone. The principle was that we should hear 'dry' sounds (wood or the piano strings with the dampers down played with felt hammers) and then hear similar pitches 'reflected' by resonance or reverberation. So a dry sound of the piano might be repeated but with the dampers raised, the reverberating sound giving us the impression of reflection. Or a dry sound on the xylophone could be echoed by the resonant, reflecting sounds of the glockenspiel or metallophone. The music accompanied the reading of the poem throughout, but an additional dimension was discovered when the reader decided to stand and face her own reflection in a large mirror. This gave the presentation an element of Theatre. To add to the mirror effect both words and music were heard first forwards and then in reverse order.

D

Improvisation sur Mallarmé II by Pierre Boulez is a setting, for soprano voice and instruments, of a rather involved impressionistic poem by Mallarmé, *Une dentelle s'abolit*. The poet is watching some lace curtains reflected in the panes of a window. The reflection appears to be opening and closing and he struggles for a word to describe this shifting impression: 'Une dentelle s'abolit ...' ... the lace dissolves ... fades ... vanishes ... vaporises ...? There is an 'engulfing white garland' which becomes indistinguishable from 'the pale window'. Now the lace appears to be floating. A train of thought starts in the poet's mind: the lace floating into focus makes him think of the process of birth, of gradually becoming. Then it vanishes into vague whiteness again, like someone who 'embellishes himself with dreams'. This 'vaporized' image is like the doubts and uncertainties of life, which is itself a great game of chance; or like an unused mandolin whose 'sleeping' sound, faded and vanished, is 'empty worthlessness'. Only by playing on the instrument could the musician give birth to the reality of music.

The images of the gently moving lace curtain and the glass of the window are counterpointed in the words of the poem. For Boulez, this is part of his initial interest in setting the poem to music: he chooses

47

instruments whose timbres will give him 'glassy' sounds and so add to the listener's awareness of the poem's impressionism. The planes of sound shift and dissolve into one another like the images of the poem, but always in the music there is the same quality of light, of reflection and of gentle movement.

Of course, there is a great deal more to the piece than a mere translation of the poet's impressionistic language into sounds. Boulez is also very much concerned with the metrical structure of the stanzas. Nevertheless, because the composer has chosen his sounds to a certain extent to heighten the thoughts about reflection and light, *Improvisation sur Mallarmé II* would be a useful follow-up to the assignment above. Some discussion of Mallarmé's poem*might be useful to show how, in looking closely at some familiar object, trains of thought are begun which can lead in many directions. Notice too, how Boulez allows the words to retain the responsibility for the detailed impressions. He does not attempt to follow the diversity of the poet's thoughts by constantly changing the sonorities and the texture, but chooses instrumental sounds that keep us constantly in mind of the central image: the window and the shifting reflections of the lace.

Chansons de Bilitis by Debussy are examples of poetry illuminated by music. In this respect readers in Britain may find some of the BBC's broadcasts for schools in the series *Living Language* useful for discussion: frequently poetry presented on this programme is 'set' into a few phrases of introductory music which prepare the listener for the mood of the words which are to follow.

---

* Anthony Hartley (ed.), *Mallarmé* (Penguin Books, 1965).

Project 5
Pictures in music

A

In Project 4 music was used to heighten our understanding of words. Music is itself a language but, unlike the language of words or of the visual arts, music can't describe. It can comment on something we see or hear spoken—as it does in ballet or theatre or in the background music for films. In these situations music might be said to illuminate characters or events. It cannot *by itself* portray these things. Nevertheless, composers do use music to tell stories and portray events. These pieces are generally called 'programme music': that is, music for which we first need to know the programme of events if we are to fully appreciate what is happening. This is not to say we can't enjoy the music without this foreknowledge: a lot of programme music is very exciting in itself and musically interesting apart from the story—for example, *The Sorcerer's Apprentice* by Dukas or Tchaikowsky's *Romeo and Juliet* overture. Nevertheless, it is the composer's intention that we should know what he had in mind.

Liszt defined 'programme' as 'Any preface in intelligible language added to a piece of instrumental music, by means of which the composer intends to guard the listener against a wrong poetical interpretation, and to direct his attention to the poetical idea of the whole'. Liszt prefaced some of his own music with quite lengthy programmes, outlining the *emotional* scheme of the works and giving the listener a series of word pictures relating to the progress of the music. Other composers will be content with a simple title and leave the listener's imagination to do the rest. Genuine programme music is concerned with the emotional content of the events. Purely imitative sounds have little place: it would not be very musical merely to imitate the noise of galloping horses with wood blocks or coconut shells, and simply to call it 'programme music' wouldn't help these sounds to qualify. On the other hand, music could give the impression of the tensions and excitements of a rider on horseback. In his opera, *The Rape of Lucretia*, Benjamin Britten has a passage of music describing Tarquin's secret ride to Rome. The tenor solo sings a narrative which relates all the hazards of the ride and the feelings of the rider, while the orchestra's music comments on these things, changing subtly in character as the story proceeds. Through the changes the rhythms of the galloping horse are kept steady until the section where horse and rider swim across the Tiber; here the galloping motifs of the orchestral music and some of the material from the singer's part are transformed to suggest the whirls and eddies of the strong river currents. When they reach the farther bank the music again takes up the movement of the horse. The river passed, we feel the added confidence of the rider as he nears his goal. They enter Rome. It is night and the horse's hooves echo in the cobbled streets. The music maintains its rhythmic patterns, increasing in excitement and tension all the time until it reaches a tremendous climax at the point where Sextus Tarquinius dismounts at the house of Collatinus and beats loudly on the door.

B

(i)   Using any instruments you have (or vocal sounds if you think them suitable) work in groups of about five, each group creating a piece of music about one of the following ideas. Choose your title first and then try to find the kind of sounds which will be of most use to you.

(1) Dusk
(2) Winter
(3) Walking through a Fairground
(4) The River
(5) Sunrise in Woods
(6) The Moods of the Sea
(7) A Tower below the Waves
(8) Empty Streets
(9) Desert Places

Tape-record your music and on another occasion listen to these pieces alongside music by other composers on similar subjects (see suggestions for listening at the end of this project).

(ii)   A group can now attempt an extended piece based on the events of a reasonably long narrative. The best kind of story for this purpose is one which has very clearly defined events and characters and a certain amount of repetition of events. As a suggestion we reprint the following legend from China. Like so many Chinese tales it is half-history, half-legend. In this version it is retold by Robert Gittings and Jo Manton.

Heartless Beauty
The young queen, Lustrous Tortoiseshell, wife of the last king of the house of Chou, had eyes the colour of topaz. Her skin was as smooth as her petticoat of

apricot-yellow satin, and when she yawned she showed the inside of a mouth coral and crinkled as a cat's. She yawned often, for she found life in the palace remarkably tedious. Indeed the king was a dull, gloomy man, whose courtiers would hide their smiles behind their wide sleeves when they saw him coming, for fear of incurring his displeasure.

It was not altogether the king's fault. Ever since he had ascended the Dragon Throne, the borders of China had been menaced by enemy horsemen, and every day he was forced to spend long hours in council with his ministers discussing their defence, until his forehead was furrowed with care. But Lustrous Tortoise-shell did not understand this, and instead of seeking humbly to please her lord, or to distract his mind from care—which all the ancient writings agree is the first duty of a wife—she preferred to sulk in her own apartments. Bored, she tore up pieces of valuable silk, her eyes glinting with pleasure at the sound. The rasp of rending embroideries set the king's teeth on edge, and made him gloomier than ever.

'Lustrous Tortoiseshell', he implored her, 'the King of Chou is your slave, but he begs you humbly not to tear up any more silk.'

For answer the queen only yawned and tapped impatiently with her little foot upon the floor. The king sent for jugglers, lute players and dancing bears; he ordered merchants to bring their most precious wares of jade and ivory and chiselled gold, yet still this spoilt beauty continued to frown. He was in despair to know how to please her.

At last one day, when Lustrous Tortoiseshell had sat sulking for two hours without a smile, the king had an idea. He gathered up his long robe, took a lighted taper in his hand, and climbed the winding stair to the highest watch-tower of the palace, where a sentry stood night and day, looking out over the plain. There upon the floor a great fire was prepared: brush-wood, pine-cones and logs of cedar-wood, all ready to flare up at a touch. It was the beacon to give warning that the enemy was at hand. Into this beacon the king thrust his lighted taper.

There was a rustle among the twigs, a sudden roar, and flames leapt like a fountain into the air. Soon, almost at once it seemed, came an answering roar from the distance. It was the sound of many hands beating on bronze war drums, as the faithful nobles of Chou led their troops out of their castles to defend the king. Winding down the valleys they came, from each castle an army of men, on horse, on foot, with banners streaming in the wind, forests of lances glittering in the sunshine, and chariots swaying from side to side in their headlong advance.

Lustrous Tortoiseshell, all boredom forgotten, watched from her window as the armies met and poured in like a mighty river at the city gate. They crowded into the court-yard of the palace, jostling for position and shouting their battle-cries. Some of the foot-soldiers, in the belief that the enemy was at hand, began to throw their firecrackers without waiting for orders, and so terrified the horses that several onlookers were trampled to death.

The chief nobles of Chou rode forward to the palace doors upon their foaming chargers. They were accoutred for war, their supple leather riding boots pulled up to their thighs, their well-flighted arrows in quivers at their sides, the vizors of their bronze helmets, grim and terrible, pulled over their eyes. They reined in their horses and waited silently at the palace steps for their king to come out and lead them.

But the King of Chou was too ashamed to show his face. In an inner courtyard of the palace he gave himself over to despair.

'Honoured sirs, honoured sirs,' called Lustrous Tortoiseshell from the window 'you may all go home to your castles of exalted virtue, and there employ the remainder of your days peacefully flying kites. The enemy is not here.'

'Not here?'

'Not here?'

Spurs and bridle bells clashed together as the nobles turned to look at each other.

'But the beacon?'

'We saw the beacon flames.'

'The Son of Heaven called us to defend him.'

'His Majesty was pleased to jest with you,' said Lustrous Tortoiseshell.

Silently, without a reproach, so great was their love and loyalty, the nobles turned away. But Lustrous Tortoiseshell, when she saw their amazement, their sorrowful looks, and all their warlike trappings hanging useless at their sides, began to laugh.

She flung back her head, closed her eyes to a cat-like slit, and laughed for joy, until the last soldier, weary and crest-fallen, had left the city gates on his homeward journey. Then she went to the king.

'At last, O King of Chou,' she cried, 'at last you have found means to amuse your wife! How foolish their faces looked when they found there was no enemy! O my husband, what a splendid pastime you have invented!'

Shame struck the King of Chou afresh at these words of an idle and worthless woman. At the council table he could hardly bear to meet the grave looks of his ministers, and he vowed that he would never deceive his faithful lords again. But the weeks passed and Lustrous Tortoiseshell grew bored once more. She wheedled and cajoled the unhappy king, she tormented him with her caprices, until in despair he set fire once again to the beacon.

This time the nobles of Chou obeyed the summons with dark looks, and when they saw there was no enemy, departed murmuring that even the king ought not so to make fools of them. When this unwise ruler lit the beacon yet a third time, the nobles chose one, the oldest and most honourable of their numbers, to plead with him. The aged lord, white-haired and venerable, prostrated himself humbly upon the steps of the throne.

'Son of Heaven, ruler of earth and sea,' he said. 'Hear, we pray you, the petition of your servants. We know your every thought is for your people's good. Nevertheless there are, around the Dragon Throne, evil counsellors, whose actions, if you but knew of them, your Majesty would never permit. It would be well, O Son of Heaven, if these persons were sent into some distant and unwholesome province. For upon the honour of our ancestors, we nobles of Chou will not be mocked again.'

'I give you my royal word,' said the king, 'that I will never again light the beacon to mock you. Go in peace.' And, laden with rich gifts, he sent them to their homes.

The very next day, as the king and Lustrous Tortoiseshell sat at rice, the watcher on the tower came running down the winding stair and flung himself in terror at their feet.

'Son of Heaven, the enemy is coming!' he cried.

'Where?' said the king, thrusting the golden goblet from his hand.

'Down the mountain-sides, through the valleys—their grey cloaks are sweeping like mist over the plain!'

'Let the beacon be lit!' commanded the king. 'Have no fear, my beautiful Lustrous Tortoiseshell, my nobles will bring their armies to defend me.'

But although they fed the beacon fire until its flames leapt as a tall tree, although they beat the bronze war drums and all the temple gongs, yet the nobles did not come. They remembered the laughter of Lustrous Tortoiseshell and feared to be mocked once more.

Then the King of Chou saw—but too late—where his weakness and folly had brought him. As the thunder of enemy horse-hooves sounded nearer and nearer across the plain, he took Lustrous Tortoiseshell by the hand and led her to the tower. When they were both inside he commanded his servants to lock the doors and heap brushwood all around. With his own hands he set fire to the silken hangings. As the first barbarian entered the city gates the king and Lustrous Tortoiseshell perished, both together, in the flames.

So ended the House of Chou.

> Nothing is gained, all is lost
> Where Heartless Beauty lives.
> The man who marries one of these
> Has witnessed his own death-warrant.

C

Sea Tower (accompanying disc, band 3): this is a piece composed by a group of children in a rural Primary School. It grew out of an imaginative discussion about a fossilised sea-urchin which their teacher had brought into school. One of the children describes what happens in their music: 'The urchin shell was like the dome of an under-sea tower, and a storm came and blew it down. The fish were swimming and then the octopus joined in. After the storm the fish swim again.'

The music begins with a quiet glissando across the lower strings of the piano (played with the tips of the fingers, the sustaining pedal depressed). This mysterious sound suggests the great depth of the sea and recurs throughout the piece as a background to the rest of the musical material. In these dark depths fishes swim gently to a tiny 'primitive' three-note fragment which describes their movements; first smooth, then suddenly darting. The octopus joins in. It has more movement than the fishes but its plaintive pentatonic melody keeps us in mind of the sea's rhythm, while the sustained low echo of the stroked piano strings is brooding and sinister. Now the pianist uses the keyboard in a carefully graduated crescendo of two note-clusters in the bass. This is built up slowly as the storm grows in strength and even the depths of the sea seem to feel it. The sustaining pedal is depressed throughout and other instruments (tambourines, castanets, drum) are built into this wall

Sea Tower

CHILDREN OF BURNT YATES ENDOWED PRIMARY SCHOOL, RIPLEY, YORKSHIRE, 1967

of sound as the storm reaches its peak. It has been so fierce the tower below the waves has been rocked and it begins to collapse. A little five-note descending figure on the xylophone gives us a picture of the falling bricks. In the background the roar of the storm reverberates and dies. The piano pedal is raised and depressed again. Once more the strings are stroked gently with the fingers and the opening music is repeated. The storm is spent; some parts of the tower still stand, and to their gently rocking and suddenly darting motif, 'the fish swim again'.

Notice how these children *used* their musical material. They give the piece unity by consistent use of the stroked piano-string sound—the music is basically about the sea, therefore it is this 'sea-sound' which must permeate the whole piece. The melodic fragments are related not only to the *action* but also to the general *feeling*—the calmness of the sea before the storm, the terror as the storm builds up, the sadness of the aftermath when the storm's destructive power is realised, the quiet return of calm waters. The form grows, of course, from the story but they are careful to repeat musical material exactly: when an idea returns it is quickly recognisable.

D

Compare the results of the Assignment (i) with other composers' work along similar lines.

Dusk and Empty Streets

Quiet City by Aaron Copland. This short piece for trumpet, cor anglais and strings conveys all the loneliness of city streets at night, their emptiness and their endlessness.

Symphony No. 2 ('London') by Vaughan Williams. The slow movement has a plaintive modal tune for cor anglais which makes an interesting comparison with Copland's use of the cor anglais in *Quiet City*. It suggests, perhaps, the quiet beauty of some of the London parks at dusk. The whole symphony is programmatic in the sense that it conveys the spirit and atmosphere of London.

Moods of the Sea

La Mer by Debussy.

Walking through a Fairground

Fourth of July by Charles Ives. Ives wrote four orchestral pieces celebrating national holidays. He described this one as 'a boy's Fourth...' It embodies the composer's childhood recollections. After a quiet beginning in which we can feel the suppressed excitement at the start of a holiday, the crowd grows and we are swept along with them as the bands play patriotic tunes from all sides. The excitement reaches a climax '... with the sky rocket over the church steeple, just after the annual explosion sets the Town Hall on fire.' (Ives' own words.) This marvellous piece of picture-painting in sound was written as long ago as 1913, though it might well be considered avant-garde today.

General Putnam's Camp also by Ives, the second of his Three Places in New England. As in Fourth of July, Ives is relating a childhood experience. He remembers the interesting effect produced by military bands on the march. They approach from different directions perhaps, playing different tunes in different keys. They merge together with other sounds of crowds and excitement, to form a new whole, and the child in the midst of it all is caught up and becomes part of it.

Tower below the Waves

'La Cathédrale Englouti' by Debussy (First Book of Preludes, no. 10). In general Debussy's music is strongly programmatic, though always in the very best sense. He never resorts to crude imitation even when as, in this famous piece about a submerged cathedral, he is concerned with bell sounds. The bells are there certainly, together with plainsong-like strands of melody which remind us of the life that once went on in the cathedral. But all these details are tightly controlled and made to serve the overall atmosphere which conveys so beautifully the pathos of the title.

Desert Places

Déserts by Varèse. This is music for orchestra and pre-recorded tape (which uses sounds gathered from many sources). It is not really programme music but the composer is concerned with desert wastes in the physical sense and also the deserts of the mind. For a thorough examination of this piece, and of the music of Varèse in general, see Wilfrid Mellers' Music in a New Found Land, Chapter VII.

Honegger's Pacific 231 would make interesting additional listening. Honegger describes himself as having 'always had a passionate liking for locomotives' and in this piece he portrays the spirit of a great locomotive hurtling across a continent. Although this is pictorial music and the orchestral instruments employ special techniques to achieve imitative sounds, the composer is careful to avoid the most obvious imitations. This is fine music in its own right.

Follow Assignment (ii) by listening to Till Eulenspiegel's Merry Pranks by Richard Strauss, the tone poem based on the legends of a

Flemish hoaxer, and *Symphonie Fantastique* by Berlioz which also has a 'programme'.

Finally (and not too seriously), if a copy of the music of Kotzwara's notorious piano piece *The Battle of Prague* can be found, it might be played as a warning against excessive literalism in programme music. There have been a number of battle pieces for keyboard composed at different times, but this piece probably reaches the lowest point of artistry. The trumpets call, the light dragoons gallop past, cannons thunder and the wounded cry for help. Kotzwara hanged himself in 1791 but this piece lived on and, in the middle of the nineteenth century, Carlyle wrote of having heard it 'done on the piano by females of energy'.

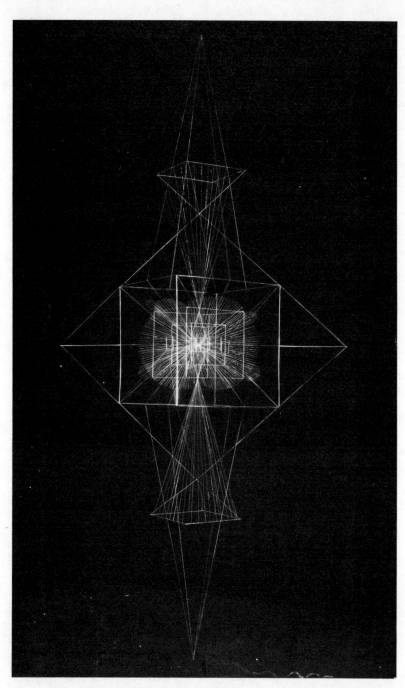

7   *Variation Number 7 : Full Moon* by Richard Lippold (Collection, the Museum of Modern Art, New York: Mrs Simon Guggenheim Fund)

Project 6
Silence

A

When we make music as we have done in the earlier projects, we tend to give most of our attention to the *sounds* we are making. We may easily forget the importance of silences in a musical continuity. The dramatic effect of silence has long been appreciated by composers (for example, the general pause in the middle of the chorus 'Have lightnings and thunders ...' in Bach's *St Matthew Passion*). In the twentieth century silence has taken on a new importance as composers have broken away from the older formulæ and looked for new ways of using the language of music.

In the music of composers such as Webern, silence is used to achieve a clear and uncluttered texture. It is also an essential element in atonal melody, producing drama at points of tension and giving the utmost sense of repose at moments of relaxation. In music of a very different kind, the American John Cage has made silence one of the raw materials of music. For him silence is the eternal background into which 'meteors of sound' explode at set points in time. The sounds have no relationship with each other beyond their co-existence in the eternal silence. Webern's music is tightly mind-controlled. Cage often uses chance operations to decide which sounds shall occur and when. Both composers make use of the positive quality of silence. In this sense silence is not non-music, any more than white spaces in a visual pattern or planned emptinesses between parts of a piece of sculpture are negative. Just as the painter and the sculptor exploit spatial properties, so the composer today exploits properties of time—which may or may not contain sounds.

B

(i)   Using percussion instruments (tuned as well as untuned) together with any other instruments used *percussively*, create a piece of music which makes extensive use of silence.

(ii)   Using the same resources as in (i) make a piece of music 'about' silence (i.e. to convey the *feeling* of silence).

Record all this music on tape and discuss the essential differences between the two pieces.

(iii)   Choose three instruments of contrasting pitch and timbre (high, middle-pitch and low—e.g. soprano glockenspiel, tenor recorder, cello). Let each player select four notes on his instrument (these might be the four open strings on the cello) and invent two or more rhythmic patterns using the four notes. The patterns should contrast with one another as much as possible. One might contain sustained notes; another short, hurried movement. One might move from note to note by step; another leap wide intervals. Try to make as much as you can from the limited materials. Experiment a great deal before making any final decisions about each figure. Clearly, the success of the final piece will depend a lot on the choice of notes and rhythmic patterns which make up the motifs on each instrument.

When the players are satisfied with these short motifs and can play any of them at will, they can create a group composition using this material. The principal aim should be to get a *transparently clear texture*. Never have more than two instruments playing at one time and think carefully about how you use silences.

C

On the accompanying disc (band 4) are two pieces made by a group of four children aged between ten and eleven years:

(1) Making extensive *use* of silence. This piece is in two sections, each containing distinct elements and therefore unrelated to one another. They are unified by the *use* of silence, here taken to mean general pauses. To a lesser extent, what is done with the sounds contributes to the unity. Both sections are built on ostinato patterns around which the other sounds move independently.

The elements of the first section are the xylophone ostinato:

a drum *scraped* softly; random, widely-spaced notes on a glockenspiel; occasional drum strokes; a quiet rocking figure on chime bars; glissandi on a soprano glockenspiel. Apart from the scraped drum all are fairly loud. This material is built into a continuity which is heard three times interspersed with periods of silence. The xylophone ostinato begins each time and maintains a steady pace throughout at about MM crotchet = 72. The other instruments enter one by one playing their various effects in roughly a cyclic order. A single stroke on a cymbal marks the end of each episode. We shall call the whole of this material A.

The elements of the second section are a chime bar ostinato:

and an ostinato on two drums:

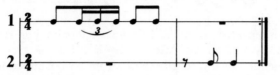

These are used independently of one another but once they have begun they continue steadily throughout an episode. The other sounds (quiet xylophone glissandi; Indian bells, clave strokes, soprano glockenspiel notes) burst around the ostinati in a random pattern. As before, a single cymbal stroke marks the end of an episode. There are three episodes, each one beginning with a quiet upward glissando on the xylophone. We shall call this material B. The continuity of the music is as follows:

A (with six repetitions of the ostinato)—4 seconds silence;
A (with three repetitions of the ostinato)—4 seconds silence;
A (with three repetitions of the ostinato).
B (episode lasting 8 seconds)—4 seconds silence;
B (lasting 5 seconds)—8 seconds silence;
B (lasting 9 seconds)—4 seconds silence;
Coda: a gentle upward glissando on the xylophone.

(2) A piece of music about silence (i.e. conveying the *feeling* of silence). An atmosphere of gentleness and calm pervades all the musical material of this piece. Silence is used. There are several short pauses, though they differ from those of the first piece not only in length but in purpose: these pauses are used to create a feeling of repose. In terms of the musical material this is a less unified piece, though the atmosphere of quiet calm leaves one in no doubt about the wholeness of the music.

It begins with a single loud cymbal stroke which is allowed to reverberate for three seconds. This provides a contrast with what follows (in discussing the music the children felt we should not fully appreciate the 'silent music' if we did not first remind ourselves of loudness). An episode follows which begins with the scraped drum, very quiet, then a single click on claves followed by a gentle downward glissando on the xylophone. A slightly more definite figure in thirds appears on the xylophone:

and this continues while the alto glockenspiel plays

The figure is repeated two-and-a-half times before it is interrupted by a single quiet cymbal stroke. After a very slight pause (a moment of repose) a gentle downward glissando on the xylophone announces a repeat of the whole of the first episode. As before this is concluded by the gentle cymbal stroke. Throughout this first section of the music the instruments have played together—not all at once but overlapping with one another, maintaining their figures while others entered, joining and leaving until the cymbal gave the signal to stop. From this point onwards we hear only solo instruments. The xylophone enters first with a passage developed from what was played in the opening episode:

After a very short pause the glockenspiel plays:

also clearly a development of its earlier material. This is followed without a break by a soprano glockenspiel variant, its gentle closing glissandi slowing down the overall movement of the piece.

The xylophone returns, its music related to what has gone before but reduced to a single line, and the piece ends with a single quiet stroke on the triangle:

All this music was, of course, made on the instruments and kept in the memory of the composers. These accounts are transcriptions of the tape-recording. The essential differences between the two pieces will need little further comment. In the first piece, the very definite use of general pauses has the effect of emphasising the sounds rather than creating any *feeling* of silence. In the second piece, silences are used equally positively but with a quite different effect: they emphasise repose and help to maintain the subdued quality which the composers felt they needed to convey the feeling of silence. Both pieces are satisfactory as musical organisations: they have unity, variety and direction. In character, however, they are very different from one another.

D

Almost any recent serial compositions would serve as useful follow-ups to the assignment. The music of Anton Webern would be particularly appropriate. Listen to his *Six Bagatelles for String Quartet Op. 9*, *Symphony Op. 21*, and *Variations for Piano Op. 27*. Notice especially the sparse textures and the use of silences. Further information on Webern's works will be found in *Anton Webern, an introduction to his works* by Walter Kolneder (Faber, 1968).

The piano music of John Cage will provide examples of sparse and 'open' textures. If possible listen to his *Music of Changes* (Hinrichsen, Peters Edition) and see the comments on this work in Wilfrid Mellers' *Music in a New Found Land*.

Perform *Music For Sleep* by Harrison Birtwistle (Novello, MT1453). Also pieces from George Self's *New Sounds in Class* and the same composer's *Nukada* (both Universal Edition).

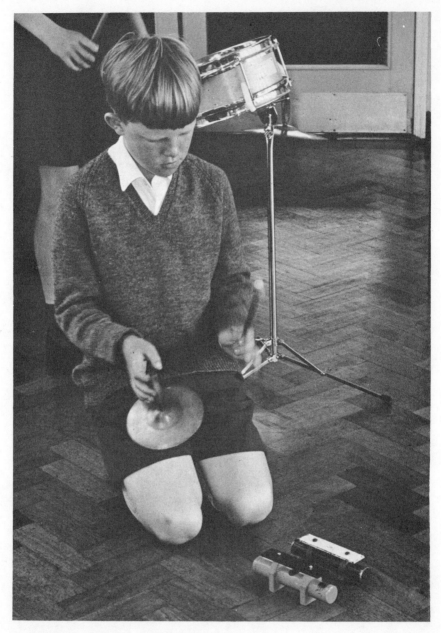

8   Making music for improvised drama (i)

Project 7
Music and drama

A

In improvised drama we often use recorded music, either as a stimulus for dramatic ideas or as additional 'atmosphere' for drama which has already been worked out to some extent. Most of us are aware of the dramatic importance of music, if only because of the impact of television. Music in a play is something totally different from sound effects. Sound effects can only imitate—thunder, horses galloping, footsteps on the stair. Music can move us and make us *feel* as the playwright wants us to feel. It can transport us and make us willing to suspend disbelief in a way that perhaps no other 'aid' to the drama can. From the musician's point of view we must be prepared to recognise that music in this situation should remain an 'aid': to be successful it must not take over. Nevertheless, in our work in the classroom or the school hall, drama may be a rich source of stimulus for creative music-making. Our sensitivity to the drama and its need of music to heighten some of its moods and characterisations will be all the more keen for having worked out the dramatic terms ourselves to begin with. Then will be the time to ask, where is music required? What will music do here or there? What kind of music? What kind of sounds, specifically? How shall we begin the music? The drama must come first.

B

(i)   Working in a school hall, let the class put themselves into groups of approximately five. Allot each group a working space at reasonable distances from one another (e.g. five groups could be placed one in each corner of the hall and one near the centre). Have a varied collection of musical instruments near the centre of the hall.

Having previously chosen some object as a stimulus to the imagination, allow each group in turn to look at this object and handle it for a few seconds. When everyone has seen it, allow approximately $1\frac{1}{2}$ minutes for the groups to make up a story using the object as their starting point. Appoint a spokesman for each group and hear all the stories in

9   Making music for improvised drama (ii)

turn, whether or not they are complete. If all the stories are good the groups might be allowed to work out their own stories in drama form. If there is any doubt, it may be better to choose one story and ask all the groups to work at this. While assisting them in their working out of the story, try to get from the groups some indication of whether or not they feel music would help them in what they are trying to say dramatically. Will they need music all the time? If not, which parts would especially benefit by the addition of some background music (taking care that we do not confuse music and sound effects)?

At this stage we might see some of the groups' work and discuss the possibilities of music with the whole class. Help them to see the opportunities, but leave the choice of sounds and the actual nature of the music to those who are going to make it. If possible each group should make some kind of music, however simple. A decision will have to be made by each group about which of its members should act and which should make the music, though all might contribute ideas to the music and, by this stage, all will have contributed ideas and action to the drama. Do the musicians drop out of the play? If they do, the action may have to be modified. If they do not, are they able to make their music part of the action so that they can play and act at the same time?

The music must be made while the appropriate sections of the drama are played out, and the process of refining the music can run alongside the refining of the dramatic action. Necessarily, with perhaps five or six groups all working in the same hall, there will be a lot of noise. The various groups working in the hall will probably be oblivious of each other so that, providing the noise does not disturb other classes in the school, we should try to let the level of sound control itself. If the groups are sufficiently absorbed by the task in hand, not only will they be able to concentrate on their own group's music but they should also be capable of judging intuitively the effect their music will have when it is heard without the noise of activity around.

The teacher moves from group to group, advising and helping where necessary. When all groups have got both drama and background music sufficiently integrated, stop the activity of the class and see each group perform. Compare versions and discuss the achievements of the work both in drama and in music.

(ii) If a play is being studied, its themes might be explored in improvised drama prior to the reading of the text. For example, a study of Shakespeare's *Macbeth* might be preceded by some improvised drama work on themes such as: light and darkness; good and evil; strength and weakness; power; ambition; kingship. At suitable points music could be introduced to deepen the dramatic experience. It would considerably help the understanding of the play, and the creative experiment in music might then be extended into the provision of actual 'background music' for some scenes of the play when the text is read and acted.

An isolated assignment on these lines might take the form of a discussion on the events of the play followed by the making of a piece of music called *Music of Darkness* for the opening of *Macbeth*.

C

Work by some children aged about $10\frac{1}{2}$ years, the 'top' class of juniors in a County Primary School. The class was divided into groups as suggested above and shown a leather moccasin. One group produced a story about the adventures of some pot-holers who, crawling through a narrow, low tunnel, came out into a cavern containing an enormous figure: 'an idol'. As each explorer crawled out of the tunnel into the cave he saw first feet of the figure (this was where the idea had begun: from having handled the moccasin). As he looked up the length of the idol he was turned to stone. The tunnel was so narrow, there was room for only one pot-holer at a time to crawl into the cavern. One by one they were petrified until all stood frozen and silent.

The story was worked out dramatically by all the groups around the hall. Many used some kind of props, such as lines of chairs through the legs of which the pot-holers could crawl as though they were in a low tunnel. Most of the groups made music for this crawling: tunnelling music, generally short, fast glissandi up and down a limited section of a xylophone or a glockenspiel. One group only chose to keep their music for the most dramatic moment in the play—the point at which each pot-holer is turned to stone. Two of the group made the music on a stand-cymbal and a pair of Indian bells. It was very simple indeed. As each pot-holer's gaze moved up the idol, the cymbal rim was stroked once gently with a metal triangle-beater. This sound was followed immediately by a single, very soft stroke of the Indian bells:

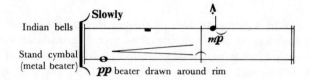

Then there was silence while the next pot-holer emerged, and the music was repeated as he in turn was petrified. This group was able to gauge the effect of their simple but very well-organised music in spite of the continual sound of the other groups working in the hall. When we saw each group's final version, all agreed on the effectiveness of this piece in particular. It was an excellent demonstration of the way in which a little music in the right place can heighten and illuminate drama. And music, of course, it was; not sound effects.

D

If background music for a play is really effective we probably shouldn't notice it too much. It will increase our awareness of the action without drawing attention to itself. However, for the purposes of discussion, arrange for the whole class either to see a film or watch a television play which is known to have had music specially composed for it. In watching, try to give more than usual attention to the music and make a note of any especially effective episodes. What kind of sounds does the composer use for these sections and how do they relate to the dramatic situations? Is music used a lot? Does the music help to convey any particular emotions? Can you classify these (i.e. sadness, despair, happiness, elation, fear, a sense of the sinister)? Which episodes had the simplest music? Which needed the most complex music (from the point of view of *texture*)?

A study of Ibsen's play *Peer Gynt*, coupled with a detailed investigation of Grieg's incidental music, might be useful (as also Mendelssohn's music for Shakespeare's *A Midsummer Night's Dream*). If you have a local theatre, members of the class might write to the musical director and try to find out about the work involved in providing music for the plays.

Project 8
Movement and music

A

Improvised drama can provide opportunity and stimulus for the creation of music. So also can movement and modern educational dance. Of course, almost any of the projects in this book would offer scope for combination with movement lessons: they would provide music which could be interpreted in movement or in dance. Some would also provide opportunities for a broad exploration of themes, following them through in three or four ways: words, visual arts (two- or three-dimensional), sound and movement. This can be well worth the effort, but it is more in the nature of combination than of integration. When we make music for drama, the music can be fed back into the play as an integral part, creating finally a new whole from the two strands of drama and music. The same can be true of music arising from ideas explored first in movement. The music can be tape-recorded and fed back into the movement work. Recorded music is frequently used for movement. There is scope here for sometimes creating our own music for movement. Moreover, if this experiment follows some preliminary work on the movement ideas, then the kind of music required will be felt all the more strongly.

B

Almost anything we do in movement can grow into music. Work on the different levels may suggest sounds of different pitch. The speed of movement can dictate the speed of music. The type of movement will direct us to this or that timbre; to dynamic qualities; to the way the music 'goes on'. For example, as a movement activity with a whole class group we might work at the following exercise on travelling and arriving.

(i) Move in any direction ... and arrive. Having arrived, maintain a stillness. Concentrate on this feeling of stillness. Consider the next direction, level, and so on. Let this lead out of the point and the manner of arrival from the previous movement. Move again ... and arrive. Continue in this way for a few minutes, everybody exploring the space through which movement is made and paying special attention to the points of stillness. It might be useful now to allow one half of the class to watch while the other half moves.

Follow on quickly by giving everyone a musical instrument. Some kind of percussion is probably best. The instruments chosen should each have a wide expressive range and offer opportunity to 'move' about them in a variety of ways. Tuned percussion (xylophones, metallophones, glockenspiels) are obviously most suitable. Claves, maracas or tambourines would be too limited and wouldn't offer the scope we need here. On the other hand, a large suspended cymbal might be useful, especially if a range of different sticks and a bow could be provided. If there are not enough suitable instruments for the whole class, then the next stage must be undertaken by small groups in turn.

Try to recall the kinds of movement made and the relationships between movement and the points of stillness. Play on the instruments (each player in her own time) in any way you like: perhaps a sudden spurt of notes rising or falling, or a more leisurely 'movement' up and down and up again. Concentrate on your own music; there is no need to move when others move. Let the feeling of movement lead where it wants to ... and *arrive*. Create a point of stillness and hold this moment quite still (even though other sounds may be moving) while you consider the next move. Once again let the music travel and arrive at another point of stillness. As we did with the movement work, we might now divide the class into two and let each half in turn listen to the overall effect of this chiaroscuro of sounds. In the movement we were able to appreciate the moment by moment alterations in the total group-shape: we can draw a parallel now between that and the moment by moment changes in the random bringing together of sounds.

The music can be fed back into the movement by recording on tape the music of ONE player and using this for the whole group's interpretation in a more unified version of the original exercise.

(ii)   Another version of (i): everyone makes a *fast* movement to the point of stillness, then another fast movement to a further point of stillness, and so on. Contrast this with *slow* movements towards a rest point, another slow movement to the next still point, and so on. As before, work at these ideas musically with suitable instruments.

73

(iii)   Movement 'conversations': working in pairs, A and B. A moves first and comes to a point of stillness; B replies, and so on. Now with *any* musical instruments, A and B conduct a similar 'conversation'. Follow this by integrating music and movement so that the 'conversation' takes place in movement with the playing of instruments at the same time. For this you will, of course, need the smaller portable instruments which will necessarily limit the music. Try to make conscious use of contrasting ideas in movement, e.g. A *Direct* is answered by B *Indirect*. Contrast levels as well. Interpret these contrasts in musical organisations that are one with the movement.

(iv)   As in (iii) but using only VOCAL sounds.

(v)   Stage by stage build up with the whole class a series of contrasting features:

(1) You are walking slowly and casually from one point to another when your attention is caught by something heard or seen. You stop suddenly;

(2) You *dash* away from whatever it was that caught your attention;

(3) From a distance you are aware that it is drawing towards you. You back away keeping your eyes on it as it comes nearer;

(4) It is now over you and presses you slowly down to the ground.

When each stage has been worked out by the whole class, let the pupils arrange themselves in groups of about five or six and work on a continuity of the whole piece. Musical instruments can be available and each group should choose suitable instruments and make music *with* the movement continuity; i.e. the music is not an accompaniment to the movement but must be thought of as part of the total working-out.

C

The accompanying disc (band 5) contains examples of music made by members of the York Children's Theatre Workshop in their working-out of Assignments (i) and (ii) above. They use temple blocks, cymbals, gong, triangle, various drums, xylophone, glockenspiel, castanets and maracas. The effect is of a constantly shifting pattern of light and dark sounds which come together at random. The total sound is controlled and beautiful, the music clearly changing in character according to the nature of the movement. It can be enjoyed for its own sake as an organisation of sounds, just as one might enjoy the overall effect of a hall full of dancers moving through the space at random yet controlled by the limits of the movement patterns.

D

From the purely musical point of view, children who have brought together patterns of percussion sound like those described in C above might be ready to appreciate the works of some contemporary composers who have been drawn to similar combinations of instruments. Parts of Messiaen's *Couleurs de la Cité Celeste* and *Chronochromie* may be of interest. *Improvisation sur Mallarmé II* by Boulez uses bells, vibraphone, piano, celesta, maracas, castanets, claves, gongs and suspended cymbals. The opening of *Le Marteau sans Maître*, also by Boulez, has the same shifting patterns of light and shade as in the piece by the York children we quote above. It is scored for flute, vibraphone, guitar and viola. Although this music by Boulez is, of course, tightly controlled, its effect is almost of random sounds. Exploration on the lines of the assignments in this project might provide a small link that would make possible an approach to the Boulez piece. However, as this project is essentially an activity which needs to combine movement and music, to follow it by merely listening to music may appear unrelated to the classroom work. There is the need for action.

A number of contemporary composers believe we must return to the total human response: seeing, feeling, hearing in complete integration. The American composer Harry Partch is one of these. He believes in an interpetation of the theatre arts which he calls 'corporeal art'. John Cage has also spoken of music moving 'towards theatre'. Harry Partch seeks a 'ritualistic reason for existence' which he feels the West has lost though it is still to be found in Eastern cultures. In Partch's music and in Cage's association with the Merce Cunningham Dance Company, there are direct links with the kind of music and bodily movement that can be found in the Japanese Nō-drama and the Kabuki theatre. It might be valuable, having worked through assignments of the kind suggested above, to hear and discuss music by composers interested in this re-union of music and the arts of movement and to hear (and if possible *see*, if only on film) some of the ancient Nō-plays. Films are available in Britain through the British Film Institute, 81 Dean Street, London W.1.

The Nō-drama is archaic and very stylised. It derives from ancient ecstatic rituals performed by masked actors. Its characteristic is a strict unity of vocal melody, word and dance performed against the playing of an independent group of musicians—usually two drums and a flute. The Kabuki theatre has obvious links in its unification of music and action, but it is a popular art and very much a live tradition. It is the Kabuki theatre which has probably been the strongest influence on the music of Harry Partch. Pieces such as *The Bewitched, Revelation in Courthouse Park* and *Water! Water!* draw heavily on the kind of musical comedy tradition of Kabuki. Unfortunately, Partch's records—he has issued them privately under his own label, 'Gate 5'—are not easily obtainable outside the United States.

Theatre Piece (1960) by John Cage has links with the philosophy of Partch. It is essentially music of action which can be performed by a variable number of musicians, dancers and mimers. There is considerable freedom in the use of the musical material. Actions are made within given time-brackets and arise from *words* chosen by the performers.

Carl Orff is another composer who has been very much involved with the theatre arts. His *Carmina Burana* and *Catulli Carmina* are both scenic-dance-oratorios employing large forces, including considerable resources of percussion.

Finally, in relation to the formalised movements and rituals of the Nō-plays, Britten's *Curlew River* will be of interest. There is an excellent stereo recording though, of course, the work should really be seen as well as heard.

Project 9
Exploring stringed instruments

A

Quite a lot of musical compositions are inspired by their own medium. The organ has 'produced' much of the music composed for it: usually by way of the composer's own technique as an organist. Hermann Scherchen, writing of Ravel's *Introduction and Allegro* for solo harp, clarinet, flute and string quartet, says:

The fresh rhapsodic character of this work is derived from the surging, exuberant timbre of the harp. The instrument's abundant richness in delicate sounds inspired the structure and episodes of the piece ... The medium which inspired him provided an incentive to create new modes of expression, and led Ravel's imagination to find an ethereal shimmering texture never before realised in music.

Which came first, the music or the instrument? In his analysis of the harp cadenza from the Ravel *Introduction and Allegro*, Scherchen says, 'All this is derived—with exquisite imaginative mastery—*from the harp's natural sound.*' Later he reminds us that Beethoven 'transformed the timpani from being merely a means of rhythmic dynamism and textural accentuation into an instrument of virtuosity and expressive power.'

Some are content to use the 'received wisdom' and look no further than what others have been able to do with a musical instrument. Others push ahead, extending the technical resources of an instrument and, having found these new possibilities, giving us textures 'never before realised in music.' Paganini's extension of violin technique led to virtuoso exploration of other instruments, notably the piano. The outcome of this was an extension of the piano's range. The exploration of the violin's potential as a sound-source continues today: the Polish composer Krystof Penderecki has worked out a lengthy catalogue of sounds, many of them so far unused, which can be produced by stringed instruments. His 'catalogue' includes the highest sound of the instrument without defining its pitch, sounds played between the bridge and the tailpiece, and sounds made by playing on the tailpiece. Penderecki has composed music employing many of these resources. By alternating and combining them with traditional violin sounds, arco and pizzicato, he is able to produced unusually colourful networks.

This project is very similar to Project 1 in which cymbals were used and 'mental catalogues' compiled of the available sounds and techniques. But whereas Project 1 aimed at the use of techniques available to anyone who could discover them, the work which follows now is designed for those who have studied the traditional techniques of stringed instruments as well as those whose knowledge will be no more than they can get by their own investigation of the instruments. If there are any of the former in the class, try to arrange for them to be distributed among the groups for some assignments and brought together as one group for others.

B

(i)   Bring to the lesson as many bowed stringed instruments as possible. Try to include all members of the string family. Experiment with the instruments and make written lists of sounds obtainable and techniques for producing them. Members of the group who have studied conventional techniques should include these techniques in their lists, even down to quite fundamental things such as 'bowing each string separately; bowing two strings together; stopping the strings with the fingers to get different notes'. When the lists are complete we can hear demonstrations of the sounds which have been found and can be controlled. Which are the best sounds? Is it really possible to answer that question? Which are the most interesting sounds? Why?

Make individual pieces of music using the sounds discovered. Work empirically from a single instrument. Those players who have studied the traditional techniques can be encouraged to use the more conventional sounds in alternation with those produced by less traditional ways of playing.

(ii)   Make further pieces individually but limit each composer to *four* different sounds.

(iii)   With the same sounds used in (ii), make group compositions employing various combinations of four instruments. Arrange some passages where everyone plays and alternate these with solo and duet passages. Remember the value of silences in music. Silence can be *positive*— like white space in a visual pattern. Silence in music is part of the composition; it is not non-music.

78

(iv)   Make a group piece (three players) using only *bowed* effects.

(v)   Make a group piece (groups as in (iv)) using only *plucked* effects.

(vi)   Make a large-group piece—any number of players—using only sounds produced by sliding along the strings (bowed or plucked).

(vii)   Make a large-group piece which employs only the lowest string of each instrument but uses a variety of bowed and pizzicato effects.

(viii)   Make a piece for strings (group or individual) called *Music of Sleep*.

C

A 'sliding' piece by a Junior School violinist:

Having decided that the music would exploit the glissando idea, it was then worked out as a pattern piece, starting on the E string and working down with more or less the same pattern on each string, ending with the sustained open G. The music was not written down by the child. It evolved as an improvisation, the contents of which were remembered and held in mind firmly enough for the piece to be repeated without variation as often as might be required.

A piece for cello using the sounds made on the strings beyond the bridge:

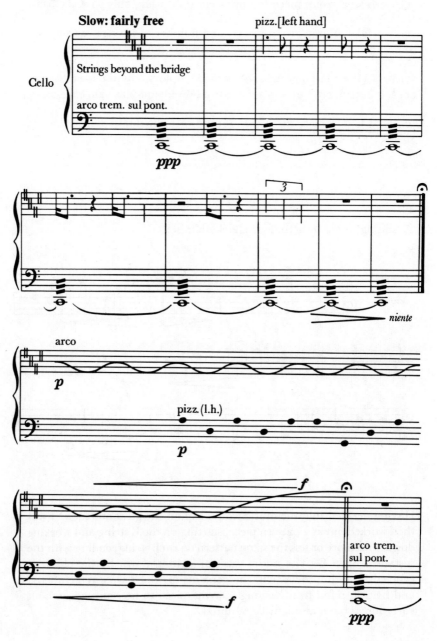

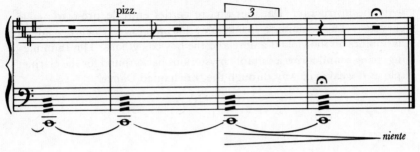

D

Listen to the opening of Britten's opera, *A Midsummer Night's Dream.*
Notice how he uses string glissandi to suggest the coming of sleep and the
merging of reality into dream.

Compare the string effects of any quartet by Haydn with one of
Beethoven's late string quartets, and again with the *String Quartet No.
3* of Béla Bartók.

Penderecki uses some interesting shifts of string sound and colour
in his *Threnody: To the Victims of Hiroshima.* Examine also the string
writing in the same composer's *St Luke Passion.*

The *String Quartet* (1950) by John Cage is an unusual and interesting
work. The players are directed to play throughout without vibrato. The
result is a curiously wistful effect. For a detailed account of this oddly
beautiful work see Wilfrid Mellers' *Music in a New Found Land*, p. 181.
A similar, though brief and fleeting, use of the non-vibrato effect can be
heard towards the end of Bartók's *String Quartet No. 5.* The mounting
excitement of the Finale is suddenly interrupted by this tiny fragment
(the indication is 'allegretto con indifferenza') which has about it a
pathetic and 'lost' quality.

Bartók's *Sonata for Unaccompanied Violin* also provides examples of a
wide range of violin effects.

A rather unusual effect in orchestral music is that of playing on the
four strings between the tailpiece and the bridge. There is an example of
this in the symphonic poem *Amazonas* by Villa-Lobos (pocket score:
Edition Max Eschig, p. 24, fig. 9). The violins, violas, cellos and basses
are divided. Half play on the strings beyond the bridge, the music
written thus

with the instruction 'Dans les quatre cordes entre le tire-corde et le chevalet'. The remaining strings play harmonics to which are added harmonics on the viola d'amore and the bowed cythara. This shimmering string sound forms a suitably mysterious background for the clarinet solo as it weaves its way through the 'Enchanted Dance'.

Project 10
Space and time

A

A lot has been said about the similarities between the visual arts and music. Drawing parallels like this may seem a little forced, especially when we remember that the visual arts are seen *in space* but music is heard *in time*. If you're looking at a small picture you can probably take it in all at once; at least to begin with. Even if the picture is very large and your attention is drawn from one part of the canvas to another, you can always go back and look at parts again in any order you choose. Music relies so much on memory. There may be a lot of repetition— that's part of the art of musical 'construction'; it also helps us to take in the composer's ideas—but you must accept the repetition when it comes. You are not at liberty to pick and choose what you shall hear and when. It will come to you in time and be gone. Your ability to understand the composer's argument will depend to a large extent on your capacity to remember the sounds and to relate those heard later in the piece to those heard near the beginning.

Nevertheless, there *are* spatial effects in music: how we place performers and where we put the audience in relation to the areas of sound. More and more these considerations are offering new opportunities to composers. Artists too, are becoming interested in the time-arts through the medium of moving lights. This project is an attempt to draw closer together in music the dimensions of space and time.

B

Using any materials you have to hand, make several pieces of mobile sculpture of different styles and size. Hang them about a room or a hall, roughly at eye level. When the arrangement is complete, move among the mobiles at varying speeds. Notice how they can be appreciated as objects *in space* but also as 'events' in time because we move among them *in time* and they also are moving and taking time to move. The experience is something like that which we get from music, because we catch fleeting moments of beauty as shape counterpoints with shape and moves on in space and time; combinations possibly never to be repeated. We see control and non-control working together. Stand still at some central point and try to take in these constantly moving 'events' in space. You may then also have the impression of the whole thing taking place in time like a continuously unfolding series of sounds.

Try to relate the experience with the mobiles to work with sounds and intervening silences. Here are some suggestions.

(i)   Collect various things which will produce sound when struck: for example, different lengths of iron bar or wood. These can be suspended on cord at points around the room as the mobiles were. One person moves among these, striking them in any order, some loud, some soft. He can move at various speeds. Can we spot anything in the course of this which we particularly like? If so, can it be repeated exactly? In this way a piece of music may gradually be constructed from the random sounds. It could be tape-recorded or notated in some space-time plan. The organisation of this music will depend upon the movements of the 'performer' in space and in time from one object to another, and the ability of the listeners to evaluate what is happening and to hold in mind the effects which are satisfying and reject those that are not.

(ii)   Repeat (i) using more than one 'performer'.

(iii)   Using either the random sounds collected for (i) and (ii) or conventional musical instruments placed at various points around a room or hall, players improvise freely on the instruments. They play as they wish, undirected, using as many different sounds, both loud and soft, as they can produce from the instruments. They may or may not react to the sounds produced by one another. One person with a microphone on a long lead moves among the players at varying speeds and in random directions, picking up on tape this sound and that sound as he draws near or moves away. You will, of course, need another person to handle the tape-recorder controls. Listen to the tape critically and repeat the experiment until some satisfactory musical continuity is achieved which bears some relation to the *visual* effect of walking among the ever-moving mobiles with which we began.

(iv)   A further development of (iii): several people create individual 'sound environments' inside large cardboard boxes or closely screened areas at different parts of the room or hall. Inside each box they suspend percussion instruments or random pieces of wood, metal or whatever that can be struck to produce sound. Alternatively, they collect together other instruments on which they can improvise. There should be an element of something personal in the choice of these sounds or instruments so that the 'sound-environment' that each creates is his or her own special environment. They now improvise at will as far as possible regardless of one another. As in (iii) a 'composer' moves among the boxes with an 'open' microphone, taking on to tape the parts of improvisation he wants as he moves around. He must listen to the whole and use his judgement about the directions he takes and the boxes into which he will place his microphone. The final tape will carry both the 'special' sounds he chooses plus the background of the other sounds, the aim in the composition being to throw into prominence certain areas of sound while at the same time keeping us conscious of the others. In this way we may create an effect comparable to seeing closely this or that mobile while remaining conscious of the general movement of other mobiles around.

(v)   A small group construct a piece of music, using any sound-sources they choose. The piece depends for its effects not only on the sounds taking place in time but also upon the spatial deployment of the instruments and players. They can also experiment with the placing of the audience (the rest of the class) when the piece is performed. The music might again be related to our experience with the mobiles if an attempt were made to create in sounds and silences the effect of moving through ever-changing vistas, each step opening up a new view of the objects around us. We should 'see' the sounds in different lights (i.e. draw upon as many different sounds from each instrument as is possible, using these at different moments in the piece and in a variety of combinations with one another).

C

In a short piece based on (iii) above, three players made sounds independently of one another on a large stand-cymbal, a xylophone and a metallophone. A fourth 'player' with a microphone moved around the room while the others played. One other person was needed to control the tape-recorder because sudden movement of the microphone towards an instrument could easily 'overload' the input. As well as moving back and forth from one instrument to another, the fourth player occasionally brought the microphone in very close to an instrument. This was particularly effective with the cymbal where the microphone could be held underneath the dome as the reverberations faded. Effects of this kind were remembered and gradually a plan was built up. Considerable experiment was necessary with the tape-recorder. The operator had to become a fifth player. In order to make a final tape which was musically interesting all distortions had to be avoided. At the same time, sudden drops or increases in level would also have spoiled the effect so that the tape-recorder 'player' had to know the order of events and the speeds with which the microphone would be brought in close to an instrument. All this meant very careful planning between the five participants after the initial period of exploratory improvisation. There can be little doubt that what resulted was a musical composition, built up with as much care as one might employ in working out a piece by more traditional means.

D

The music of Karlheinz Stockhausen provides a number of examples of musical effects dependent on spatial arrangements, sometimes of instruments and, perhaps more frequently, of loudspeakers relaying tape-recorded sounds. *Gruppen* is a piece for three orchestras in which the stereophonic effect of ideas flung from one orchestra to another is essential to the composer's design. In his *Mikrophonie I* (1964) Stockhausen provides for a group of four performers to play on one tam-tam in many different ways: two of the group have microphones which they move in various directions around the tam-tam, sometimes touching it. The sounds are amplified and then 're-fashioned' by being passed through electronic filters by other performers who operate the equipment and transmit the final versions of the sounds through a pair of loudspeakers. As with the assignments above, this music is created directly through its own techniques. It is made out of ways of using (or acting upon) the materials.

Kontakte, also by Stockhausen, is scored for piano, a large group of percussion instruments and tape-recorded electronic sound. As with *Gruppen*, the spatial idea is important. The tape part has four tracks, transmitted through four loudspeakers placed to the right and left and to the rear of the audience and among the instruments. The tape sounds can be made to pass around the hall in many directions. At various points in the work the electronic sounds on the tape 'make contact' with the live sounds of the instruments. Stockhausen's concept of 'moments'—complexes of sound standing as *events* in space and time—might be compared with the results of Assignments (iii) and (iv) above where the final composition on tape, though not perhaps stereophonic in itself, will depend on the stereophonic awareness of the 'composer' moving with his microphone among complexes of sounds in space.

Project 11
Patterns in nature

A

One way and another, many artists and poets find ideas or starting points in nature. Perhaps it is a view of a landscape or a seascape which is especially moving. It may be one object in the landscape—an animal or a tree—as in Graham Sutherland's picture (p. 88), where his imagination works around the trees, leaves and shadows at the entrance to a lane.

Then again, it might be some tiny detail, never before truly seen. A composer, like any other artist, may find ideas in this way. Occasionally, he will find inspiration in a poem or a painting or photograph made by someone else. In this case the stimulus to make music is, as it were, second hand.

In this project we try to follow an idea through from something looked at to something heard, and begin by finding our inspiration close at hand, in the immediate environment.

B

Go out and find one natural object which you like. Don't choose too hastily. Have a good look around but bring back one thing only. It could be a leaf, or a stone, a shell or a piece of wood. Make up your mind what there is about it you especially like. Examine the patterns on it carefully. We are going to copy these patterns on paper. Use any materials you have: charcoal, paint, ball-point pen, chalk. If possible try using different coloured papers as a basis. Choose the materials carefully: they must be appropriate to the pattern you are copying and working; they must help you to get the right feeling into your work. If the pattern is made up of fine lines, you will need the thinnest equipment (a ball-point pen may be just the thing for this). If the pattern is soft and blurred you may need charcoal which you can rub, or chalks combined with charcoal, or paint which is allowed to run.

Work the pattern; develop it all over the paper. Fill the paper to the edges, letting whatever it is about the pattern that attracts you go where it wants to go and develop as it seems to want to develop. This is not just

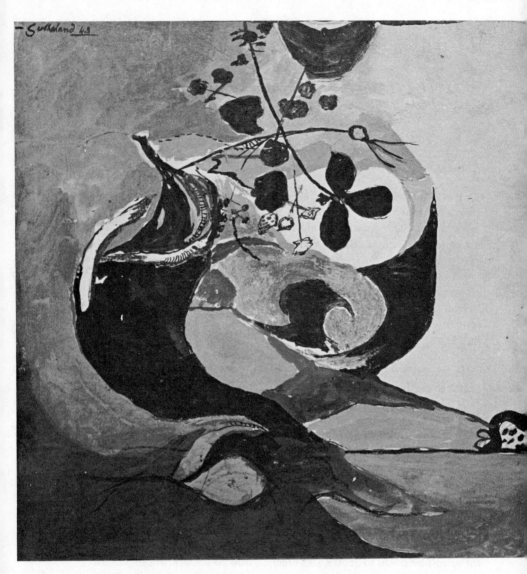

10   *Entrance to Lane* by Graham Sutherland

a copy of your object; it is taking an idea from the pattern *on* it. Ignore the outside edge of the object: that will only hem in your ideas.

Perhaps *pattern* is a misleading word because for many people it means wallpaper or a shirt. We could find another word. *Rhythm* may be better. Rhythm carries an idea along. Rhythm is movement. Rhythm goes somewhere, it leads onward. When we have been thinking of the pattern on the object, it is this quality of movement onwards which we have really been focusing upon. Take a section of this; transfer it to your paper, creating more rhythm with dark, light, spotty movements—whatever the natural object suggests to you.

This directional thing we call rhythm—the feeling of going from one place to another, of wanting to go there or needing to move onward—is found in all art, whatever the medium. It carries the poet's ideas from here to there. We can see it in the work of sculptors as well as painters. It is of course an important characteristic of music. Rhythm in a work of art may be regular or it may be nervous and irregular. Regular rhythms suggest repeated patterns, ticking of clocks, or machines. They may become monotonous. Rhythms in nature tend to be irrational and irregular, stretching or compressing time as it is dictated by the clock. Perhaps this is why nature is never dull. The rhythm you have derived from your object and which you have now developed to fill the paper, may be just such an irregular rhythm. It is no less rhythmic; no less a *pattern*.

Now that you have worked it thoroughly, does your visual rhythm suggest an organisation of sounds and silences? Is there an immediate impression of the *kind* of sound? Which instruments will you choose? Does it also suggest a way of using these sounds? Are there wisps of sounds, delicate lines weaving here and there or fanning out from a central point? Are there strong, firm lines moving on ponderously? How are these directional forces grouped? Is there some overall arrangement, such as a spiral, which might provide a skeleton form for the music?

Just as you filled your paper with an idea from the object, take an idea from your paper and fill a space of time with an organisation of sounds and silences based on the same qualities. Take these sounds in the same kind of directions that you felt the lines and shapes needed to move in. Try to catch that same quality of movement using your visual work as an idea on which to improvise. You need not stick slavishly to what you have on your paper: you are not trying to *translate* what is seen into something heard but you should be following-through an idea which you began to work on in visual terms and now extend into musical terms. Listen to the sounds. Judge carefully the lengths of silence between the sounds. Remember the effects you like. Reject those you don't like or those which don't 'belong' and so take away from your original idea. When you have finished you may want to find some way of writing your pieces down. There are many ways of doing this and they need not involve the use of traditional musical notation. You could invent your own. If you don't want to do this, tape-record your piece. The pattern from nature was merely a peg on which to hang subsequent ideas: a starting point. What we have now is music, and it stands or falls as music, not as another way of looking at the original object. If it is satisfying as music it's worth preserving.

C

The piece of music which follows was evolved by a group of three students working from a visual pattern (opposite) drawn by one of the group. The pattern itself arose from *feeling* the surfaces of a fungus. The resulting shapes in chalk and charcoal are clearly influenced by the smooth rounded top and the furrowed underside of the fungus.

The pattern was used as a 'score', its various sections and ideas translated into a musical continuity. The hard furrowed shapes became the sharp rhythmic ostinato alternating foot-taps with the striking of a section of bamboo. The tambourine trills and the vocal curves grow out of the ostinato just as the sweeping curves of the pattern are extensions of the zig-zag lines. These sounds we have had to show on the score in graphic form. Similarly with the guitar sounds. These were made by tuning the two extreme strings down as low as possible and, at each pluck of the string, turning the tuning peg with the left hand to tighten the string and quickly release it again, giving the effect of four short glissandi and a fifth longer up-and-down glissando. This is heard first on the lowest string, derived from the dark charcoal loops of the pattern, then on the highest string; an interpretation of the series of parallel white-chalk loops (lighter = higher). A repetition of these high guitar sounds is followed by more vocal 'loop and curve' sounds, this time to the syllable 'd'lan' ('the noise the children make in their games of cowboys ...'). There is no slackening of tempo and the piece ends abruptly just as the visual pattern does. Simple as it is, there is nevertheless *musical* organisation of the sounds; an organisation that was only possible for the group by way of the visual pattern which prompted not only motion and continuity but also timbre.

11   *Pattern* by Jean Phillips

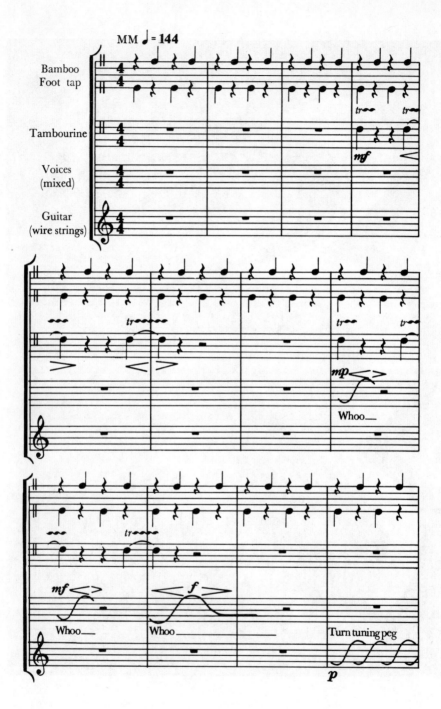

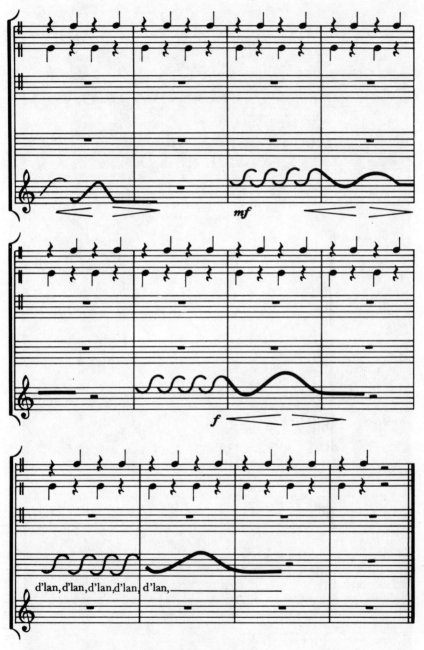

SHEILA BADGER, CHRISTINE BRANT, JEAN PHILLIPS, 1967

93

12   *Reclining Figure No. 5* by Henry Moore

D

Books which may be useful both before and after the assignments are: C. Postma, *Plant Marvels in Miniature—a Photographic Study* (Harrap, 1960), and Wolf Strache, *Forms and Patterns in Nature* (Peter Owen, 1959).

The picture on the opposite page, of Henry Moore's *Reclining Figure No. 5* (1952), like other made at the same time, is based on the outlines and veining of dead leaves. The skirt takes on the leaf-like sweep and gives the whole figure a feeling of direction.

Look also at reproductions of paintings by Paul Klee—he is included among the artists whose work is published in the *Express Art Books* (Beaverbrook Newspapers Ltd, 1958)—and if possible listen to *Seven Studies after Paul Klee* by Gunther Schuller. Denis Apivor is another composer who has been visually inspired by the work of Paul Klee: his *Overtones Op. 33* written in 1962 consists of nine pieces based on paintings of Klee, each piece prefaced by a short evocative prose-poem.

Distinguish between overall rhythmic *direction* and articulated rhythm patterns. Listen to the *Concerto for Double String Orchestra* by Michael Tippett. Notice, especially in the first and last movements, how the music has a tremendous feeling of onward progression which the composer maintains throughout both these movements as a key feature. The music moves on with inevitability. We find this same inevitability in the onward-moving curves of Moore's *Reclining Figure No. 5*. This is rhythm.

Project 12
Short sounds and long sounds

A

It is part of a composer's job to reveal to the listener aspects and properties of music's raw materials, sounds and silence. Some instruments, such as claves, bongos, and wood blocks can produce only short sounds. Other instruments are capable of producing both sustained tones of varying lengths and short, sharp sounds, whatever the composer or player chooses. We shall exploit this feature in making a piece of music about short sounds and long sounds.

B

The following are assignments for individuals or for small groups. Naturally, you will have greater flexibility with more than one player. A group of four would be a reasonable size. On the other hand, group composition arising out of group improvisations calls for group decisions. The pros and cons will have to be weighed carefully. Experiment with both arrangements if possible.

(i)   Using any instruments you have (but *not* voices), explore the production of long and short sounds. Which instrument is able to produce the longest sound? What technique will give the shortest sound? Concentrate on the relationships between sounds of different length and silences of different length. Notes of any pitch may be used: it is the 'shortness' or 'longness' of the sounds which matters. Create a piece of music out of these sounds and silences.

When you are satisfied with the order of events and have practised the piece several times, invent some means of recording the composition on paper. This will probably turn out to be some simple graphic notation. You could use dots for the short sounds and dashes of different lengths for the long sounds. Silences between the sounds will, of course, appear as blanks. These will be of varying lengths according to whether it is a long or short silence which is intended. Remember, we are not bothering about pitch at the moment: the notes played may be high or low at the discretion of the performer. What matters is that the players make the sounds short or long, and leave short or long silences between sounds, according to their final design for the piece. Try to make the notation as accurate as possible. Your eye is the judge. Arrange for a performance of the finished piece by a player or players other than the composer(s).

(ii)　Make another piece on the lines of (i) but this time indicate the pitch of the sounds in general terms (high, middle, low) so that some freedom is still left to the performer(s). Let the notation be as before but add this rough indication of pitch.

(iii)　All our pieces in this project are primarily concerned with short or long sounds or silences, and with each piece we are becoming more definite about the nature of what happens. This time the instrument(s) to be used should be specified and an attempt made to define the exact pitch of the notes used (with tuned percussion this will not be difficult as the names of the notes generally appear on the sounding-bars). It could present problems to a non-pianist improvising on a keyboard: he could either be quickly instructed in the names of the notes on the keyboard or find some other way of defining the sounds he selected.

(iv)　The four characteristics of music are pitch, timbre, loudness, and duration. We have succeeded in making pieces which are for specified instruments (timbre), using notes of specified pitch. So far, though, we have left *duration* of the sounds and silences to the judgement of the player(s), even though this judgement may have been considerably assisted by the dots and blanks of the notation. *Loudness* we have not considered. For this next piece we shall try to control the four aspects of music. Which instruments are used will need careful consideration: should they make a unity by being all of the same family (strings for example, or all tuned percussion)? Should they offer opportunity for contrast so that we may have, say, an ensemble of glockenspiel, cello, cymbal, recorder? The composition will be built up as before by experi-mental improvisation, evaluation, selection and rejection. When a final decision on the events has been agreed, the *actual* notes played should be carefully noted. This time note also the *loudness* of each sound. When the piece is complete, tape-record it and then with stop-watch or stop-clock, carefully note the exact length of sounds and silences in seconds and incorporate this information into your final notation. What is the overall length of the piece? Perhaps you could divide up the paper on which you are recording your music so that it shows seconds in equal proportions?

97

(v)   Reverse the procedure adopted in (iv): using graph-paper to indicate seconds of time, create a piece of music *on paper* which exploits long sounds and short sounds, long silences and short silences. As you proceed try to imagine the kind of sounds you will be making. Indicate the instrumentation carefully. Make up your mind before you begin on the kind of effect you want the music to make. Perform the completed piece and tape-record it. If you have a tape-recorder with three speeds, record your music at 3.75 inches per second (i.p.s.). You can now *halve* all the time values by playing it at 7.5 i.p.s., or *double* all the time values by playing it at 1.8 i.p.s. Does this change the character of your music? What happens to the pitch when you change the speed?

(vi)   Can you create a piece as in (iv) but using *voices* instead of instruments?

C

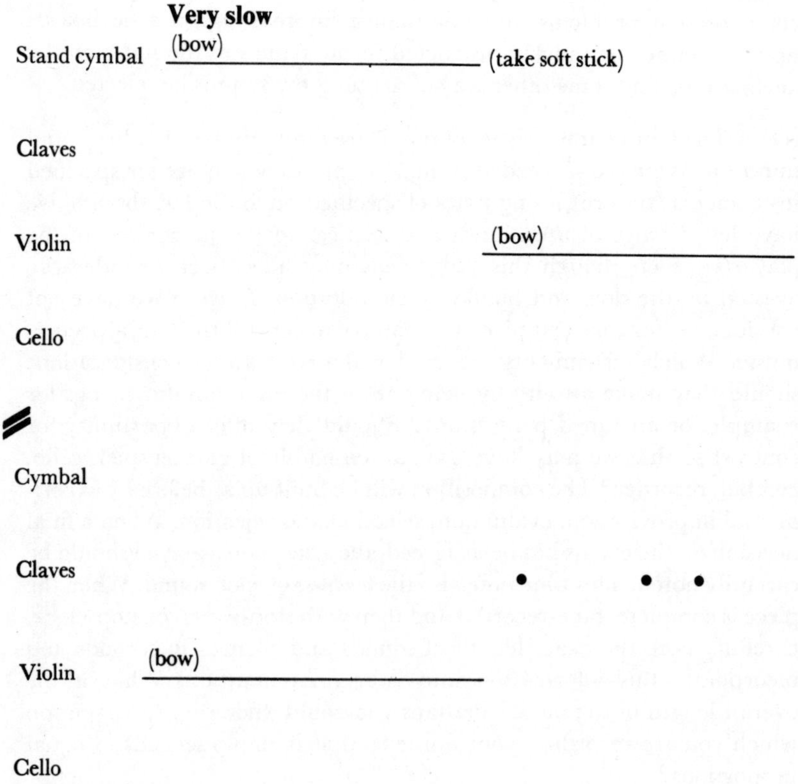

Very slow

Stand cymbal   <u>(bow)</u>—————————————— (take soft stick)

Claves

Violin   <u>(bow)</u>————————————

Cello

Cymbal

Claves   •   •   •

Violin   <u>(bow)</u>————————————

Cello

98

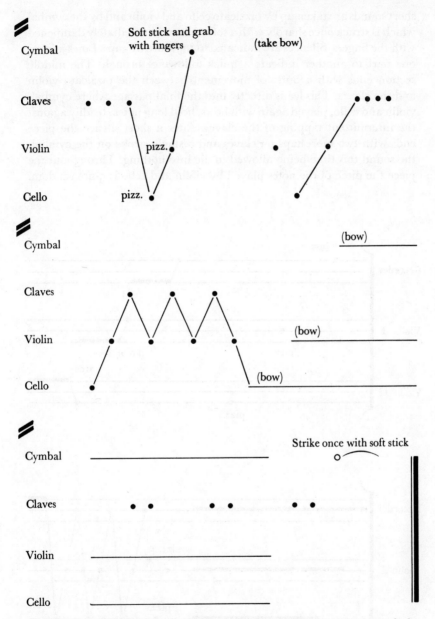

The piece falls into three sections. In the opening passage, cymbal, cello and violin each sustain long bowed notes in turn with short silences between them. After a pause the claves initiate the middle section. The short sounds are taken up by pizzicato cello and violin and by the cymbal which is struck once sharply with a soft stick and immediately dampened with the fingers. Silences are indicated in the score by gaps. Lines joining one part to another indicate a quick following through. The middle section ends with a burst of movement between the pizzicato violin and the claves. This leads directly into the final passage where cymbal, violin and cello, played again with bows, hold long notes steadily against the intermittent tapping of the claves. After a short silence the piece ends with two more taps on claves and a single stroke on the cymbal, the sound this time being allowed to die into nothing. Throughout the piece the pitch of the notes played by violin and cello is quite random.

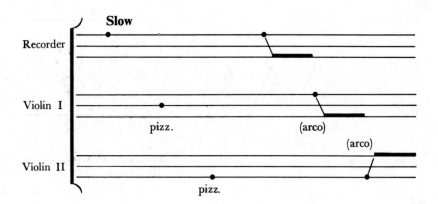

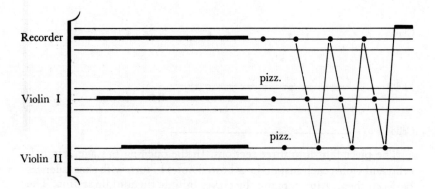

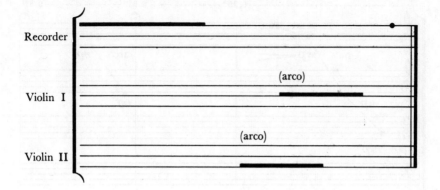

A piece for three players. Here pitch has been roughly defined in the score; the three-line stave for each instrument indicating high, middle, low. It is understood that within each of these rough divisions notes of different pitch may be played; so that, for example, the fact that the recorder part opens with two 'high' notes does not mean they must be the same two high notes.

Piece for String Quartet

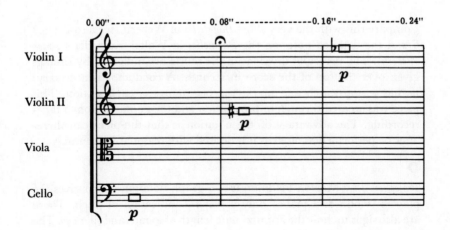

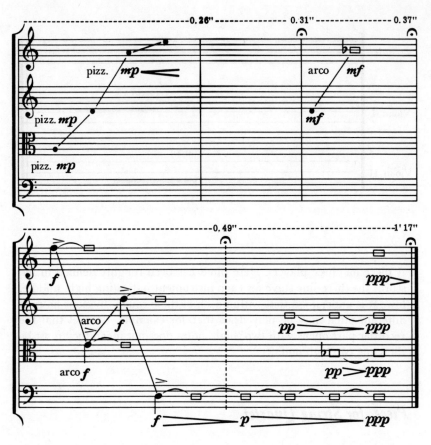

Compare this with the very short *Bagatelles* of Webern (see also Project 6 and the detailed notes on the *Bagatelles* in Walter Kolneder's *Anton Webern*). The principal divisions of the music are indicated by timings given over the top of the score in seconds. A conductor is necessary: he has a stop-watch and marks the beginnings of each section. This piece was created through improvisation and then notated from a tape-recording. The advantage of the notation is that the piece can thereafter be performed as often as it is desired with reasonable accuracy.

D

Projection 4 by Morton Feldman uses a graph notation which gives the players (violin and piano) only a general indication of pitch. There are also signs to show the approximate length of sounds and silences. The score is really to be treated as a basis for improvisation and no two performances can be exactly alike.

Two other pieces by Feldman which may be of interest in connection with this project are the *Piece for Four Pianos*, in which the players begin simultaneously, reading from identical parts, but having begun each takes his own time independently of the others; and *Durations* where Feldman applies similar techniques to an ensemble of wind and stringed instruments. The assignments in this project could provide a useful approach to some serial music (see Project 22). The techniques suggested above have, of course, no relationship with serial techniques, but the resulting *textures* may take on some of the characteristics we find in the textures of Webern's music. Experiment with short sounds and long sounds on stringed instruments, for example, could produce sparse and 'open' textures. We have already suggested that a group of pupils who produced music like that in the last example above might begin to appreciate the *Six Bagatelles for String Quartet* by Anton Webern. Once the approach was made, it could be followed by detailed work on serial composition, perhaps on the lines we suggest in Project 22.

Project 13
Exploring the piano (1)

A

A composer's creative imagination is sometimes stimulated by the different ways in which instruments can be made to sound. It is also given impetus by his own techniques with these sounds. Stravinsky, for example, often composes at the piano because he believes that it is a thousand times better to compose in direct contact with the physical medium of sound than to work in the abstract medium of one's own imagination. In general Stravinsky may use the piano to translate his thoughts immediately into music, but there have also been occasions when these very thoughts arose and took shape as a result of the mechanical properties of the instrument. The *Petrushka* motif, two superimposed arpeggios, one in C major the other in G flat:

may have been suggested by the arrangement of the black and white keys of the piano. In his *Chronicle of My Life* Stravinsky writes about the composition of *Piano-Rag Music* (1919) and tells how he was fascinated by the way in which various sections were the result of the fingers' dictation. He warns us that we should not despise our fingers, for they can in themselves inspire by contact with a musical instrument. Ideas that come to life at the keyboard may otherwise never enter our heads.

B

Begin with Stravinsky's point of departure for his *Petrushka* motif: the keyboard and its arrangement of black and white keys. Even if you've never played the piano before you can put your fingers on the keys, look at the patterns they make and see if your hand wants to fit naturally into any particular shape. Many people enjoy 'playing on the black notes': the fact that these notes stand up as they do seems to invite us to use them. We can forget the others and limit ourselves to the black notes with their obvious pattern of twos and threes. You might begin by exploring the 'black-note pattern'. Go on from there to find other patterns on the keyboard, patterns which are suggested by the way your hand lies on the keys. What can your fingers do? Music will take shape if we can remember sound-ideas we have discovered and can repeat them exactly or perhaps very slightly changed ('developed' maybe). It is surprising how often it is possible to repeat an idea without it becoming dull. Suppose you put your fingers on the notes C E and G. They fit easily under one hand. Play them separately in descending order—G E C. Now shift your hand up one note and play the same shape on the notes A F D. Shift one note up again, and so on, repeating the simple pattern of three notes higher and higher. This could make interesting musical material in itself. You could try making it a little more interesting by using your left hand at the same time. Go back to the original notes G E C. As your fifth finger strikes the G, play C sharp with your left hand. Make the rising pattern as before but this time as you shift your right hand up a note each time, move your left hand to the next black note, like this:

Experiment with this pattern. Repeat it in various parts of the keyboard, high and low. Play it softly; play it loudly; play it as fast as you can. Try starting it at a different point and leaping over gaps, for example:

Rearrange the placing of the left hand note in its relation to the right hand notes. For example, instead of striking the left hand black note *with* the first note of the right hand pattern, play the black note by itself first, hard and short, and follow it quickly with the three notes in the right hand:

Can you make other arrangements of this pattern? If you repeat it all over the keyboard, sometimes soft, sometimes loud, at a consistent speed you will find you can build up a convincing piece of piano music. Using the arrangement of notes from the example above we might evolve something like this:

Allegro leggiero

Piano

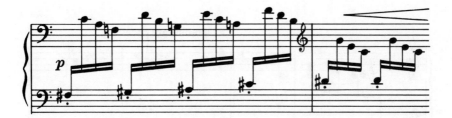

That piece grew from the tiny germ-cell C E G—a pattern which arose from the instrument itself and the fingers placed in a natural shape on the keyboard. Try to find other patterns and repeat them in various ways, building them into consistent pieces of music. The pattern and its repetition creates a unity; it makes the piece hang together. In one sense this is what this kind of music is about: an exploration of a pattern which we see, feel (through our fingers) and hear.

C

A 'pattern piece' based on triads and octaves. The composer, aged eighteen, had made himself familiar with the keyboard by 'doodling', but in no sense could he be called a pianist and he had certainly never had any instruction. The original notation was in literal symbols.

ANDREW WOOD

This is uncomplicated music but it does reveal a sense of design. Notice how the whole continuity derives from the bass notes of the opening four bars. The triadic formation and the octave leaps are the primary materials. The descending sequential figure is also arrived at by way of the octave leap. The cycle of upward moving triads and descending sequences finally arrives back at the note C on which the piece began. Notice too the preoccupation with the low rich sonorities of the bass, the changes of rhythmic emphasis, and the acceptance of some delightful harmonic subtleties, such as the augmented fourth in bar 20, which occur because of the composer's self-imposed restriction of making his pattern on the 'white notes' only. These things are, of course, intuitive but it would nevertheless be profitable to discuss them with the composer.

VALERIE MILLS

This is a piece based directly on the suggestions made in B above. There are, however, developments. Notice how this music differs in character from the examples. The style has been used to produce an aggressive, almost violent, piece. Notice the forceful rhythms at the points where the triadic note-groups are sounded as staccato chords. The composer might appreciate some of the piano music of Béla Bartók (in particular the *Allegro Barbaro*, parts of the *Piano Sonata* (1926), or 'Chase' from the *Out of Doors* Suite).

D

As we have suggested above, the piano music of Bartók will provide a number of useful examples. Debussy's piano music is also a fruitful source. If possible, copies of the following pieces should be examined and the patterns in the music discussed in relation to hand-shape before the pieces are heard: 'Doctor Gradus Ad Parnassum' (from the *Children's Corner* Suite); 'Jardins sous la Pluie' (from *Estampes*); 'Feux d'artifice' (Second Book of *Preludes*). Even if the printed music cannot be usefully studied, it would be profitable for pupils who have made 'pattern pieces' to hear the music on recordings. Listen also to Stravinsky's ballet music *Petrushka*. The passage referred to in A above is at the beginning of the Second Part (revised 1947 version). It was originally part of a Concert Piece for piano and orchestra. In this the composer had tried to portray a puppet, endowed with life. The puppet music was in the piano and grew from the motif which itself arose from the arrangement of the keys on the keyboard. At the suggestion of Diaghilev, Stravinsky used music from his Concert Piece as a basis for the score of *Petrushka*. At the start of the Second Part the puppet motif is played by two clarinets (fig. 95).

Project 14
Exploring the piano (2)

A

The modern piano is a very different instrument from the piano of 150 years ago. Then it was a fairly weak-sounding instrument, a development of earlier domestic keyboard instruments and only just beginning to be regarded as something more than a mere alternative to the harpsichord. Now, after extensive developments, the piano has a much wider use and composers are discovering and using piano sounds which would have been unthinkable 100 years ago. In the twentieth century they have brought it into the orchestra, exploiting it as a *percussion* instrument, sometimes using clusters of notes played with the fist or the forearm, and even with lengths of wood. In Project 13 we explored patterns arising from the arrangement of the keys and the ways in which the keys would lie under the hands. This produced a type of pianism which has obvious links with older keyboard techniques. Now we shall begin to look at some of the other techniques possible with piano sound. This project takes the *percussive* nature of the piano as a starting point.

B

(i)   With your fingers close to one another, strike together as many notes as you can get under the fingers of one hand. Do this at any point on the keyboard and then, keeping your hand in the same shape, move to another part of the keyboard and play a similar cluster of notes. Now use both hands to play note-clusters. How many different effects can you find with this one hand shape? You can strike the keys with both hands at once with the hands wide apart, or both at once with the hands close together; you can strike the keys with one hand after the other; you can play note-clusters in different parts of the piano with the sustaining pedal held down all the time. This will give you a big 'back-wash' of sound. Keep your foot on the pedal and listen as this sound dies away. Begin again and after a few clusters have been played, listen as before while the sound dies. Try this a number of times, playing loudly for some and softly for others. Build all these effects into a continuous piece of music. When the music is completed and you can repeat it, give it a title.

(ii)   Experiment with other percussive effects. If you have a good piano, the sound should cut off as soon as you take your hands off the keys. Use your clenched fist to play groups of notes. Strike sharply the clusters of notes which fall under your fist, lifting your hand off quickly. Notice how the sound makes us *feel* the silence that follows. Build up a piece which exploits this technique.

(iii)   Make a piece of music which uses large clusters of notes sounded simultaneously by playing with the whole forearm. Extend this idea by using rulers or other pieces of wood of different lengths to depress groups of keys. Make a duet piece, one player using lengths of wood or forearm note-clusters while the other player intersperses these sounds with pattern-figures similar to those found in Project 13 but used in short spurts rather than extended phrases.

(iv)   Hold down without sounding, any three notes in the lower part of the piano range. Strike sharply another group or cluster of notes, lifting the striking hand off quickly but keeping the original three notes depressed. You should be able to hear quite clearly the harmonics of your three notes sounding 'in sympathy' with harmonics of the notes you struck sharply. (See also Project 3.) Use this effect in a piece of music for piano.

C

Refer again to Section C of Project 5 and its accompanying disc. The piece *Sea Tower* uses note-clusters played with the flat of the hand in its 'storm' section.

Band 6 of the accompanying disc contains extracts from three short pieces of improvisation by a child of ten. In the first the flat of the hand is used and the player stands, moving rapidly from one end of the keyboard to the other, the piece becoming almost dance or Theatre (see Section D of Project 8). Notice how the piano's percussive qualities are exploited but the music varies in volume; the quieter effects are not ignored. Rhythmic patterns develop from time to time, sometimes increasing in speed, sometimes slackening speed. The piece quietens at the end and the final cluster is sustained a long time.

In the second extract the player works in short episodes of loud note-clusters, each episode ending with a sustained cluster which is allowed to die before the music goes on. There are attempts at repetitions within the episodes. The notes are played with the fingers close together.

The third extract uses a mixture of techniques: the flat of the hand, the fingers close together, and the forearm. It has more design than the first two pieces. The player begins with her hands as wide apart as possible. After three chords (hands striking together the extremes of the keyboard) she dives for the centre of the piano and holds this cluster while it dies. Again her hands go to the extremes of the keyboard and repeat the opening sounds. This time, however, instead of the cluster at the centre of the piano, a rhythmic figure begins about middle pitch: the note-clusters are played with less ferocity and with a slightly dreamy air. This is interrupted suddenly by a short, hard rhythmic fragment. The improvisation ends where it began, the final section returning to the first idea; comparing the extremes of the keyboard with clusters at middle pitch and ending with a sustained chord played with the hands as wide apart as possible.

D

Look at the piano writing in the 'Danse Russe' from Stravinsky's *Petrushka* (revised 1947 version, Boosey and Hawkes pocket score, p. 39). Notice the way in which the hand shapes remain fixed in the passages between figs 64 and 66, and again at fig. 72 and at fig. 82.

Charles Ives employed telescoped chords and note-clusters in a number of his pieces. The piano can be heard amid the frenzied orchestral excitement of *Fourth of July* playing forearm-clusters which romp from one end of the keyboard to the other. On p. 25 of his second piano sonata (the *'Concord' Sonata*) Ives directs that the note-clusters shall be 'played by using a strip of board $14\frac{3}{4}$ inches long and heavy enough to press the keys down without striking'. There are more note-clusters on p. 40 which Ives tells us will be 'better played by using the palm of the hand or the clenched fist'.

Another American composer, Henry Cowell, also experimented with the percussive qualities of the piano. Cowell had very little conventional musical education, but he published his first piano compositions in 1911, when he was fourteen years old. Among these, *Lilt of the Reel* and *Tyger* make extensive use of note-clusters played with fist or forearm.

Much of Messiaen's piano writing tends towards the percussive, though the principles on which his music is based differ greatly from those of Cowell or Ives. Listen to *Oiseaux Exotiques* and *Couleurs de la Cité Celeste*.

Project 15
Exploring the piano (3)

A

In the search for new sounds, new colours for the palette, twentieth-century composers find the piano a very rich source. Of course, this has been happening for some time now. Henry Cowell, living in a shack with little else apart from an old upright piano and his own spirit of adventure, found lots of unusual sounds and used them in piano pieces published before World War I. He played with note-clusters like Ives; he took the front off the piano and stroked or plucked the strings with his fingers. What Cowell did with the piano made a path for the music of John Cage. Cage invented the idea of the *prepared* piano. To prepare a piano we select certain notes and put pieces of wood, glass, rubber or metal between the strings. We must be careful not to push the pieces in so far that they stretch the strings and alter the pitch. Screws work well: they can be turned in between two strings quite gently, gradually changing the sound of the string when it's struck. Coins also work well. The muting of strings in this way produces harmonics. The principle is roughly the same as with violin harmonics: there the string is touched *lightly* at a certain point rather than being pressed right down on to the finger board. In the prepared-piano music of John Cage the sounds rarely resemble the normal piano tone; they are closer to the metal and wood sounds of the Balinese gamelan. Cowell and Cage both found inspiration in oriental musics. The prepared piano may seem like gimmickry—and indeed it could easily become just that—but Cage's music for it is often very beautiful. Wilfrid Mellers describes the idea as 'a highly ingenious means of producing a one-man percussion band of the most varied and sensitive sonority'.

B

(i) Prepare any four notes on the piano and, limiting yourself to these notes, improvise freely. Use plenty of silences so that the new sounds can be relished! Choose the best ideas from this improvisation and build

13   'Preparing' a piano

them into a continuous piece of music which you can remember and repeat. Find some way of notating the music.

(ii)   Make another piece using the same four notes but incorporating other notes which have not been 'prepared'. Use the un-prepared notes sparingly as a foil to the 'prepared' sounds.

(iii)   Choose four drums of different pitch and make a drum interlude to be played between (i) and (ii). This could be a free improvisation by four players.

(iv)   Using ideas from (i), (ii) and (iii) and extending the preparation of the piano, construct a long piece which alternates between prepared-piano and drum interludes. In addition to the drums, use sounds obtained by knocking and tapping the wooden surfaces of the piano. These can also be varied by depressing the sustaining pedal to add resonance when it is needed.

(v)   Hold down without sounding any combination of notes you can manage with one hand. With the other hand stroke the strings inside the piano at the point at which your other hand holds the keys. The pedals should not be used. The hand on the keyboard can gently be shifted to change the shape of the chords, though care must be taken not to strike any of the notes and so spoil the mysterious harp-like effect. Create a whole piece using this effect.

(vi)   Some very beautiful effects can be obtained by rubbing the strings of the piano lengthwise with the fingers, or dragging the finger nails along the strings. A grand piano will be most suitable. Work from the end of the piano furthest from the keyboard. Another person can sit at the keyboard end and help to vary the effects by using the pedals. The strings can also be plucked or played with hammers of different qualities. Harmonics can be obtained by pressing lightly on the strings with the fingers about the mid-point of the string. While the hand is held on the string, the note is struck with the piano hammer in the normal way. This is particularly effective on the lowest strings of the instrument. Use these effects, either on their own or in combination with other instruments, to make a whole piece of music.

C

An example based on Assignment (i) above. Four notes of an upright piano were prepared thus:

| a short ruler | a screw | a large coin | a small coin |

The small coin produced an attractive vibration between itself and the string. This has become a feature of the music as can be seen below: there is a tendency to dwell on the B flat wherever it occurs, allowing the vibrations to die before proceeding. The B flat also becomes the cardinal note in the final chordal passage. The piece was performed with great sensitivity, the dynamics and the rhythmic variety all being carefully gauged to create moments of tension and relaxation. The limitation of the four notes naturally gives the piece unity, added to which there is a tendency for the notes to be used in a cyclic form retaining the original order (see also Project 22).

ROWENA ROUTLEY

The following example, *A Piece for Percussion*, by Catherine M. Alexander and C. Leslie Gregory, this time arises out of exploration like that suggested in Assignment (vi).

Composers' introduction

Stimulated primarily by external naturalistic forces, this piece of music came into being as an extended fraction of the original idea. Our major concern was with sound rather than rhythm, and we attempted to use every facet of the instruments at our command—namely, the piano, timpani and the bass drum.

After listening to a recording of Henry Cowell and looking at part of the score of Stockhausen's *Zyklus*, we were prompted to experiment with the different surfaces of the piano. We had listened to Cowell playing the strings of an open piano lengthways and we found that the most pleasing sound for our purpose was produced by plucking and strumming across the strings.

Leslie kept the sustaining pedal depressed throughout the piece and produced most of the piano sound by making stroking movements with the finger tips across each string area. This is shown in the score by the symbol ✳. We numbered each area of the piano thus:

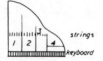

When individual notes were played, the first finger of the right hand was used to pluck the appropriate string. The symbol we used for this was ∓. Usually the strings were stroked from left to right and the sound allowed to reverberate— ♪ . To produce a sharper, more definite sound, the strings were plucked in quick succession from right to left—\.

We experimented with different use of percussion too: bowing the cymbals, using the rasp against the metal side of the drum and making whipping motions in the air with the metal brush, producing high-pitch sound vibrations. Yet after improvising with this variety of instruments we found that we had produced a seriously unconnected and unassociated series of sounds, and in order to make these at all meaningful we had to select and prune.

We reduced the piano playing to vertical string-strokes and plucks (see above) and made a more conventional use of the timpani and the bass drum. Occasionally, rather than strike the face of the drum, Catherine stroked it with the drum stick, producing a quiet swishing sound— Ⓖ ; and to make a sharp explosive noise she depressed the drum skin silently with her fingers and then released them suddenly with a sharp upwards gesture — ⟋ .

We have shown which drum is struck by the position vertically of the circle in the box and the time the drum is struck by the horizontal position of the circle. The circle which is filled in—●—means that a muffled drum stick is used, therefore ⬚ means that first the small timpani is struck once and then

the bass drum struck three times with the muffled drum stick. The size of the circle shows the volume of the drum beat.

Two other symbols need explaining: ▷ the sound is allowed to fade away fully before playing is continued; and ∿—the drum is played very lightly until the next specified drum beat.

The speed of playing is slow and unhurried. We have not attempted to specify a time factor, for we hope that within the framework of the score there is a certain amount of freedom to explore the relationship between the sounds of piano string and drum, and produce, as we tried to do, a balance between the ethereal nebulous quality of the string playing and the menacing build-up of the drum beat: the instruments should complement each other rather than contrast.

A Piece for Percussion

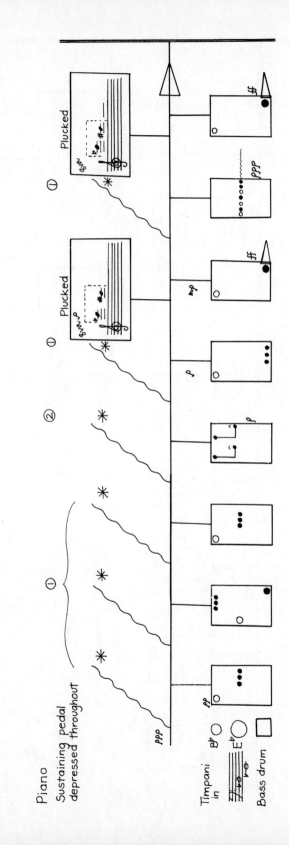

Piano

Sustaining pedal
depressed throughout

Timpani
in

Bass drum

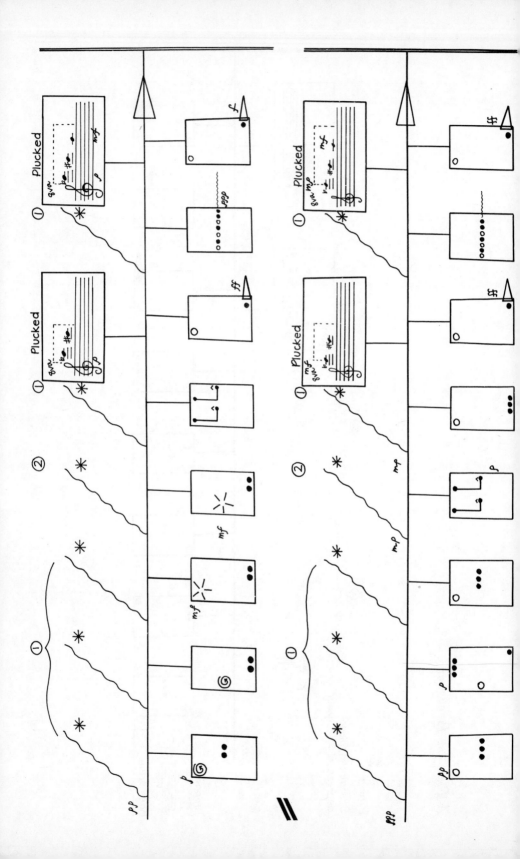

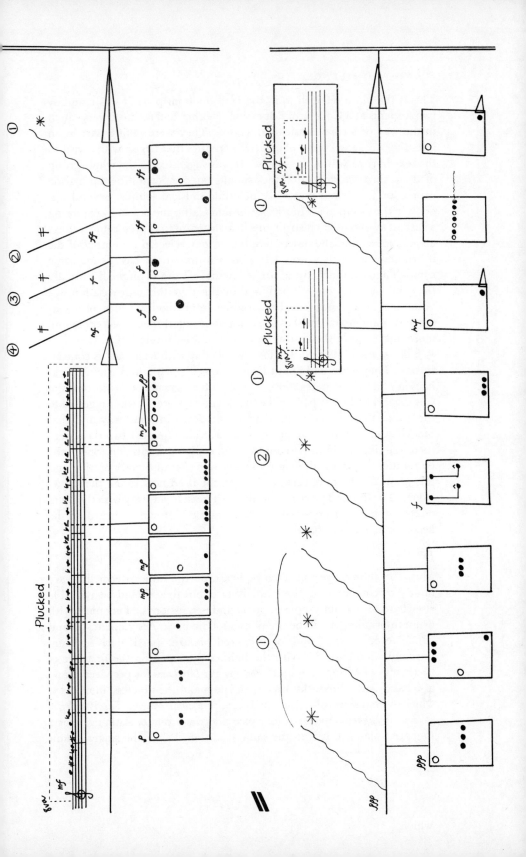

This is the piece referred to in the Introduction, p. 1. It was made by two students at a College of Education. Neither had received very much in the way of formal musical education. They were taking part in an intensive weekend course of creative activities that began with a visit to the sea-shore to watch the sunrise. It was suggested to the whole group of about thirty students that they should explore possibilities for artistic expression in various materials including musical sounds. Several students in the group made music. Leslie and Catherine began by exploring a vast array of musical instruments in an attempt to express some feelings about the sea and the dawn. Gradually they rejected a number of the instruments until they were left with two timpani, a bass drum, some cymbals and the plucked and stroked strings of a grand piano. Eventually the cymbals too, were rejected, and by this time the improvisation was becoming firmly ordered. The original impressionistic idea of a sea-scape was also abandoned as the composers found themselves more and more interested in the abstract qualities of their music.

They worked at the music for a whole day with tremendous concentration. They were told about Henry Cowell's piano music and Stockhausen's piece for percussion, *Zyklus*. They listened to recordings of Cowell and looked at part of the Stockhausen score. It was suggested to them that they should write their music down in some way and that Stockhausen's methods might provide a lead. The next two days were spent refining the improvised music and evolving a notation (one of the two students had a rudimentary knowledge of traditional notation and this grew a little more certain through the need now to use the knowledge). The finished piece is reproduced here in its entirety with the notes on its composition provided by the composers. It can be heard on the accompanying disc (band 7).

D

Music by John Cage can often be heard on the radio. Recordings are mostly by companies in the United States but they should be available elsewhere. *Amores* for prepared piano and percussion is a long piece with drum interludes. It will be useful as a follow-up to Assignments (i) and (ii). The opening section for prepared piano is particularly oriental in sound. Compare this with the Balinese gamelan on the first disc of 'A History of Music in Sound'. *Sonatas and Interludes* for prepared piano also has oriental links, this time with India and the timeless 'monotony' which is characteristic of much Indian classical music. *The Wonderful Widow of Eighteen Springs* is for voice and *closed* piano. Although not a prepared piano, this is in the same tradition. While the singer chants the words (from James Joyce's *Finnegan's Wake*) in her lowest register, her accompanist taps and knocks on various parts of the piano case. The closed-piano sounds are sometimes dry or dull, and sometimes resonant with the use of the pedal.

There is an excellent Folkways recording of piano music by Henry Cowell. Pupils who have worked at Assignments (v) and (vi) will probably find this record interesting. In addition to the music, Henry Cowell can be heard talking about his compositions and the album includes some printed notes and photographs of considerable interest.

Project 16
Shapes into music

A

'Revolutionary' composers appear at every stage of musical history. In the main they build upon tradition. The avant-garde of this mid-century, however, aim at the formation of a completely new musical language which sweeps away all convention. Some have begun to call upon performers' powers of improvisation and in the process they often have to reconsider musical notation as we know it, especially the extent to which traditional notation dictates what shall happen in a piece.

At the humblest level, notation is a method for recording compositions. Later it becomes a means of extending the composer's view of a piece *during* its making, allowing a more extensive manipulation of the materials because he is able to see what is happening over a larger period of time. Then again, the *look* of music on paper can stimulate a composer's imagination, providing him with leads and openings for development.

In the eighteenth century composer and performer were often the same person; even if they weren't, performers were used to acting in part as composers and elaborating on sketchy notations. We are returning in some ways to this position. The art of improvisation has gradually been coming back, first through jazz and now in other kinds of music. Composers are using unusual arrangements of traditional notations and coupling these with graphics as stimuli for the performer. The player *re*-creates the music according to his interpretation of the graphics or the spatial arrangements of the notational devices. As improvisation plays such a big part in the re-creation of avant-garde music, no two performances of any one work need be the same. A lot is left to chance.

Some composers have gone the whole way, even arriving at the signs they put on the paper by chance means. This new field of so-called 'aleatory' music, is perhaps a reaction against the extremes of organisation found elsewhere in twentieth-century music (see Project 22). Even so, the aleatory music of the present avant-garde has characteristics of style which are very like other contemporary musical styles. It uses a full chromatic range; it uses irregular rhythmic figuration; and it aims to eliminate metre.

By using graphics with staves and clefs as stimulus for improvisation we can keep some ties with traditional music. Before going on to the assignments, it may be helpful to look at one or two scores. For example, *Mobile for Shakespeare* by Roman Haubenstock-Ramati (Universal Edition), *Zyklus for Percussion* by Karlheinz Stockhausen (UE), Earle Brown's *Available Forms 1 and 2* (Associated Music Publishers Inc.), and *Octet 61 for Jasper Johns* by Cornelius Cardew (Hinrichsen Edition). The chance element in these pieces is the interpretative powers of the performer who may also have to be an 'arranger' (see Cardew's notes on *Octet 61*).

B

This project retains some reference to traditional notation by using staves with treble and bass clefs. These simple features can of course be explained if they are not already understood. There is no reason why the assignment should be restricted to the more advanced performers, though it is bound to offer more scope to those who are thoroughly at home with a musical instrument. Include the instruments with the simpler techniques. Once the implications of the staves are understood, anybody can use the stimulus for improvisation.

(i)   Choose any piece of furniture which is not too large and impose its 'portrait' on two staves of a music chalk-board. If we chose a music stand and turned it sideways, drawing around the stand as it was held against the board, we might produce something like this:

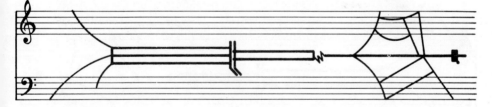

Arranged across the staves in this way, the shape has points of reference with traditional musical ideas. Does it suggest a procedure for improvisation? How many instruments should play? Do they all play at once? Does the shape suggest divisions of the musical content? (i.e. are there points at which new things happen?) Is there a point of climax? Experiment with various combinations of instruments. If there is a good pianist he can interpret the shape as a piece for piano solo using a variety of techniques (see Projects 14 and 15).

(ii)   Doodle interesting shapes and patterns on a *stave without a clef*.
Don't make them too complicated but try to get some kind of progession.
Players can now improvise freely on any instruments, taking their
stimulus from the shapes. The nature of the shapes offered must determine whether the general lie of the sounds should be high, low, or middle
pitch. Don't forget to leave silences at appropriate points.

(iii)   For those with a reasonable knowledge of conventional notation:
Look at the shapes in Cardew's *Octet 61 for Jasper Johns*. Most of them
stem from traditional notation symbols. Cardew seems to be interested
in calligraphy: try something like this for yourself. Start with notes,
clefs, time-signatures, key-signature, and construct a 'score' for interpretation. Give it to a group of players and let them use it as the basis
for a piece of music.

C

An interpretation of Assignment (i): the instruments were guitar, piano,
bass xylophone and two violins. A gong was used to mark the changes of
event. The group improvised on each section until the gong player
decided the point was reached at which the next event should begin.
The pianist interpreted the whole pattern. In the first and final sections
the violins played only what was suggested by the lines on, and associated
with, the treble stave. The lines associated with the bass stave were taken
up by guitar and bass xylophone.

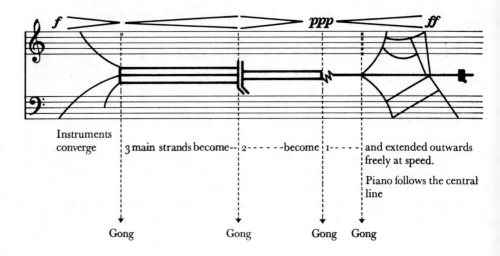

Band 8 of the accompanying disc contains another example of music which grew from a response to shapes. This was part of a project on Mexico. Some photographic slides were to be projected showing patterns taken from ancient Mexican stone carvings. The group responsible decided they wanted to accompany these slides with some music and created their own piece based on the elaborate zig-zag pattern. The pattern suggested an arrangement of three drums, two timpani and a side drum, used throughout in a 'triangle' order:

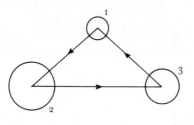

A 'triangle' hand-shape on the keyboard produced some interesting and jagged-sounding chords:

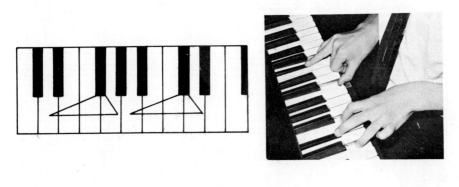

Zig-zag glissando patterns were added on xylophone and rasp with a repeated pattern on two skulls and a triangle. After a mysterious opening section composed of vocal hisses and a slow triadic pattern on a chordal dulcimer, a steady movement begins on the drums. One by one the other instruments are added as the piece builds into a ritual-like dance of great intensity.

Mexico

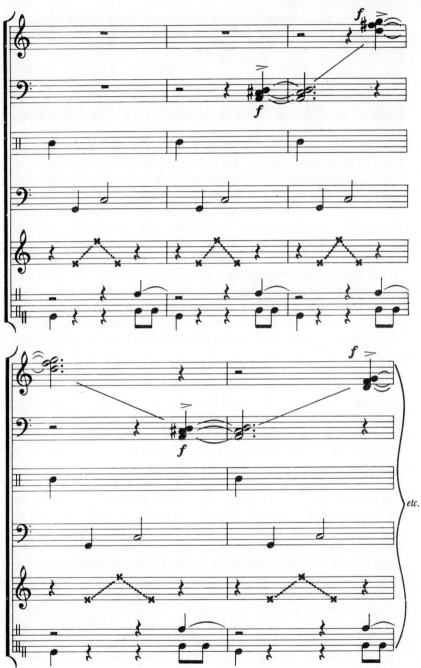

This music, heard in conjunction with the pictures of the Mexican religious carvings, seemed completely appropriate and added a great deal to the presentation of the slides.

D

Try to hear a performance of Stockhausen's *Zyklus for Percussion*. If possible, study the score (Universal Edition, 1960; no. 13186 LW). Written as a test piece for the instrumentalists' competition at the Damstadt Summer School of Music in 1959, this remarkable virtuoso work is for a single player. Its richly varied instrumental resources include a marimbaphone, a vibraphone, gueros, two African tree drums (each giving two pitches), a suspended bunch of bells, a tambourine, a high-pitched side drum with snares, four tom-toms, two cymbals, a hi-hat cymbal, at least two very high-pitched triangles, four cow bells, a gong with a raised dome, and a tam-tam. Sounds are produced in a variety of ways. The player must have hard sticks, soft sticks, and an iron beater (for the cow bells). Sticks used to play glissandi on the marimbaphone and the vibraphone must be 'as sharply differentiated as possible'. The striking point on the two cymbals must be varied continually and the hi-hat cymbal can be played with its pedal or struck with a stick at the centre or the rim, open or closed. Single strokes on the triangles are to be played with heavy sticks; tremoli can be produced with 'very thin metal sticks'. It is all very carefully worked out. A multitude of new symbols must be learned and copious notes on their interpretation are provided for the performer's guidance. In spite of its apparent complexity, the printed score is really a vast abstract pattern. It uses few of the conventions of musical notation and leaves the player an unusual degree of freedom. He can choose which parts of the pattern he will play, which way up to play the score and on which page he will begin the performance. Sections of the score are related to one another in time proportionally along a continuous line (see the second example in the previous project, which also uses this device). Musical material is printed in boxes, providing the player with stimulus for improvisation throughout the duration of the box. The whole is laid out on large sheets of card. Each page is a complete section, and the player may begin anywhere, proceeding through the pages in order and returning in a cycle to the place where he began.

The character of *Zyklus* is essentially improvisatory, the player reacting section by section to the visual stimulus of the patterns. One is struck by the virtuosity of both composer and performer, but this is also a very beautiful work. The many subtle ways in which sounds are combined or lead into or out of one another could only be achieved through the great care with which the material has been laid out for the player.

Study Cornelius Cardew's *Octet 61 for Jasper Johns*. The composer provides notes to show how the score may be realised. Any number of instruments and players are possible but they must first prepare a performing version by working out their own interpretation of the symbols Cardew offers on the score.

A number of composers have in recent years turned towards concepts of music which allow the performer to be actively involved in taking decisions about the progress of the music. This may be a revolt against the way in which the composer over the last 100 years has created for himself the image of absolute dictator. It may also be in part the result of influences from jazz and classical Indian music. Discuss both types of music in relation to the art of improvisation.

Project 17
Sounds on tape

A

So many schools now have tape-recorders that it's reasonable to include this equipment among the 'musical apparatus'. It would be a pity, though, if we restricted its use solely to preserving music we wanted to hear again. We can also use a tape-recorder to *make* music. Many composers today are turning to electronic devices in their compositions and we can learn about their music by experimenting with this medium ourselves.

In 1937 the American composer John Cage, writing on *The Future of Music*, said, 'I believe that the use of noise to make music will continue and increase until we reach a music produced through the aid of electrical instruments which will make available for musical purposes any and all sounds that can be heard'. Over the years this has been happening. Eleven years after John Cage's prediction, Pierre Schaeffer, working in Paris and with the help of Radio-diffusion Française, introduced the idea of *Musique Concrète*. He began by using musical or natural sounds from existing recordings which he re-arranged and altered by changes of speed and by reversal. Since 1950 Schaeffer has used tape-recorders of increasing complexity. *Musique concrète* is so named because it starts from sounds which already exist. More recently composers have begun to use sine-wave generators and other completely electronic means of sound production. All this experiment has given us vast new resources for music. It has widened the available range of sounds and timbres, and produced new techniques of composition.

In this project we shall concentrate on *musique concrète*. This is not 'electronic music', of course, but it is a step in that direction and a relatively simple point at which to begin. Sounds can be produced from any source: musical instruments or anything else which will make a noise. These are recorded on tape and then played back in a variety of ways to bring about interesting changes in the sounds. If, as we experiment with sounds and tape-recorders, we can remember the results and the effects we particularly like, it should be possible eventually to use these techniques to build up a predictable musical continuity.

134

B

(i)   Find out first what your tape-recorder can do. A machine with only one speed will not be a great deal of use. Changing the speed of the tape is the simplest 'effect' that we shall need. All but the smallest tape-recorders made for the ordinary market have two or three speeds (usually, $7\frac{1}{2}$, $3\frac{3}{4}$, and $1\frac{7}{8}$ inches per second). This immediately gives us a number of possibilities. We can record sounds at $7\frac{1}{2}$ i.p.s. and play them back at $3\frac{3}{4}$ i.p.s. which will double the length of time and lower the pitch an octave. If we play the same sounds back at $1\frac{7}{8}$ i.p.s. they will take four times longer than the original and be two octaves lower.

If we record at $3\frac{3}{4}$ i.p.s. we can increase the speed and raise the pitch by playing back at $7\frac{1}{2}$ i.p.s., or slow the sounds down and lower the pitch by playing back at $1\frac{7}{8}$ i.p.s.

By recording at $1\frac{7}{8}$ i.p.s. we can raise the pitch and increase the speed twice by playing back at $3\frac{3}{4}$ i.p.s. or $7\frac{1}{2}$ i.p.s.

With two tape-recorders it is possible to lower or raise the pitch of sounds many times over. For example, on machine A record sound at $7\frac{1}{2}$ i.p.s. and play back at $3\frac{3}{4}$ i.p.s., at the same time transferring this sound to machine B which is recording at $7\frac{1}{2}$ i.p.s. Now play back the tape on machine B at $3\frac{3}{4}$ i.p.s. recording this sound on machine A at $7\frac{1}{2}$ i.p.s. Continuing in this way will lower the pitch of the original sound octave by octave. Even to lower the pitch one octave can produce from, say, the sound of a large cymbal, the most beautiful gong-like reverberations. Lowering the pitch many times can reveal a completely new world of sound.

Another relatively simple but often beautiful effect can be obtained by playing taped sounds backwards. If it is a percussive sound this can be quite startling: you hear first the sound as it was when it was dying away and then move quickly to the moment of impact. To play tapes backward you really need a *single track* (or 'whole track') tape-recorder, but these are not generally available on the ordinary market. However, there is a way of playing tapes in reverse and getting a reasonably good result. You will need to bring together a two-track ('half-track') recorder and a four-track ('quarter-track') recorder. Record on the two-track machine, turn the tape over and *play back on the four track machine*. Although you will lose a certain amount of quality, you will hear the sounds in reverse.

But if you are really going to construct pieces of music from these new sounds you will need to be able to do a lot more than simply record and play back. You will need to be able to select sounds from different parts of tapes, to cut them and join them together in a variety of ways. We call this process 'editing' the tape. You can cut tape with scissors, but you'll find it a lot more manageable if you buy an 'editing block'. This has a groove along the top. The groove holds the tape firmly while you cut it by drawing a razor-blade across a diagonal slit. To join bits of tape you put the two diagonally cut ends together in the block and stick about an inch of joining tape across them.

To find the precise place to cut the tape you will have to locate the 'playback head' on your tape-recorder. On some tape-recorders this point is marked with a line and it is here you should cut, either just before or just after the sound you want according to how you intend to use it. Lift the tape up from the head and mark the spot with a chinagraph pencil, then put the tape into the editing block and cut. By cutting off a small piece of tape—say, two or three feet—and joining the ends you can make an endless loop. Record on to this loop so that the sounds recorded can be repeated as often as you need them. The loop is placed on the machine so that it passes the heads but does not go round the spools. Take up the slack by passing the tape round a pencil or the stem of a music stand. Repeating patterns of sounds on loops could be run simultaneously on several tape-recorders, stopped and started at will, made louder or softer, and so built up into a continuous piece of music. You can record the finished piece on to a master tape through a centrally placed microphone, though the final result will be much better if sounds are transferred from one tape-recorder to another by direct link. A mixer will be useful in helping you to put together sounds from two or three loops. Record all your 'final versions' of sounds on to the master tape and then 'edit-out' the gaps or noises that are unwanted so that you have a continuous and smoothly joined series of musical effects. The editing process also gives you the opportunity to have second thoughts about the position of sounds in the continuity. You can remove passages or transfer them to other points where their effect will be more telling. In this way it is possible to create points of climax or moments of relaxation.

When you become skilled at editing you might try cutting off the beginnings of sounds and using what remains as material for music. The effect is interesting: it removes much of the essential character of the instrument making the sound; for example, the sound produced at the moment when the bow makes contact with the string of a violin, the breathy sound which is characteristic of the start of a flute note, or the initial 'contact' sound of the piano-hammer hitting the string.

All the 'new' sounds you create can be altered even further by changes of tape-speed. You can get speeds other than those allowed for on the tape-recorder by taking either spool off the machine and putting it on the turntable of a record-player at one side.

Any sounds will do as original sources, though musical instruments will give you the widest range of expression. Limit the sound material you are going to use: if you don't it may become unmanageable. When you have found some interesting sounds, construct a musical fabric with them, recording the final version on to a master tape. This might be impressionistic music aimed at creating an atmosphere (perhaps to enhance the reading of a poem); it might, on the other hand, be a structure of interesting sounds for their own sake. Either way this is *musique concrète* and a performance of the piece will be simply a playing of the master tape.

Electronic music is a development of *musique concrète*. Here the original sound-sources are themselves electronic (audio-frequency wave generators) and the techniques are generally a great deal more complex, especially in the methods of 'performance' which often demand tapes of several simultaneous tracks and a number of widely-spaced loudspeakers for relaying the sounds. However, audio-frequency wave generators are not uncommon, and if one is available in the school physics laboratory you could try producing some simple electronic music. Find out what you can do with the generator. If it has a switch to change from sine wave to square wave, notice the differences in sound between the two. The sine wave is a pure tone. The square wave includes the fundamental and the odd-numbered 'harmonics' of each frequency. Experiment with alternations of sine and square waves. You can have fun picking out well-known tunes by turning the dial-knob on the front of the generator, but there are also opportunities for using these sounds in completely new ways. It would be a waste to employ electronic sounds simply to play music which would in any case be better performed on a traditional instrument. Experiment with the generator as a sound-source. Select from its range sounds and manipulations of sounds which you find interesting. Record these sounds on tape and then edit the tape using this material to create a musical structure as you might do with any other sounds.

Further projects

(ii)   If you have a tape of *Music for Cymbals* made as we suggested in Project 1, listen to this at different speeds. Now, using a limited number of cymbal sounds discovered during that project, create a piece of *musique concrète* which relies for all its effects on changes of tape-speed.

(iii)   Using the piano as a sound-source (see Projects 14 and 15), make a piece of *musique concrète* which relies for its effects on speed changes and, if possible, tape-reversal.

(iv)   Take any one instrument and select ONE sound on it. Record this sound and by using additional tape-recorders build up a large collection of alterations of this one sound. Employing all the tape techniques at your disposal, use these sounds to create a musical structure which is recorded on to a final master tape for performance.

(v)   Make a piece of *musique concrète* using only *vocal* sounds.

(vi)   Using notation similar to that suggested in Project 12, work out *on paper* a piece of *musique concrète*. You will have to judge 'in your head' the results of what you put on paper. Use anything you like as your sound-source(s) but before you begin decide first on some simple design for the music: perhaps it could be based on gradations of volume. Plan the effects you want to get by means of tape-techniques. Now, using squared paper to represent seconds of time, plot the actual 'events', that is what happens and when. The score should show what each instrument does and what changes in the original sound will be made and by what technique. Indicate the precise nature of tape-edits, as shown in the following example.

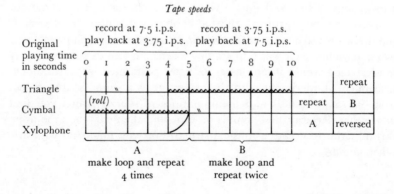

You can create moments of repose by causing the sounds to move slowly (i.e. stretching them out over longer periods of time). Tension can be achieved by fast-moving sounds and increase in volume. Arrange the *final* playing times carefully so that climaxes may be placed at suitable points in the piece. What is the effect of a large number of repetitions of a tape-loop? What is the effect of a single hearing of a short phrase?

To construct this piece you'll need more than one tape-recorder. Try to use a variety of effects but be careful to preserve an overall unity. When it's completed, the final tape must sound like one piece of music. Avoid the impression of having simply joined together several pieces of tape which have nothing to do with one another. If, at the outset, you have some plan of the general direction the piece will take, your job will be made easier.

(vii)   Make a piece of music for cymbals, drums, and glockenspiel and pre-recorded tape. Create the tape sounds first. Any sounds will of course do for your original sources though, if you have an audio-frequency wave generator, you might like to use true *electronic* sound-sources which would provide a bigger contrast with the cymbals, drum and glockenspiel. Space the taped sounds widely and make a feature of *silences*. When the tape is complete, continue the creative experiment by improvising on the cymbals, drums and glockenspiel *against* the playing of the tape. The processes of composing 'from the sounds' (i.e. evaluating and establishing material as you go along) will be the same as in other projects you have tackled except for the presence of the fixed musical material on the tape. Listen carefully to this as you proceed and let your instrumental sounds *complement* the sounds from the tape. The larger silences will give you opportunities for extended improvisations on one or more of the instruments, rather like cadenzas in a concerto. Arrange these so that they dove-tail in with what is happening on the tape. Silences of definite and pre-arranged lengths can be put into the tape at any point by simply splicing in a length of 'leader-tape': so many inches for so many seconds, at whatever speed the tape is running; for example, 5 feet = 8 seconds at tape-speed $7\frac{1}{2}$ i.p.s. Try to keep in mind as exactly as possible the music you work out for the instruments and its relationship to the taped sounds. When you are satisfied with the wholeness of the piece (tape + improvisation) it might help if you worked out some kind of notation: graphics may be sufficient.

C

Band 9 of the accompanying disc contains a short example of *musique concrète* made with a minimum of apparatus. Two tape-recorders were used; one two-track and one four-track. Both had three tape-speeds. A mixer was not available. To begin with it was decided to limit the original sounds to a cymbal, claves and a metallophone. Experiment revealed an interesting sound from a side-drum standing in the same room. This drum vibrated in sympathy with the middle C of the metallophone and so it was decided to make use of this 'accidental' material. Three tape-loops were made as follows.

Loop A: 3′ 8″ long: a cymbal roll increasing in volume with intermittent taps on claves. This was recorded at $7\frac{1}{2}$ i.p.s. After the recording a small piece was cut out of the loop and the ends rejoined so that the cymbal roll would cut off at its climax point;

Loop B: 24″ long: on to this was recorded a short ostinato phrase played on the metallophone:

There were eleven repetitions of this ostinato on the loop. The recording speed was $1\frac{7}{8}$ i.p.s.;

Loop C: 23″ long: the sympathetic vibration of the snare drum was recorded at $3\frac{3}{4}$ i.p.s. The loop was then slightly shortened to remove any trace of the original metallophone sound and also the start of the sympathetic reverberation. The final loop then held only the hum of the drum note C from a moment immediately after it had started to vibrate to a point where it was dying away.

The loops were used to build up a continuous piece of music. The plan was to begin and end with sections low in pitch and without a great deal of movement in them. The middle sections would be short, change frequently and move higher in pitch increasing all the time in intensity. The following table shows how the final master tape was built up. A, B, and C are the loops. O indicates the original direction of the loop, R the reversal of the loop. The figures following multiplication signs (× 1 ; × 4) show the number of revolutions of the loop. The tape-speeds indicate the speed at which each part was played as it was re-recorded onto the master tape. Combinations of two loops were recorded through a microphone. Other material was transferred from one recorder to another by direct link.

1. AO × 2, $1\frac{7}{8}$ i.p.s.
2. AR × 1, $1\frac{7}{8}$ i.p.s.
3. AO × 2, $7\frac{1}{2}$ i.p.s. (original speed)
4. CR × 4, $7\frac{1}{2}$ i.p.s.

5. CO × 1, $1\frac{7}{8}$ i.p.s.
6. BR × 1, $1\frac{7}{8}$ i.p.s. (original speed)
7. BR × 1, $3\frac{3}{4}$ i.p.s.
8. BO × $1\frac{1}{2}$, $7\frac{1}{2}$ i.p.s.
9. BO × 1, $1\frac{7}{8}$ i.p.s. (original speed)
10. BR × 1, $1\frac{7}{8}$ i.p.s. and AO $3\frac{3}{4}$ i.p.s. *combined*
11. CR $1\frac{7}{8}$ i.p.s. and AO $3\frac{3}{4}$ i.p.s. *combined*
12. BR $1\frac{7}{8}$ i.p.s. and AO $1\frac{7}{8}$ i.p.s. *combined*. Fade

D

Pierre Schaeffer's own *musique concrète* compositions include *Symphonie pour un homme seul, Concert de bruits* (1948), *Suite pour quatorze instruments* (1949), *Variations sur une Flûte Mexicaine* (1949), and an 'experimental opera' called *Orphée 53*. Schaeffer has also written about his aims in a book entitled *À la recherche d'une Musique Concrète* (Paris, 1952). Karlheinz Stockhausen is the foremost European composer working with tape-recorded sounds (see Project 10 for a note on his *Mikrophonie I* and *Kontakte*). The latter might be useful as a comparison with results from Assignment (vii) above. The record which contains *Kontakte* also has the same composer's *Gesange der Junglinge*, a piece based on tape-mutations of recorded children's voices.

Musique concrète and electronic sounds have found their way into the pop world. The Rolling Stones' song *Two Thousand Light Years from Home* makes use of both, in association with traditional musical sounds. The 'otherworldly' nature of much electronic music lends itself well to 'space age' ideas.

The Beatles have used techniques similar to those of *musique concrète* in songs such as *I am the Walrus, A Day in the Life,* and *Strawberry Fields Forever*. These include not only the alteration of sounds by speed change, tape-reversal and so on, but also the bringing together of many other sounds such as speaking voices, animal cries, and sections of other pieces of music: a technique known as 'sound-montage'. This technique is employed by John Cage in his *Williams Mix* (1952) and *Fontana Mix* (1958). *Fontana Mix* can be heard on the disc 'Electronic Music' (TV 4046) which also contains *Agony* by Mimaroglu, and *Visage* by Berio. This last work uses a tape based on the voice sounds of Cathy Berberian together with electronic sounds.

Other recordings which might be useful in connection with this project are: *Cain and Abel*, electronic ballet music by Henk Badings; *Poème électronique* (1958) by Varèse; and *Déserts* by Varèse.

Project 18
Exploring melody (1):
Runes and incantations

A

Music is about feeling: it is a response to things that happen to us. The most immediate sound-response we can make is a vocal one—a high-pitched yell of excitement or a low moan of fear or sadness. Music happens when a sound like that is worked on consciously and built up into a large-scale symbol of what we feel.

Primitive peoples always thought of music as being in some way associated with their everyday life, so that the earliest music was tied to the great and important things which needed to be said: wonder, fear, excitement, and the rituals of magic and religion. Remnants of this music can still be found in runes and incantations which have been handed down by word of mouth for centuries.

In this early music, the borderline between singing and the natural inflections of speech was blurred. Short musical phrases would be chanted over and over again, the voices rising and falling in pitch only as much as the words themselves demanded. Generally this produced tiny two-note fragments which could hardly be called melodies, though very gradually they did extend themselves naturally into melody-proper as the singers learned to alternate one two-note phrase with another two-note phrase of different pitch. For a very long time melody was linked to speech inflection, expressing and communicating. Many of these ancient chants were associated with laborious tasks which took men hours to accomplish. Others grew out of laments and dirges. In some parts of the world even today, when someone dies, it is still possible to hear 'professional' mourners dragging out lengthy and monotonous dirges on two-note or three-note repeated patterns, usually very low in pitch.

This project will explore melodies that arise naturally from the words of runes and incantations.

B

(i)   An assignment for a group of about four people: *chant* this old rhyme together:

> There was a man of double deed
> Sowed his garden full of seed.
> When the seed began to grow,
> 'Twas like a garden full of snow;
> When the snow began to melt,
> 'Twas like a ship without a belt;
> When the ship began to sail,
> 'Twas like a bird without a tail;
> When the bird began to fly,
> 'Twas like an eagle in the sky;
> When the sky began to roar,
> 'Twas like a lion at the door;
> When the door began to crack,
> 'Twas like a stick across my back;
> When my back began to smart,
> 'Twas like a penknife in my heart;
> When my heart began to bleed,
> 'Twas death and death and death indeed.

Repeat your improvisation a few times: notice how soon the chanting becomes half-speech, half-song. We often speak of someone reciting in a 'sing-song' voice. Try to make use of this tendency when you chant the rhyme, but keep the pitch low as befits the mystery in the words. Work on this to make it into a definite 'dirge-chant', perhaps accompanied by solemn drum beats.

(ii)   A slightly more hopeful mood is set in the following words:

> A soul! A soul! A soul-cake,
> I pray, good misses, a soul-cake!
> An apple, a pear, a plum, or a cherry
> Any good thing to make us merry!
> One for Peter, two for Paul,
> Three for Him who made us all.
> Up with the kettle, and down with the pan
> Give us good alms, and we'll be gone.

This ancient begging-rhyme comes from Staffordshire where it was chanted by groups of singers around the villages on St Clement's Day, 23 November. In folk-lore the whole month of November is sacred to the memory of the dead; hence the references to 'a soul' and the custom of 'souling' (begging for food on these special days). Originally, apples and beer were begged as a way of getting supplies for a communal Feast to the Dead. It isn't a dirge, though you must give it a certain solemnity. One of the group should work out a tune by reading the rhyme over several times out loud, then beginning to chant it until it takes on a 'sing-song' fashion and finally develops into a tune. Keep the melody simple. Just chant each line to the same kind of tune over and over again. The oldest tunes used only two or three notes and were rather monotonous like the playground skipping games that small children play today. Try to make yours a 'primitive' tune with that same kind of monotony. When you've thought it out and can remember it, get the other members of the group to join in. When everyone has got hold of it, you can elaborate it a little by making some kind of accompaniment. The simplest, and one of the most ancient ideas for accompaniment, would be to have a couple of singers intoning a 'drone' while the main group chant the rhyme. If the drone group take whatever turns out to be the *lowest* note of the tune and sing that only in long, sustained notes underneath the melody over and over again (perhaps to the words 'A soul——! A soul——!'), you'll have a satisfactory drone. Think of the sound of bagpipes. Drones are found in a lot of ancient and oriental music, especially in songs about heaven or hell or the spirits of the dead, possibly because drones symbolised eternity.

You can try more elaborations on this chant. Keep the drone going underneath but let one other singer from the main group add simple harmonies *above* the tune, like a descant, as people sometimes do when *Abide with me* is sung at a football match. You can make the drone more bagpipe-like as well. Think of the note on which you are droning already as *doh*; now divide the group who are singing the drone and let half pitch the note *soh* (five notes above the *doh*). With the group divided, keep the two notes going side-by-side on the words 'A soul——! A soul——!' Add a simple and regular drum beat as a group of singers might have done in the past, trudging from village to village.

(iii)   Make a version of this work-song:

> Stormey's dead, that good old man—
> *To my ay, Stormalong!*
> Stormey he is dead and gone
> *Ay, ay, ay, Mister Stormalong!*
>
> Stormey's dead and gone to rest—
> *To my ay, Stormalong!*
> Of all these skippers he was best—
> *Ay, ay, ay, Mister Stormalong!*

We dug his grave with a silver spade—
To my ay, Stormalong!
His shroud of softest silk was made—
Ay, ay, ay, Mister Stormalong!

I wish I was old Stormey's son—
To my ay, Stormalong!
I'd build a ship a thousand ton—
Ay, ay, ay, Mister Stormalong!

I'd load her deep with wine and rum—
To my ay, Stormalong!
And all my shellbacks should have some—
Ay, ay, ay, Mister Stormalong!

This very beautiful old song is, of course, a sea-shanty. Like all other work-songs, shanties helped men to pull together or to tackle other forms of hard manual work which required a concerted effort. Try to get this feeling of strength into the italicised lines. This refrain would have been sung by the main body of workers (in this case sailors) while the shanty-man sang the first and third lines alone. Most of the old shanties had melancholy tunes, perhaps arising out of the loneliness of those who sang them. You can find the same sad loneliness in the work songs and spirituals of the American Negroes.

C

The following is a setting of the *Souling Song* in Assignment (ii) above. It was made by an eleven-year-old child in the top class of a Junior School. The child read the verse through once or twice and was encouraged to cultivate a sing-song manner of reading ('as you might recite a skipping rhyme'). At the third reading the voice began to focus around middle C for the main part of each line, dropping to a low sound of indefinite pitch for the final syllable:

A soul! A soul! A soul - cake, I pray, good miss - es, a soul - cake,

With a bit of encouragement the low note began to take on a more definite pitch and soon became the low G:

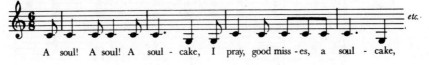

A soul! A soul! A soul - cake, I pray, good miss - es, a soul - cake,

145

Another voice was added, descanting above the original 'primitive' two-note melody. Notice how the second voice naturally pulls right down to the low G rather than remaining a third above the original melody as one might at first expect:

Various elaborations were made:

Finally a drone was added and a drum beat:

D

You can hear some ancient chants on the first record of 'The History of Music in Sound'.

'Frost and Fire: A Calendar of Ceremonial Folk-songs' is a fine recording of the Watersons, a group of folk-singers from the North of England. This disc will provide a number of interesting examples for following-up the assignments. Track 3 on the second side has an old setting of the *Souling Song*. Its little three-note tune is described as 'one of the most primitive we have'. The words differ slightly from those of the version we give in this project. The final song on side one of 'Frost and Fire' is

Hal-an-Tow, a song for the procession which was once part of the old May Games ushering in the summer. The song is accompanied by a drum and will make a useful comparison with results from Assignments (i) and (ii).

Project 19
Exploring melody (2):
Pentatonic patterns

A

The indefinitely repeated two-note and three-note chants which are the oldest melodies we know eventually moved into another stage where the short phrases were extended, by a natural process of growth, into sequences of pitches which *go on*. So a tune made out of the notes A C D might be extended by singing the same phrase a little lower on the notes D F G.

Then these three-note patterns spread into five-note patterns.

This five-note formula is found in ancient music from many different parts of the world, and although there are many forms of the pentatonic (five-note) scale, they all have certain characteristics in common, chiefly the absence of semitones and a 'gap' of a third somewhere in the series. This formula became a world language—the first *classical* music. Of course, the music came first, not the scale. Like all other scales, this one arose from the phrases men and women sang naturally.

Apart from the stabilising of world music in the pentatonic formula, another important discovery had been made when men developed this power of creating sequences of notes. They could now unfold one phrase from another, making the music go on in decorative and symmetrical structures which were delightful in themselves. So we had melody proper. This was indeed a cultural advance on the older work-songs and ritual chants which could only repeat tiny phrases endlessly and which were often tied to the rhythm of the work or the monotonous body-sway of the mourners or dancers. This breaking away from the metres of ritual and dance produced music of endless melodic unfolding and elaboration, unfettered by repeated rhythmic patterns. The melody flowed onwards with the words, or simply with the urge to create *musical* structures. We can find numerous examples of this kind of thing in the music of India as well as in Hebrew and Gregorian melodies.

In recent years composers in the West have looked to the Orient for a new source of melodic inspiration. Of course, it's really a very ancient source but our western development of harmony has tended to obscure the artistic possibilities in music which *grows* in lines of notes not generating harmonic tensions and which is unfettered by metres of the kind we've become used to.

B

(i)   Make a long, 'unwinding' melody for the recorder (or oboe, or clarinet, or flute) using only the notes C D E G A. You can repeat any of these notes in the upper octaves so that in all you have these notes to use:

Let the melody *flow*, starting low in pitch and gradually rising to make a climax on a high note. Then let it fall again gradually, coming to rest at a low pitch. Try to get a sense of continual unfolding and let the music take you where it wants to go.

(ii)   Play this pentatonic scale on the piano.

If you started on F♯, which other notes would you need to make a pentatonic scale which has the same sound-pattern as the one which begins on C? Find this F♯ pentatonic scale by trial on the keyboard and, when you've found it, see if you can use it to play the following well-known tunes. They're all pentatonic tunes so you'll need only the five notes you've found. Pick the tunes out and memorise them:
  (1) *The Skye Boat Song*
  (2) *Auld Lang Syne*
  (3) *Ye Banks and Braes O' Bonnie Doon*
  (4) *The Campbells are Comin'*
  (5) *The Hundred Pipers*

Which country do these songs come from? You'll find most of them in the New National Song Book. If you don't already know them, learn them from the book and then see if you can pick them out on your F♯ pentatonic scale. You may occasionally need a note that isn't in your scale but these odd notes are only decorations: all these tunes are basically pentatonic.

Here are some more songs (also in the New National Song Book). They are all essentially pentatonic, though some have occasional 'decoration notes'. If you are able to read the music, work out from the notes the pentatonic scale which each song uses. For example, in this song, *I'll bid my Heart be still*

the note B which occurs three times is only a decoration. The first phrase then gives us c′ (B) A G E D (D E G), which we can see is the pentatonic scale on C—C D E G A, and the rest of the song is built on this. Can you find the scales of these songs:

(1) *The Flowers of the Forest*

(2) *A Man's a Man for a' that*

(3) *Leezie Lindsay*

(4) *Will ye no come back again?*

(5) *Remember the Glories of Erin the Brave*

(6) *O Bay of Dublin*

(7) *The Songs Erin Sings*

Make a collection of pentatonic songs. If they are truly pentatonic you'll be able to play them all on F♯ pentatonic notes.

(iii) Experiment with two different pentatonic scales at once. You could use C pentatonic and F♯ pentatonic on the piano, perhaps making a duet improvised by two players. Alternatively, two players could make a duo for recorder and glockenspiel. You would need the fully *chromatic* glockenspiel so that the player could use the 'black' notes only while the recorder used, say, the C pentatonic.

(iv) Make pieces for two chromatic glockenspiels but this time let both instruments draw on notes from either or both pentatonic scales. The following notes will be available:

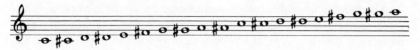

If you have instruments with removable bars it will help to take off all Fs and Bs. If you can't take the bars off, stick small pieces of paper on to these notes to remind you not to use them. First make a piece which unfolds and unwinds like the recorder tune you made in Assignment (i). Let it start quietly with both parts low in pitch, rising gradually to high climax notes and then curling downwards, getting quieter as it comes to rest on low notes once more.

Then make a piece where one player starts and the other follows using the same rhythm patterns (though not necessarily the same notes). The second player starts after a short phrase by the first player and must listen hard to the rhythmic patterns of player 1 so that he can 'imitate them 'in canon' as he goes along. Work on this piece and see if it is possible to remember exactly where it goes so that you can repeat it.

(v)   In Project 18 we used drones as accompaniments to simple tunes. Play C and G together on chime bars or metallophone and keep this going as a drone while someone else improvises on a xylophone using C pentatonic, for example:

Now play the same two-note drone in *repeated* notes on the xylophone while someone else improvises on a chromatic glockenspiel using F♯ pentatonic. For example:

Another ancient form of accompaniment was the OSTINATO. This word means obstinate or persistent. It refers to a short phrase of a few notes only which is repeated persistently, giving the impression of an obstinate refusal to move on to anything else. This is a pentatonic ostinato:

If one player keeps that going over and over again, another (or more than one) can improvise over it using a pentatonic series: the whole thing will fit together like a primitive band.

(vi)   Here are some other pentatonic scales. Use them to make music. Do you find any particular instruments more suited than others for making music in these scales?

Japanese pentatonic scales:

C

An example of a long melody from Assignment (i):

An example from Assignment (iii):

D

A great many folk-songs, especially those from Scotland and Ireland, are pentatonic and might be used as a follow-up to the assignments. They could be learned by a group of singers and arranged with accompaniments (also pentatonic) for tuned-percussion with vocal drones or stringed instrument drones.

Further ideas for extending ostinato accompaniments will be found in Carl Orff's *Music for Children* (intended for small children but easily adaptable for use by older groups).

Play the pentatonic pieces in Bartók's *Mikrokosmos* (Boosey and Hawkes): vol. II, p. 27; vol. III, p. 22; vol. V, pp. 10 and 13. Reasonably advanced pupils might take these as models and compose (by improvisation first) similar short piano pieces.

There are some oriental pentatonic melodies on the first record of the 'History of Music in Sound'.

Many twentieth-century composers have turned to pentatonicism and other oriental-sounding scales in order to break with western harmonic traditions. This often produces a freshness and vitality, a clarity of line and texture which other western music lacks. Debussy's piano music will provide some examples ('Jimbo's Lullaby', 'Serenade of the Doll'—both in *Children's Corner;* and 'Pagodes' from *Estampes*). In the music of John Cage there are examples of a modern composer's use of 'primitive' techniques, including ostinati and pentatonic-oriental tonalities. For further references to Cage and others, see Wilfrid Mellers' *The Resources of Music* (*Life Cycle* contains pentatonic passages, notably the second movement 'Sun-Song').

There are a number of pentatonic melodies in pop music. Two recent examples that come to mind are *Tomorrow Never Knows* by the Beatles and Dylan's *The Mighty Quinn*.

Listen also to *Syrinx* by Debussy and *The Lark Ascending* for violin and orchestra by Vaughan Williams. Although these are not pentatonic pieces, the long, unwinding melodies may serve as useful comparisons with the assignments above.

Project 20
Word sounds

A

The voice is the oldest musical instrument and speech-melody (tiny fragments of song growing from the natural inflection of spoken words) the oldest music. In Project 18 we experimented with these ancient forms of two-note and three-note melody. Working along somewhat different lines we shall now try to use word-inflection, and other vocal sounds arising from words, as a source of *material* for music, not in a harking-back to primitive cultures but in a search for new sonorities. We shall use this new material in much the same way as we might use selected sounds from a cymbal or a violin or a group of 'prepared' notes on a piano (see Projects 1, 9, and 15). In a sense this will be music for 'prepared' voices because we shall choose certain sounds in accordance with a pre-arranged limitation. This limitation will be the subject of the music *expressed in one word*. The word will provide a variety of sounds and these sounds will become the basis of the musical material.

B

(i)   An assignment for the whole class group: make a piece of music for voices on the subject of WINTER. Choose a word which can be agreed by all taking part as characteristic of winter; for example, the word 'ice'. By experiment, build up a catalogue of all the ways you can find of uttering this word (high and low pitch, loud, soft, whispers, drawn out, snapped off, and so on). Eliminate any that seem unsuitable as an expression of coldness; for example, you may feel that low-pitched utterances of the word 'ice' are too warm in feeling. Is there any correlation between coldness and sharp, high-pitched sounds? Arrange the class in any number of groups, each group taking a different version of the word as their 'sound material'. The groups may be arranged in a circle around a hall or large room (the spatial effect of sounds coming from different parts of the hall could prove musically interesting: see also Project 10). One person can now stand in the centre of the circle and create a musical continuity from the available material. He can call on sounds from any group by pointing. They can be made to 'sound' separately or together. He can experiment with this material as he might with any other sounds, building up his composition step by step from what he hears, selecting and rejecting, revising and confirming as he goes along. Remember the value of silences. Alternatively, the whole pattern could be worked out by class discussion, trial and error; everyone contributing ideas, the teacher guiding the gradual building-up of the music.

When a continuity of satisfactory wholeness has been worked out, the piece should be performed and tape-recorded so that the total effect may be appreciated by all taking part.

(ii)　If there is movement work in the curriculum, the result of Assignment (i) could be used as a starting point for a movement piece about winter. Better still, the sound and the movement could be evolved together, each small group working out its movements and sounds as a unity and the whole class then building up a large-scale piece. The movement and the sound should be integrated, not simply combined; that is, you should try to avoid working out the movement and then adding the sounds as an accompaniment.

(iii)　Make another piece as in (i) or (ii) on the subject of DARKNESS. Extend the expressive resources by using a tape-recorder and altering the sounds with tape-speed changes (see Project 17).

C
Halloween

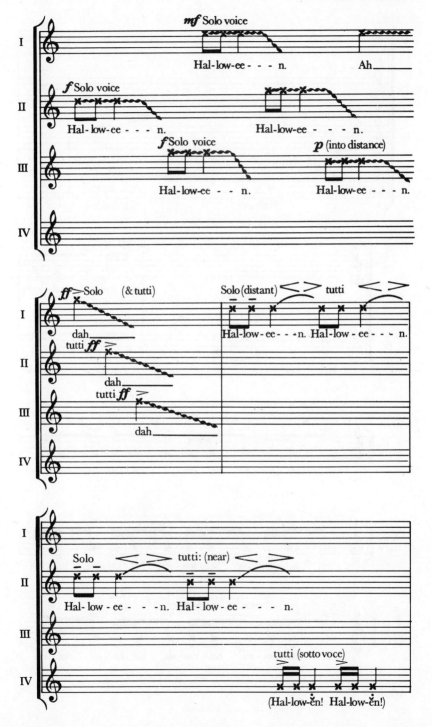

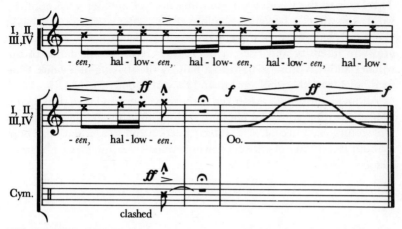

MISS MARGARET HORSLEY AND CLASS 3x, FARSLEY FARFIELD C.P. SCHOOL, PUDSEY, YORK-SHIRE, NOVEMBER 1966.

This score shows the vocal sounds in a large-scale piece of sound and movement made by a class of children in a Junior School near Leeds. The piece is really Theatre and should be seen to be appreciated fully. However, the organisation of the sounds is completely musical so that it is possible to consider this aspect on its own.

A story was evolved in movement. It concerned various groups of witches meeting at night, casting their spells and finally disappearing as dawn comes. The musical organisation grew out of the movement. It was decided to limit the sounds to vocal noises. A further limitation was imposed by looking for one word which would sum up the feelings of the dance. The word *Halloween* was chosen and this became the musical material in much the same way as one might choose a cymbal or a drum. Various ways of saying the word were developed to fit in with the movement which was already being fashioned. The final version falls into two sections. The first opens with a howl from the whole group. After a pause, four 'soloists' snarl the word 'halloween' in high pitched and quavering voices. The sounds come from different parts of the hall, exploiting both the spatial effects and the echo. The last, distant 'halloween' becomes a high-pitched yell into which all the other voices are joined as it slides down in a long sweep. This leads to the second section in which solo voices alternate with chorus groups, stretching the word 'halloween' across upward and downward glissandi. After four of these, a group of boys' voices is joined into the pattern, inter-jecting 'halloween' several times in a short, sharp and breathy style.

This leads to the whole group snarling out yet another version of the word: this time it becomes, 'halloweee'*nă*'. After a silence, all begin chanting 'halloweenhalloweenhalloweenhalloween ...'. The chant grows in intensity and rises in pitch. This is the ritual dance of the witches and it is only brought to a halt by the striking of a clock. One final howl from the whole group and they are gone.

Although the sounds are linked to the movement and used principally to heighten the witch-like effect of spell-casting, the pattern made by these sounds has musical form. It has direction and recapitulation. There is about it a feeling of wholeness which makes the sound-pattern satisfactory in itself.

Project 21
Notes, modes and rows (1)

A

The first indispensable requirement of music is a series of notes which stand in some recognisable relation to one another in respect of pitch.

PARRY

The old scales on which most of our music is based grew naturally out of the fragments of melody people sang. Looking back in time it is clear that at certain periods many different peoples used similar scale patterns. We can see, for example, that the pentatonic formula (see Project 19) was the first real world-language of music; but to say that all these people 'used the pentatonic scale' is an abstraction after the event. To the people who used it, that arrangement of sounds into a pattern was instinctive.

The beginnings of high civilisation carried music beyond the instinctive stage and made it subject to the reasoning of mathematicians and philosophers. They gave the theory and practice of music a new basis: the basis of numerical ratios. Pythagoras is said to have been among the first to establish this mathematical view of music by experiments with strings and their divisions to produce the octave, fifth and fourth. This eventually produced the twelve semitones commonly in use in western music. Primitive musicians apparently had instruments which could produce a very large number of different pitches, but it seems they most frequently *selected* from these extensive resources the five notes of the pentatonic formula. Presumably they did this intuitively. The mathematicians showed that it was possible to build scales logically and use these as musical material. It is simply a matter of making patterns of tones and semitones. Either way, of course, the selection is dependent upon the human will: the only truly *natural* scale is the harmonic series.

The twelve semitones give us a wide range: from them we can arrange a number of different modes and scales. The commonest arrangement in western music is the *major scale*:

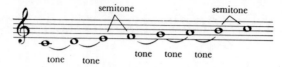

This has been the European standard since some time in the seventeenth century. It developed from the church modes of medieval Europe, which in turn grew out of the old Greek scales. Another well-established arrangement is the *minor mode* version of our major scale:

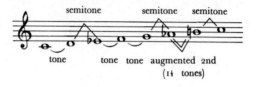

If we place some of these scales and modes side by side we can compare their different patterns of tones and semitones:

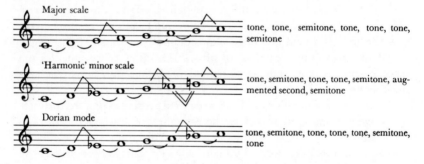

Major scale

tone, tone, semitone, tone, tone, tone, semitone

'Harmonic' minor scale

tone, semitone, tone, tone, semitone, augmented second, semitone

Dorian mode

tone, semitone, tone, tone, tone, semitone, tone

There are, of course, many other possible arrangements of tones and semitones. One very ancient Persian scale began as a kind of combination of what we should call major and minor scales:

As it developed, this scale grew to include divisions smaller than semitones until the octave consisted finally of seventeen notes. In the assignments that follow, we shall experiment with arrangements of tones and semitones and use these new scales as material for music.

164

B

(i)   Find out by experiment the names of the notes in a scale which goes from C to c′ in steps of WHOLE-TONES (that is, there will be no semitones). Work this out on a chromatic glockenspiel or on a piano keyboard, then select the notes in your scale from a set of individual chime bars.

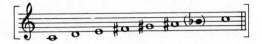

Notice that this scale imposes a further limitation because it has only *six* different notes to the octave instead of the seven notes we have in the more common scales of western music.

(ii)   With the chime bars (or the bars of a chromatic glockenspiel, metallophone or xylophone) arranged in the whole-tone scale started on C, experiment with melody-making. You'll find this scale has a beauty quite unlike any other scale. It has the vagueness and lack of tension we find in the pentatonic scale, but greater melodic scope. Individual pupils can make short whole-tone melodies and write them down; for example:

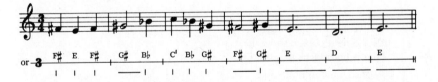

Continue by setting words to whole-tone melodies. Read the words over carefully and rhythmically, then, keeping their rhythms in mind, invent a tune on the chime bars arranged in a whole-tone scale. To start with you could complete the setting of the following words:

> I am of Ireland,
> And of the holy land
>   Of Ireland.
> Good Sir, pray I thee,
> For of saint charité
> Come dance with me
>   In Ireland.
>
> ANON., *14th century*

I am of Ire - land, And of the

ho - ly land of Ire - land. Good Sir,

* The dotted bar-lines have been inserted to simplify the rhythmic structure of the melody. In fact the rhythm should be as free as possible. A rigid accent on the first beats of bars will destroy the essential flow of the poetry.

Notice how appropriate the whole-tone scale is for a verse like this one. The music has that same distant and slightly mysterious quality that we find in the words.

Here is another ancient poem, this time about the Virgin Mary and the Christ-child. It's a lullaby. Set it to a gentle whole-tone melody:

> I saw a fair maiden
> Sitten and sing.
> She lulléd a litel child,
> A sweté lording:
>
> *Lullay, mine liking, my dear son,*
> *mine sweeting,*
> *Lullay, my dear heart, mine own*
> *dear darling.*
>
> Angels bright they sang that night,
> And saiden to that child:
> Blessed be thou and so be she
> That is both meek and mild.
>
> Pray we now to that child
> And to his mother deare,
> Grant them his blessing
> That now maken cheere.

The rhythms of the verses differ in each case. Your melodies can be fairly free, simply following the word rhythms. The *Lullay* refrain comes after each verse and this can have the same melody at each repetition. You might even make some simple harmony with your whole-tone notes by 'doubling' the melody three notes lower throughout the refrain, like this:

Lul - lay, mine li - king, my dear heart, mine sweet - ing

166

This would provide a contrast with the verses, for which you should keep to single melody lines:

I saw a fair maid - en sit ten and sing.

(iii)   Use the whole-tone scale to make a more extensive musical pattern. Don't necessarily aim to make a 'tune': there are many ways of combining sounds to make music. This could be a group piece where three or four players set out to improvise together and then deliberately to construct a musical continuity using the sounds of the whole-tone scale in more or less the same way as we used the sounds of cymbals in Project 1.

(iv)   We've been using a whole-tone scale which starts on C. From the twelve semitones of our complete chromatic scale it is possible to make only two different whole-tone scales.* We have used this one:

Can you discover by experiment the notes of the other one?

(v)   Make a piece of music for two chromatic instruments (glockenspiels, xylophones, metallophones) using the *two* whole-tone scales. Let one instrument use one scale and the other use the second scale.

(vi)   Construct a scale which uses alternate tones and semitones. Begin on any note you like. Make first a scale which goes tone, semitone, tone, semitone. Then make a scale which is arranged in the pattern semitone, tone, semitone, tone, etc. Continue your pattern in each case until you arrive at the note an octave above the one on which you began.

* The scales can begin on any note. Your scale could go from G to g or from E to e in whole-tone steps.

For example, beginning on G:

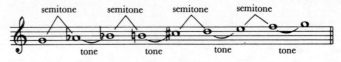

Use your scales to make melodies and write these down. Combine with someone else to make a duet piece using the scale you have worked out. Give the piece a title and tape-record it.

(vii)   The Spanish composer, Oscar Esplá has evolved a scale which he uses as a basis of his own music. Starting on C this scale has the following notes:

What is its arrangement of tones and semitones? Make some melodies or other music of your own using Esplá's scale.

C

An example of a piece using the scale given in (vi) above. It was evolved at a keyboard but could be played by any two melody instruments of appropriate compass.

Circle

Sempre legato

D

The different effects of the various modes should be demonstrated through folk-songs and Gregorian chant. Volume I of Bartók's *Mikrokosmos* contains a piece in the Dorian mode (no. 32) and another in the Phrygian mode (no. 34). *Mikrokosmos* vol. II has a piece in the Lydian mode (no. 37) and a piece in a Yugoslav mode (no. 40); there is also 'Triplets in Lydian Mode' (no. 55). All these should be played and their scales arranged on chime bars for discussion. This might be the point to call attention to the differences between major and minor scales and Bartók's study in *Mikrokosmos* vol. IV (no. 103) could be useful. *Mikrokosmos* also contains several chromatic studies, and it would be helpful to look at these and discuss the chromatic scale. Pupils might be encouraged to use the Bartók pieces as models for imitation. Debussy's music will provide numerous examples of whole-tone music. There are some whole-tone pieces by the nineteenth-century Russian composer, Rebikov, which are worth looking at. Again, Bartók gives us an example of whole-tone music: *Mikrokosmos* vol. V (no. 136).

Examples of music built on scales of alternating tones and semitones will be found in *Cinq Rechants* by Messiaen and in the anthem *God be*

Merciful Unto Us (SSATB and organ) by Peter Aston (published by Novello). In the cantata *My Dancing Day* (also by Peter Aston; Novello hire library) one movement is based on a scale alternating tone-semitone and another movement on a scale alternating semitone-tone.

Study the song *O my love, how long*, number 1 of 'Four Greek Folk Songs' by Matyas Seiber (Boosey and Hawkes, 1947). The melody consists of a short phrase repeated over and over again using the mode:

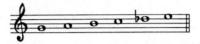

The American composer Harry Partch has made a study of many ancient scales, and out of this study has evolved his own scale, a microtonal scale with forty-three notes to the octave. He has constructed special instruments on which these arrangements of notes can be laid out. These are described in his book, *Genesis of a Music* (University of Wisconsin Press, 1949), which also gives the mathematical background in great detail. A survey of Partch's ideals and music will be found in Wilfrid Mellers' *Music in a New Found Land*, Chapter VIII. The music is recorded privately and issued on Harry Partch's own label, 'Gate 5'. There are occasional broadcasts and other performances in Great Britain. Of particular interest in connection with this project are his *Study in an ancient Phrygian Scale* and *Study in the ancient Enharmonic Scale*. On the recording both are played by Partch on the harmonic canon, an instrument he devised for playing in a number of unusual scales.

Discussion of scale arrangements could easily lead to some investigation of microtonal music. If a monochord is available experiments could be carried out, dividing the string at different points to produce a variety of notes and divisions smaller than a semitone. Listen to Alois Haba's *Duo in the Sixth-Tone System* for two violins. If your ear is sufficiently acute, quarter-tones can be played on stringed instruments without much difficulty.

An instrument something like the harmonic canon of Harry Partch could be made using as a basis the chordal dulcimer, for which plans will be found in *Musical Instruments made to be played* by Ronald Roberts (Dryad Press, 1965). Instead of stringing the instrument with a series of different strings, use the *same* gauge of string for eight pegs (guitar A string, no. 5 would be the best one). Tune all eight to the same note, D. Construct seven small moveable bridges which can be placed, one beneath each string after the first, on the table of the instrument between the two fixed bridges:

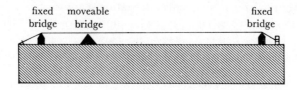

These small bridges can now be set at different points along the lengths of the strings to produce the notes of any scale desired. The relative pitches of notes in a scale are usually given by reference to the vibrating lengths of strings as ratios of whole strings. We can therefore show the individual pitches of the notes in a scale as a series of ratios. For example, here is a Chinese scale, dating from the third century B.C.:

$$\frac{1}{1} \quad \frac{8}{7} \quad \frac{6}{5} \quad \frac{5}{4} \quad \frac{4}{3} \quad \frac{3}{2} \quad \frac{5}{3} \quad \frac{2}{1}$$

The upper figure of each ratio shows into how many parts the string is divided; the lower figure indicates the number of those parts which are free to vibrate. In the scale we quote, the first note is obtained by vibrating the whole open string (string in one part: that one part vibrating); the second note is obtained by dividing the string into eight equal parts, dampening one part and vibrating the remaining seven parts. If we subtract the lower figure from the upper figure of the ratio and place the result *above* the upper figure of the ratio, this will give us the fraction of string to be measured off and dampened, leaving the remaining length free to vibrate and so produce the required note:

ratios:	no. of parts of whole string	$\frac{1}{1}$	$\frac{8}{7}$	$\frac{6}{5}$	$\frac{5}{4}$	$\frac{4}{3}$	$\frac{3}{2}$	$\frac{5}{3}$	$\frac{2}{1}$
	no. of parts to be vibrated								

fractions of string to be measured off and dampened $\qquad 0 \quad \frac{1}{8} \quad \frac{1}{6} \quad \frac{1}{5} \quad \frac{1}{4} \quad \frac{1}{3} \quad \frac{2}{5} \quad \frac{1}{2}$

Applied to the chordal dulcimer, we should measure off lengths of string as shown in the diagram below to obtain the notes of this ancient Chinese scale; these would then be the points at which to place the moveable bridges:

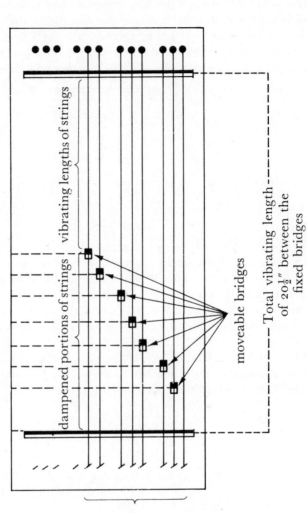

Ratio indicating notes of the scale: $\frac{1}{1}$ $\frac{8}{7}$ $\frac{6}{5}$ $\frac{5}{4}$ $\frac{4}{3}$ $\frac{3}{2}$ $\frac{5}{3}$ $\frac{2}{1}$

Length to be measured off (from L.H. bridge) :   0 $2\frac{9}{16}''$ $3\frac{5}{12}''$ $4\frac{1}{10}''$ $5\frac{1}{8}''$ $6\frac{10}{12}''$ $8\frac{2}{10}''$ $10\frac{1}{4}''$

vibrating lengths of strings

dampened portions of strings

moveable bridges

Total vibrating length of $20\frac{1}{2}''$ between the fixed bridges

Eight pegs strung. All open strings tuned to D

Our suggested tuning of the open strings on the harmonic canon to D is, of course, quite arbitrary. The ratios indicate the intervals between notes. This makes possible the setting up of quite complicated scales, if necessary using quarter-tones and even smaller divisions of the gamut. Here are two more ancient scales, a Lydian mode and a Mixolydian mode:

$$\frac{1}{1} \quad \frac{9}{8} \quad \frac{81}{64} \quad \frac{4}{3} \quad \frac{3}{2} \quad \frac{27}{16} \quad \frac{243}{128} \quad \frac{2}{1}$$

$$\frac{1}{1} \quad \frac{14}{13} \quad \frac{7}{6} \quad \frac{14}{11} \quad \frac{7}{5} \quad \frac{14}{9} \quad \frac{7}{4} \quad \frac{2}{1}$$

and a Greek pentatonic scale of the sixth century B.C.:

$$\frac{1}{1} \quad \frac{8}{5} \quad \frac{3}{2} \quad \frac{6}{5} \quad \frac{9}{8}$$

By moving the small bridges to the appropriate places on the strings, these scales could be set up and melodies improvised on them.

A very simple version of the instrument could be made with one string. Mark the positions of the various notes in pencil on the table of the instrument. A glass rod, large enough in diameter to fit tightly between the string and the table, can be moved from one note-position to another with the left hand. The string is plucked with the right hand. Some pleasant glissando effects are obtained as the glass 'bridge' is moved from one note to another. Listen to some Japanese Koto music on the 'History of Music in Sound', record two.

Project 22
Notes, modes and rows (2)

A

The maker of anything must impose certain limitations on himself to help channel his imagination. The first limitation will be his choice of materials. Then the materials themselves will restrict him. If he works in clay there are some things clay simply will not do and these limitations will remain constant all the time the artist works with that material. This is as true of music as it is of any other art. The composer's intuition will tell him what needs to be said (you can call that 'inspiration' if you like); *how* it is to be said will depend on the materials he chooses and his imagination and skill with these materials.

The materials of music are in some ways less definite than the materials of the potter's art. Moreover, the ways in which a composer can work, especially in this century, are so unprescribed that it is all the more necessary for him to limit the extent and use of his materials. In fact, it would be fair to say that in one sense it is when the artist or composer is most bound, most tightly organised, that he has the greatest artistic freedom.

We've already explored some forms of limitation in earlier projects making music for specified voices or instruments within certain well-defined organisational patterns. To work in a particular scale or mode might be a sufficient limitation. This piece, we might say, needs to be in a major key, or for this piece we will use the Dorian mode or the whole-tone scale, and so on. The Spanish composer Oscar Esplá limited himself, for much of his music, to a scale selected from the twelve equally tempered semitones like this:

* And see Project 21.

Of course, he could broaden the scope by *transposing* the scale, but the essential character of the music would always remain the same because, whatever note you begin the scale on, the distances (intervals) between the notes remain the same. In the case of Esplá's music, he sought the character which he found in the folk music of the eastern Spanish coast and he achieved his aim by his *choice of material*—his 'Levantine' scale.

Serial music is something like that. The composer selects a series of notes to form a new 'scale' and then composes within the limits of that 'scale'. This gives the music its character. The material is fundamentally the same as composers have always used: the twelve semitones of the chromatic scale. For each composition the composer arranges these notes in a certain order and imposes on himself some further limitations in the techniques of using his series.

Serial music (that is, music composed with a series of notes known as a tone-row or a note-row) avoids the 'homing' feeling present in traditional western music. By using a note-row in which each of the twelve notes of the chromatic scale appears only once and no one note is repeated until all the others have appeared, the feeling of key centre is obliterated: there is no one note as a focal point. Both melody and harmony are derived from the series, the notes being used always in the original order.

The particular arrangement of notes chosen for the series may be based on some mathematical or symmetrical principles: it may make a pattern. On the other hand, it may arise, as Arnold Schönberg said it *always* did for him, 'in the form of a thematic character'; that is, the composer makes a twelve-note melody which uses all twelve semitones and this order of the notes is then fixed as the basic note-row on which the rest of the music will be made. Whatever the origin of any particular series, it is important to remember that the note-row is *not a theme* but only a sequence of notes which will form the basic *material* of the music. You make a new series for each composition.

In all music one of the major problems for the composer is to make his music 'go on'. He generally solves this by using his material in two ways; one (involving repetitions) to unify and the other (inventing new material or new ways of using existing material) to give variety. In traditional western music the chief characteristic is rhythmic symmetry: phrase balances phrase. The phrases and their rhythms are related to the harmony which itself has a feeling of direction, of moving onwards, one chord *leading* to another until the inevitability of the final 'homing' chord is achieved. In music that has no key centre (usually known as 'atonal' music) rhythmic patterns become very important. They have to do what harmony does in tonal music: propel the music forward to the points of climax or lead the music into periods of relaxed tension. Rhythmic patterns can provide the variety while the note-row gives unity. And silence will of course be important. Silence will help us to make dramatic climaxes. It will also produce calmness and so relax the tension of the music.

B

(i) *Twelve-note melody:* using chime bars (or chromatic glockenspiels, metallophones, or xylophones with removable bars), arrange the twelve notes to form a new pattern. For example, you might put all the 'white' notes first and follow them with all the 'black' notes:

or

For another pattern you could start with the lowest C and take every other white note up to B, followed by all the black notes descending, and ending with the three remaining white notes:

If you are familiar with musical notation it might help to 'fix' your note-row by writing it down once you have decided on the arrangement of the notes. Other arrangements, especially if you aim to make symmetrical patterns of notes, may more easily be seen on paper: for example the following note-row which is built up of three groups, each of four notes. The pattern of the first group—a leap upwards of a note plus a semitone followed by a descent in semitones—is repeated three notes higher for the second group and three notes higher again for the third group:

The distances between the notes are very important because it is these intervals which give the particular character to the series, and this character becomes part of the music made from the series.

Now we can begin to make melodies. This assignment is for a group of four players. Divide your note-row into four groups of three notes each and allot a group to each player:

Add to these notes their upper and lower octaves (where available) so that players have the following sounds available:

Now the group of players can between them improvise an extended twelve-note melody using this material. Limit each player to *three sounds* each time his part of the row appears. Players must follow what each other does so that they can continue the melody without unintentional breaks. Remember that the row itself gives the music unity: aim therefore for rhythmic variety. For example, each player's section should contrast rhythmically with what happens immediately before it. At the same time the whole group should have some idea of where the total improvisation is leading. Try to build towards a climax: you can do this by using wide leaps between your highest and lowest notes and making the notes short and fast. Follow the climax by a gradual relaxing of the tension: you can achieve this by avoiding leaps, moving to notes close to one another in pitch, and using longer and slower moving notes. You may, of course, go round the row as many times as you like. The *order* of the notes should remain always as in the original row, but your melody may end on any note in the series; that is, you must not feel compelled to finish your melody on note 12 of the row. After a few improvisations, let the four players work together to create by improvisation a melody which they can recall and repeat. If possible the completed melody should be written down in traditional notation (though if that is too complicated a process, letters could be used with some convenient indication of the rhythm). The result might be something like this:

or this:

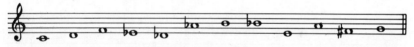

(ii) Individual players make note-rows and compose their own melodies to be played on suitable instruments. The rows could be made out of consideration for the patterns and arrangements of notes as in (i) above, or you might begin by making a melody just twelve notes long, using each note of the chromatic scale once only and then taking the notes in that order to form a basic row from which the original melody could be extended (see (iii), (vii), and (viii) below for other ways of extending the use of a note-row). For example, we might start by making (on an instrument) a lyrical twelve-note melody like this:

Flute (or tenor recorder)

which gives us a note-row:

Now we can take our original melody and extend it by repetitions of the row. Notice how points of climax are made with the help of sudden upward leaps or fast-moving notes, and repose is achieved at the end by using longer note values and less abrupt movement:

Flute (or tenor recorder)

179

(iii)   Make more melodies as in (i) and (ii) but expand the resources by sometimes using the note-row in reverse (this is known as the RETRO-GRADE form of the series).

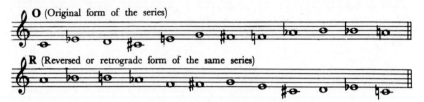

Extend your techniques by occasionally repeating notes, but try to avoid repeating rhythmic patterns. For example, using the same series as in the examples above, we might repeat the first two notes of the row before going on to the third note:

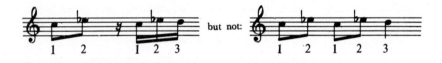

(iv)   *Twelve-note harmony:* divide the series between three players. Add octaves as in (i):

The players improvise chord sequences using chime bars or other suitable arrangements of tuned-percussion (you can hold two beaters in each hand, which makes it possible for one player to sound four notes to-gether). Each player should play either one four-note chord or two two-note chords before handing on the sequence to the next player (these 'rules' are simply to get the improvisation started: once you've experimented with chord sequences it will obviously be possible to think of further arrangements and organisations). With experience you will learn to judge the effects of chords and so be able to give 'shape' to your music. As a rough guide, notes close to one another produce more tension than notes widely spaced. Notes moving at speed produce tension and help to build towards climaxes; notes moving slowly relax the tension. Keeping these points in mind, we might get a sequence of chords like this:

(v) *Twelve-note melody and harmony*: make a piece of music for chime bars and recorder. You must take care to avoid as far as possible sounding notes in the recorder part which are being sounded at the same time by the chime bars. This may be difficult to spot in improvisation, though it should be possible to notice it in more detailed working out. Where it does happen that the two parts have the same note, leave that note out of one part and take the next note in the series. It might be easier to avoid these 'doublings' if the chime bar player(s) create a chord sequence using the original form of the series, while the recorder player's melody uses the retrograde form of the same series.

(vi) Make a note-row and divide it between six players of any instruments (i.e. each player will be restricted to two notes of the series). Try to get a variety of different timbres. Make a series of dynamic markings (*p*, *ff*, *pp*, etc.) and associate these with the players, for example:

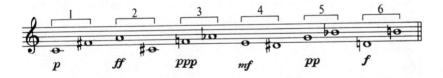

Add a further series of non-melodic percussion instruments:

Cymbal	Claves	Maracas	Rasp	Triangle	2 Indian Drums
1a	2a	3a	4a	5a	6a

The players are paired (one having a melodic instrument, the other a percussion instrument) and they sit in a semi-circle with a gap between each pair. A director stands at a central point:

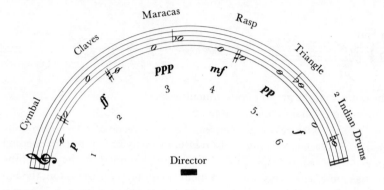

The director has in front of him the pre-arranged layout in a diagram like the one given above. From this he can see the basic material. He builds up an improvised piece by indicating which of the pairs should play and for how long. Two or more pairs may play at the same time (the whole ensemble may play together) but *the order of the series should be maintained.* With his left hand the director indicates which pairs play, while with his right hand he 'holds' a pause. During the period of this pause the pair(s) concerned improvise freely with their musical material (the notes of the series and the qualities of the percussion instrument(s)) but always at the level of volume indicated for their group(s). The director can make climaxes by careful use of silences and those points in the series where the louder dynamic markings occur.

(vii)   You can add even further to your resources by *transposing* the note-row. For example, if your original row is:

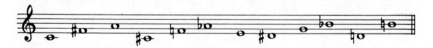

you could transpose this down one whole tone: C becomes B♭, F♯ becomes E, and so on:

The intervals between the notes are the same, of course, and it is this which gives the row its individual character. You can use the transposed row together with the original row. You also have the retrograde form of each. You could transpose the row up or down to start on any one of the twelve notes and each of these transposed versions would be available in its retrograde form. Can you work out how many versions you can produce of the one original series? The more you have, the more material you can draw upon but the greater become your difficulties of handling the notes, and the greater your difficulties of choice! Work out some ways of using four versions of the same series.

(viii)   If you know how to reckon intervals between notes, you can add further to your material by *inverting* the note-row. Starting on C the *upward leap* of an augmented fourth in the original series becomes a *downward leap* of the same interval:

The inverted form of the series can be used backwards (retrograde form). So, from any note-row you have the possibilities of the original version plus any of the other eleven transposed versions, and all of these can be inverted and used backwards. How many possible forms of a series are there? Make a piece of music using as many forms of a series as you can control.

C

A suggested opening for the piece proposed in Assignment (v) above: the figures refer to the position of the notes in the original series.

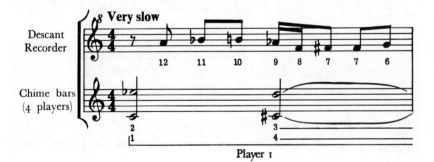

Player 1

Player 2   Player 3   Player 1

Player 2   Player 3

A simple piece for two flutes:

Duo for Two Flutes

SARAH RABAN

D

The music of 'The Second Viennese School', with its emphasis on chromatic structures, has become the current 'classicism' and is therefore readily available on records. The results of any of the suggested assignments might be compared with sections of the following pieces:

SCHÖNBERG

Variations for Orchestra Op. 31 (Score published by Universal Edition (London) Ltd.)

Survivor from Warsaw

Six Little Piano Pieces Op. 19 (Score published by Universal Edition (London) Ltd.)

Five Pieces for Orchestra Op. 16 (Peters Edition no. 3376a.)

WEBERN

Six Bagatelles for String Quartet Op. 9

Symphony Op. 21

Variations for Piano Op. 27 (Universal Edition.)

BERG

Violin Concerto (Universal Edition.)

Lyric Suite for String Quartet (Universal Edition.)

For advanced students, Reginald Smith Brindle's *Serial Composition* (Oxford University Press, 1966) will be useful. Further individual experience of twelve-note composition should be followed by a detailed study of some of the pieces listed above.

Project 23
Music and numbers

A

Primitive music was a closed system. It had limited resources and, because it was entirely intuitive, could do little to expand these resources. The scientists and mathematicians of the first high civilisations drew attention to nature's logic. It was the application of this logic in the development of forms and patterns which caused music to move forward. The beginnings of all art are intuitive, but reason and logic are required to put the intuitive ideas into forms that can grow. The maker can then give coherence to his imagination, and by his artifice we have art.

At every period of history since the beginnings of civilisation, musicians have absorbed mathematical ideas and used them to form scales and rhythmic patterns. Not only does mathematics give impetus to musical construction, moving it on in a variety of patterns, but doors are opened to those musicians who, like many other artists, find delight in symmetry and construction for its own sake: a delight which in turn increases their sensitivity to the materials they are working with.

Of course, the logic and the symmetry are in nature's patterns in the first place. They are present intuitively in Man's most primitive art forms because these forms draw upon nature: it is there we find the wellsprings, the sources of inspiration. In this project, however, we shall be primarily concerned with the reasoned application of symmetry, and with mathematically organised rhythmic constructions. Rhythmic patterns organised on proportional bases were fairly frequent in medieval music. In the twentieth century, composers have revived interest in this kind of construction.

B

(i)   An assignment for individual players: make a short piece for piano solo. It should be a single line of melody. Use *any* notes (they can be quite random when the piece is first improvised) but keep a steady pulse in mind all the time (say, MM ♩=144) and maintain a proportional structure of these pulse beats in the pattern 2 : 3 : 5 (these numbers indicate the *length* of each sound in pulse beats, i.e. the first note lasts for two pulse beats, the second note for three pulse beats, the third for five pulse beats, the fourth for two pulse beats, the fifth for three pulse beats, and so on). For example:

Before you begin, practice counting '1.2/1.2.3/1.2.3.4.5.' over and over again at a steady pace. In the first instance your piano piece should go on without a break as an improvisation. Listen carefully to the sounds and try to control your response so that you can arrange climaxes and bring the improvisation to a satisfactory conclusion. After this you can try making a more definite piece of music by improvisation and evaluation, remembering as exactly as possible the effects you like and working on them till they become fixed and you can repeat them. You might make some of your pulse beats silences. Try to grade the loud passages and the quieter passages in the piece in relation to your points of climax.

(ii)   An assignment for a group of four players: using any melodic instruments you have, make a piece based on the same principles as in (i). Use the same proportional rhythmic structure. All the players should start together and keep their counting together, though the notes they play may be completely random. Each player plays only a single line of notes.

(iii)   As in (ii) but with each player beginning at a different time. This will bring about an interlacing of cross-rhythms. It will require a considerable effort of concentration to maintain individual rhythmic patterns and at the same time to be aware of what the others are playing, but it is important that the group listen to one another as they play so that the improvisation can be built up into one whole piece.

(iv)   As in (iii) but based on a pre-arranged note-row (see Project 22). Each player should have the complete row and keep to the order of the series in either its original or its retrograde form. As this is an improvisation it will be difficult to avoid 'doublings'. Even so, it should be possible to work over the improvisation: players can enter at different points and work to achieve a clear texture by using silences (but these must be in the proportional rhythms too which, in the rhythm we've been using, will mean silences of either two pulses, or three or five pulses. A silence must be followed immediately by sounds, otherwise the structure will be broken).

(v)   Make a proportional piece for non-melodic percussion with any number of players. Some players can use the rhythmic pattern in reverse, i.e. 5:3:2.

(vi)   Choose instruments which contrast in sound. They can be either melodic or non-melodic. Make a large-scale piece of improvised music (using random notes on the pitched instruments) to an extended proportion-pattern of 2:3:5:8:1:9:10:7. Keep the pulse at a steady MM ♩=120.

(vii)   Arrange two semi-circles of four players each. You may use any instruments you like, but try to get a contrast of sounds between the two groups. At the same time keep a *unity* of sounds within each group. One group works to a rhythmic pattern organised on the proportions 2:1:3:4. The other group uses the pattern 7:11:6:5. The players improvise, selecting notes at random on melodic instruments. Each player is allotted *one* pulse group (i.e. in the first group, player number 1 has a two-pulse group, player number 2 a single pulse, player number 3 a three-pulse group, and so on). There are two directors, one for each group of players, and they decide who shall play and when. The continuity of the music is in the directors' hands while the content is still with the players. The directors should listen carefully to the results of each other's direction, reacting to what they hear and deciding whether their group should play or be silent. Once a group has started to play, it should continue (and in the order of the proportional rhythm) until its director indicates silence. He may start the rhythm pattern at either end of the semi-circle (i.e. the pattern can be reversed). The pulse remains steady throughout. Experiment with different pulse speeds, some fast, some slow.

(viii)   Write on a blackboard a proportion pattern as follows:

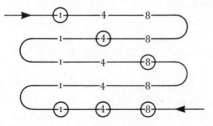

Any number of players can take part. Evolve as many ways of using this pattern as you can. Here are some suggestions:

(1) On the 'ringed' numbers, everyone plays sounds lasting for that number of pulses. The unringed numbers are counted as silences. The series is used forwards and then immediately reversed (as the arrows indicate), ending where it began;

(2) Melodic instruments play on the ringed numbers, non-melodic percussion play on the unringed numbers. The notes are all single sounds held for the length indicated by the numbers;

(3) As in (2), but melodic and non-melodic instruments change places when the series is reversed;

(4) Melodic instruments play on the ringed numbers but instead of holding a single note for the given number of pulses they improvise freely on any notes within the period of the number. Non-melodic percussion play on the unringed numbers single sounds as in (2). The instruments do *not* change places when the series is reversed;

(5) As in any of the above, with the additional 'rule' that the higher the number the louder the sound, giving three grades of dynamic which should be sharply differentiated, i.e. *ppp mf fff* rather than *p mf f*.

Tape-record all improvisations so they can be heard and appreciated fully by all taking part.

(ix)   Indian music is based on proportional rhythms. A pattern is beaten out on a pair of hand-drums called tabla. This pattern, known as a *tala*, is a measure of time with fixed number of beats, some of which are more accented than others. For example, in an overall time-measure of nine beats, the first, fourth and sixth beats may be emphasised:

or the proportions may be beaten out as *durations* (as we have done in the assignments above):

The tabla player marks the time-measure while a melody instrument improvises, usually around a limited number of notes arranged in what is known as a *raga*. The *ragas* are not scales but really melody-*patterns*;

short but distinctive phrases which can be elaborated by the player. There are more than 200 of these *ragas*, each one expressing a specific feeling. Many of the *ragas* are associated with particular times of day and, according to the very strict conventions of Indian music, may only be used at those times. The basic concept of Indian music is a continual *unfolding* of patterns within the limits of the chosen *raga* over a background of the time-measure played on the tabla together with an unchanging drone, usually played on a stringed instrument called a tambura. The traditional melody instrument is the sitar, a complicated lute-like instrument with movable frets by means of which the scale of the *raga* can be set in much the same way as scales can be set on the harmonic canon (see Project 21, Section D). Decoration plays a big part in Indian music. The tabla player 'decorates' the basic *tala* by striking his drums in different places, either with the whole hand, or with the ball of the thumb, or with separate finger strokes; he will also sub-divide the individual beats of the measure, weaving increasingly complicated patterns as the music progresses. There is usually a kind of 'rhythmical contest' between the tabla player and the sitar player, who elaborates rhythmically as well as melodically on the notes of the *raga*.

Listen to some Indian music to catch its flavour. The scales used are not so very different from our own but there is a tendency to delight in melodies which revolve around intervals such as

which, on the whole, traditional western music has tended to avoid.

Experiment with music in the Indian style. Choose two small drums of different pitch for tabla (bongos would do, though strictly speaking the two drums should have between them about five notes difference in pitch). A violin or cello could provide a drone note on an open string. The short melodic phrase on which you will improvise should, perhaps, begin on the same note as the drone. If possible let it also contain those characteristic intervals we mention above. It might be a phrase like this:

Now, while your drummer beats out the time-pattern (with elaborations if he wishes) and the cellist plays the drone C, you can improvise melody variations on a recorder or a glockenspiel, perhaps something like this:

C

The following example shows a piece for four players. It could be performed on any instruments of suitable compass, though it would probably be most effective if all the instruments were of the same family (e.g. all strings or all winds). It was in fact evolved by four players on chime bars. They began by dividing a selection of chime bars between them in more or less random fashion (though it will be seen that players 1 and 2 took mostly 'black' notes and players 3 and 4 confined themselves to 'white' notes). The division was not equal in number: players 1 and 4 had six bars each, player 2 had five and player 3 had four.

With the limitations of their note-groups set, each player evolved a melodic pattern in the proportional rhythm 2 + 3 + 5 with the 2, 3, and 5 taken as durations:

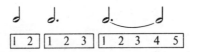

For example, player 1 divided the note-group into two sub-groups of three notes each and made a two-bar melody pattern which repeats throughout the piece. On the other hand, player 3 tried to vary as much as possible the order of the four notes in her group. Once all the patterns

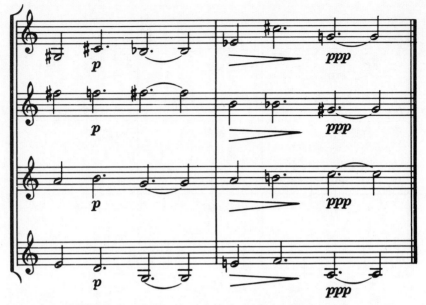

were established, the players put them together and decided as a group how they would use their material and what the length of the finished piece should be. It must be emphasised that all this was done by working from the instruments and the sounds. Nothing was written down at the time of making the piece. The music was remembered and notated by one or two of the group at a later date.

D

Organisation and the desire to make symmetrical patterns can be a great stimulus to composers, but ingenuity will not by itself automatically make good music. If the organisation of the materials is too obvious, the chances are that the piece may have little else to recommend it. In the end, all music stands or falls *as music*. It is the sound which moves us or excites our imagination, not the ingenuity of the composer, although we may indeed admire his skill. With this said, it is nevertheless useful practice for us to examine as closely as we can the ways in which organisation and symmetry stimulate composers to produce music. We have tried to do this through creative experiment. Further exploration through the works of professional composers may depend on the pupils' capacity to study printed scores in detail. As we have said, if the music is good the organisation will not obtrude: we shall have to look for it in the notation.

Canto di Liberazione by Dallapiccola is based on proportional rhythms.

The score is published by Edizioni Suvini Zerboni, Milan, and details of the music will be found on pp. 162–3 of Reginald Smith Brindle's *Serial Composition* (Oxford University Press, 1966).

Some of the assignments and examples above use the series of numbers known as the *Fibonacci Sequence*. In this series, each expression is the sum of the two preceding numbers, and the pattern formed is a numerical version of the proportional principle we call the *Golden Section* or *Golden Mean*. Not only has this principle been used both consciously and unconsciously by artists and musicians since the dawn of civilisation, but it is to be found everywhere in nature, in things seen and in things heard. Not surprisingly it has often been associated with magic, especially as expressed in the magic shapes of the pentagon and five-pointed star.

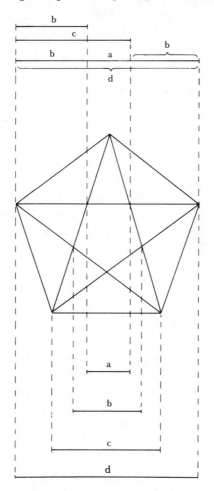

The Golden Section is found in every proportion of these figures: d:c=c:b=b:a=1:0.618. We can find this same pattern in the most ancient forms of the pentatonic scale which, of course, men evolved intuitively not logically. If the sequence 2, 3, 5, 8 is seen as a sequence of numbers of semitones, a melody pattern emerges: 2 semitones=major 2nd, 3 semitones=minor 3rd, 5 semitones=perfect 4th, 8 semitones =minor 6th. This same melody pattern is the basis of pentatonicism:

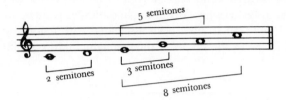

As so much primitive music is connected with ritual and magic, it would not be unreasonable to suppose a fundamental link between Man's spiritual gropings and pentatonicism, which is one of music's intrinsic laws.

However that may be, some composers, particularly composers in our own time, have made extensive use of the principles of the Golden Section and the Fibonacci Sequence. In a fascinating and exhaustive study of the music of Béla Bartók,* Ernö Lendvai has shown that the order conveyed by these principles was as natural to Bartók in the formation of every detail of a composition as 4- and 8-bar periods were to Mozart. Lendvai demonstrates how, in the *Sonata for Two Pianos and Percussion*, every unit, from the whole work to the tiniest section, is divided structurally according to the Golden Mean. For example, the first movement is 443 bars long: 274 is the Golden Section of 443:† the recapitulation, which Lendvai describes as 'the centre of gravity of this movement', begins exactly at bar 274. There is evidence that this kind of organisation came naturally to Bartók; that is, it was not so much a logical, reasoned process as an unconscious one. It occurs in so much of his music. Again, Ernö Lendvai demonstrates with an analysis of the first movement of the *Music for Strings, Percussion and Celesta*. The move-

---

* 'Duality and Synthesis in the Music of Béla Bartók', *The New Hungarian Quarterly*, vol. III, no. 7 (Corvina Press, Budapest; July–Sept. 1962), pp. 91–114.

† Golden Section = 1:0.618; 443 × 0.618 = 274.

ment is 89 bars long: the dynamic climax is reached at bar 55 (55 is the Golden Section of 89):

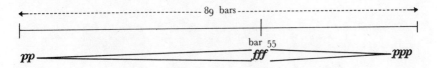

The two sections thus formed are themselves sub-divided by the Golden Section and events of importance occur at these points:

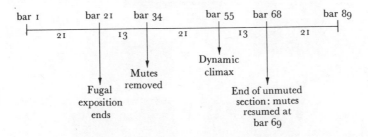

All the numbers which emerge from this analysis are, of course, part of the Fibonacci Sequence 2, 3, 8, 13, 21, 34, 55, 89 ... Bartók's melodic construction is so often based on the most ancient traditions of Hungarian folk music which, in its pentatonicism, is linked to this numerical pattern so fundamental to nature's own ordering. In his article, Lendvai draws our attention to the logarithmic structure of the cochlea of the ear and suggests that this may account for the attraction which children and primitives have for the pattern

From this pattern stems the pentatonic formula which, like the pentagon, is a closed form devoid of the 'direction' and functional attraction we have now become accustomed to in *major* tonality. Bartók drew on the ancient sources saying that 'only by going to the truly old can we create something truly new'.

14　*Collage with Squares Arranged According to the Law of Chance* by Jean Arp
(Collection, the Museum of Modern Art, New York)

Project 24
Music by chance

A

Music delights us and gives us pleasure, but beyond that it has another
function: it is more than mere entertainment. Like all the arts, music
embodies the reactions of its makers to life as they live it and as they see
it lived around them. Of course, a musical work does not have to be an
obvious piece of social commentary, although, in a sense, this happens
inevitably. By its own nature music makes a comment. This is why the
music of our own day is more relevant to us and to our situation than
music of any other time. To understand the art of the present is to understand ourselves.

In the twentieth century, music, broadly speaking, has developed
along two paths. One has given us the music of Schönberg, Berg, Webern,
Boulez and other 'serial' composers. For all its revolutionary nature,
their music has roots securely in the past and grows naturally out of the
music of their immediate predecessors. It enables the composer to
express personal feeling. By increasing the scope of musical material as it
does, serial composition broadens the range of expression. In addition,
the tight 'mind-control' of such music makes it possible for composers
to define with absolute clarity the nervous energies and tensions of
twentieth-century living. These they express *for us* in their music. They
are part of that mainstream of composers reaching back to the renaissance. They bear, on behalf of society, the burden of expressing feeling
and human reaction.

The other path begins with Debussy and Satie, and takes us into the
world of the present avant-garde. The newness of their music lies not
only in the unusual sounds it makes; not only in what is admissible as
'music', but also in its underlying philosophy which is fundamentally
different from the 'expressing and communicating' philosophy of most
post-renaissance composers. These composers seek a music which is not
controlled by the human will. Man's 'consciousness' has led him into
such perilous situations that it may be better now to turn back to the
unconscious, to trance-like states of will-lessness. In musical terms this

meant in the first place turning away from western forms to the ritual and magical formulae of eastern music: the trance-inducing monotony of the Indian *tala*; the music of Java and Bali, with its 'gapped' pentatonic scales lacking all tension. The path leads back through oriental and primitive musics to that state where 'music was born independently of man'. For musicians like John Cage, music has become less and less a matter of *composing* sounds into humanly devised orders. Instead, Cage has 'let things happen'. All the sounds around can come in and be part of our music. This is perhaps not such an odd point of view after all. For a long time poets have used phrases such as 'the wind's song' or 'the music of the sea'. We recognise a strange mystical beauty in the *random* sounds of nature: we might find similar qualities in other random sounds.

From the philosophies of John Cage a new branch of music springs: 'aleatory' music, produced by chance operations such as the tossing of a coin or the throwing of dice. Can music produced like this express and communicate anything? Does it need to do either of these things? Can we any longer talk about music as 'an organisation of sounds *for expressive purposes*'? Perhaps the composer's own decision to make his organisation subject to chance operations *expresses* something in itself. As we have said, music makes a comment by its own nature. It is arguable that the movement led by Cage expresses mankind's need to become less conscious of itself, and this can only be expressed by a music in which the human will plays the smallest part. In practice the composer usually retains control of certain aspects. For example, he chooses the materials: the dice tell him how the materials shall behave.

In Europe, composers such as Stockhausen and Nono have worked on similar developments, drawing closer together the two paths of twentieth-century music. 'Pop' music too has moved towards the expression of comparable philosophies about Man's condition, principally through its lyrics, but also, from time to time, by including some musical evidence of its sympathy with Cage and Stockhausen. Consider the passage in the Beatles' *I am the Walrus*, where random voices, radio sounds, snatches of melody and whatever are brought together in the manner of Cage's *Imaginary Landscape* for twelve radios.

Another interesting development in the field of 'chance' music is 'indeterminacy'. The composer provides musical material from which performers may choose. This is not to be confused with improvisation on a theme. The performer does not invent new material or even elaborate what is given: he is allowed to make a choice but it is to be made without a rational basis. Of course, the nature of the resulting music is conditioned by the materials provided, but it will also be 'expressive' through the performers' natural reactions to the sounds. In the course of this project we shall be combining the creation of music by chance operations with music which is indeterminate in performance.

B

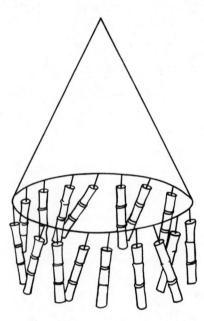

(i) Wind-chimes like these have been made for centuries in Japan. The small bamboo sticks hang in a circle so that they strike one another at random when the wind blows them.

Make wind-chimes or any instrument of a similar kind which will produce random sounds when hung in a window or from a tree. Tape-record the music the instrument makes. Listen critically to the tape. Do you think the sounds are beautiful? Are some more beautiful than others? What makes us say they are beautiful?

(ii) Choose four instruments contrasted in timbre, and select a note on each of them. Let the four notes be different from one another. Represent two of the notes by the head and the tail of a large coin and the other two by the head and the tail of a small coin. Toss the coins alternately and

write down in order the notes they select. You may get something like
this:

Now take this series of notes and make it the subject of an indeterminate
performance. Here are some suggestions:

(1) The notes, deployed as they are between four instruments, are
taken as a piece of music complete in itself. The four instrumentalists
perform the piece by playing the notes in the given order but making

rhythm patterns in any way they wish as they play. The piece might begin like this:

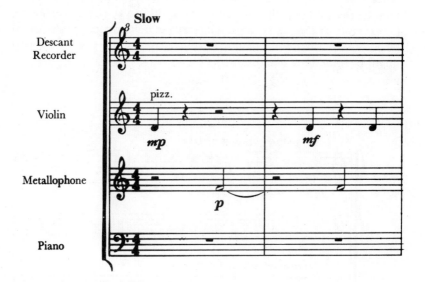

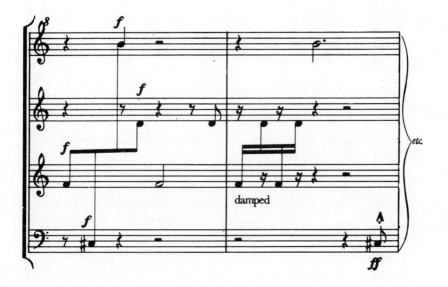

As the piece is indeterminate, no two performances will be alike;

(2) Take the same succession of pitches and apply them to *one* instrument. Let one player now use the notes to make a piece as in (1);

(3) As in (2) but with two players, each having the entire series of pitches to play on his instrument. They begin together, but thereafter they are free to choose their own durations within a given general tempo, for example 'fast' or 'very slow'. The series of notes we give above could be played like this on two pianos, in which case the effect of the opening might be something like this:

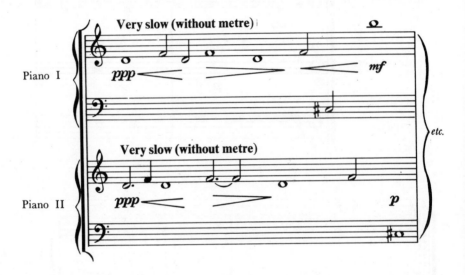

(iii)   Taking the same succession of pitches as in (ii), organise their duration by chance operation. Set a pulse of, say, MM ♩=60, and take the numbers on a dice as representing durations. A throw of 4 would mean 4 crotchets duration; in other words, a semibreve. Throw for the duration of each note in turn and notate the results to form a piece. The pitches are deployed among the four instruments as in the original selection. Add dynamics and, when the piece is completely notated, the four players can perform it from the score. The piece might begin like this:

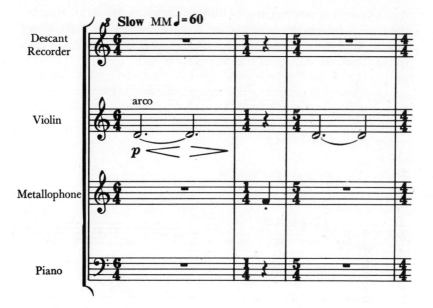

(iv) Choose at random any six different notes on the piano. Number the notes 1–6 from lowest to highest. By throwing a dice, make a long succession of these notes from the chance numbers appearing at each throw. Thus, if the original selection of notes is:

the result of dice selection might be:

Extend the range of this series by allowing each note named to be played in any one of four octaves. Number the octaves 1–4 from lowest to highest. Throw the dice to determine in which octave any given note shall be played. (In this case, of course, 5 and 6 on the dice will not count: throw again.) The result might be:

Clearly, this music will have to be performed on instruments capable of producing these pitches. It could be a piece for piano solo, or you could select a number of instruments and score the music accordingly.

Throw the dice again to determine the duration of each note. Work as in (iii), but this time let the numbers on the dice represent *half*-beats of the pulse. With crotchets as the standard pulse, a throw of 5 would give a note value of ♩♪; a throw of 3 would give a note value of ♩.

Arranged for piano solo, our piece might begin like this:

Is there anything we might add to this music which could also be deter-mined by chance operations?

(v)   Work again as in (iv), but make two successions of notes and run them simultaneously. Devise a system for determining different dura-tions of *silence* at certain points in the music.

(vi)   Devise chance operations by which you may determine timbre, pitch, duration, volume, and the order of succession of notes in a piece of music. Notate the piece exactly according to the results of your dice-throwing, or whatever means you devise, and arrange for the piece to be played.

(vii)   *A game for at least six players.* Using chance methods as in (iv) above, determine a fragment of musical material and notate it in a 'box'. Do this for six boxes and arrange them around a circle. In the centre of the circle place a seventh box containing *one* note only. The following example shows a completed 'score'.

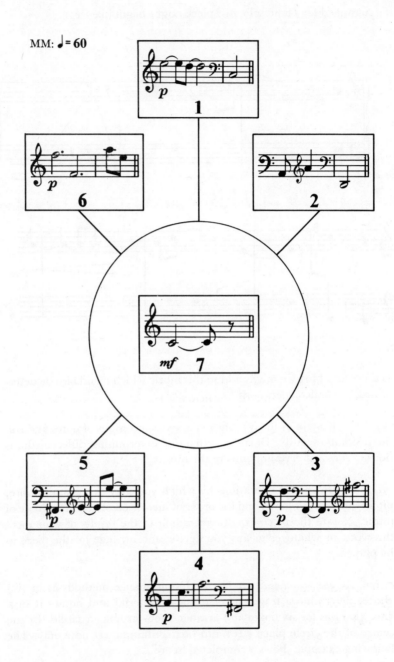

MM: ♩ = 60

The number of players will depend on the range in pitch of the instruments chosen (though you could start the other way round and limit the possible results of your dice-throwing to the pitch ranges of whatever instruments are available). In the example we print, the material in box number 1 could be played by one person on a piano; alternatively it could be divided between two players, one with a recorder, the other with a cello. Box number 6, on the other hand, could be played by any treble instruments but, as it contains no notes below the treble stave, bass instruments would be excluded.

Having decided which material can be played by which instruments, boxes 1–6 are each allotted to one or more players as 'starting boxes'. Box 7 is not occupied.

The game begins with everyone playing the succession of notes once round in the given order of boxes 1–6. Try to avoid gaps between the boxes but adhere strictly to the rhythmic patterns which have been determined by the dice. Players must be alert to what is happening in the box preceding their own, and be ready to follow on without a break.

As soon as the last note of box 6 is played, the field is open for any player to jump in with the *opening material* of any box, if that material is at a pitch suitable to his instrument (i.e. it must not be transposed). The other players must try to spot this opening 'clue' and complete the box without disrupting the rhythmic pattern. Again, this must be done without transposing material so that the notes to be played must be within the compass of a player's instrument or else he keeps silent. As soon as that box is completed, the field is open again and any player may be ready to continue with material from the beginning of another box. This in its turn is completed by those with appropriate instruments who are able to spot the clue. If two or more players begin different boxes at the same moment, they should stop and begin again.

Box number 7, however, does signify 'simultaneous attack'. Its pitch has been determined by the same chance methods as the notes in the other boxes, and this pitch is fixed. The instruments which can play it, therefore, may be limited in number. Playing box 7 is the signal for the game to end. As soon as they recognise it, all the other players must return immediately to their 'starting boxes', play their original fragment through once, and stop.

The game can, of course, be simplified by inventing material for the boxes rather than determining the notes and durations with dice. If you invent material you can restrict the pitch range in any way you wish; you can also make the fragments as distinctive as you wish and thereby make it easier to distinguish one from another.

A game of this kind is not as frivolous as it might at first appear. The players must develop considerable powers of memory and be able to react quickly to the clues as they hear them. This is the kind of concentration we expect in a competitive sport. When we see it in football we applaud. Composers such as Morton Feldman, Lukas Foss and Christian Wolff have shown us that a demand for similar kinds of concentration and speedy reaction can be as important musically as other kinds of musicianly skill. Devise games for yourself.

C

The following example shows a piece for soprano and alto glockenspiels made according to some of the suggestions in (v) above. The alto glockenspiel was a fully chromatic one, but the soprano glockenspiel was diatonic only. To begin with four notes were selected on each instrument: on one instrument the notes were numbered 1–4 leaving 5 and 6 on the dice to represent silences, on the other the notes were numbered 1, 2, 5, 6, with 3 and 4 representing the silences in this case.

Dice were thrown for the succession of notes and silences, and then thrown again for durations. Finally, the piece was scored for the two instruments. The chance-devised material extends to the half-way point of bar 14; from this point on the soprano glockenspiel part is mirrored while the alto glockenspiel part is repeated exactly as before.

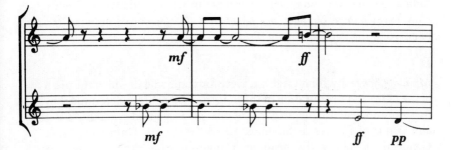

The dynamics were determined by dice using a five point scale (6 indicating an extension of whatever was thrown immediately before it).

A performance of the *Game for at least six players* can be heard on band 10 of the accompanying disc.

D

Music of Changes by John Cage is a piece for piano solo in which the pitch of the notes and the duration of the notes and silences are determined by *I-Ching*, an ancient Chinese game of chance. Cage writes about *I-Ching* and *Music of Changes* in his book *Silence* (Wesleyan University Press, Connecticut) under the heading 'Composition as Process'. He also deals with indeterminacy and describes a number of indeterminate compositions. Try to hear some of the indeterminate music of Christian Wolff, Morton Feldman and Earle Brown. In particular, Feldman's *Durations* would be a useful follow-up to Assignment (ii.3) and Earle Brown's *Available Forms 1* (1961) is also of interest. There is a good account of aleatory music with descriptions of works by these composers in *Twentieth Century Music: An Introduction* by Eric Salzman (Prentice Hall 'History of Music Series', 1967). Further descriptions of indeterminate music similar to the *Game* in (vii) above, will be found in back numbers of *Perspectives of New Music* (Princeton).

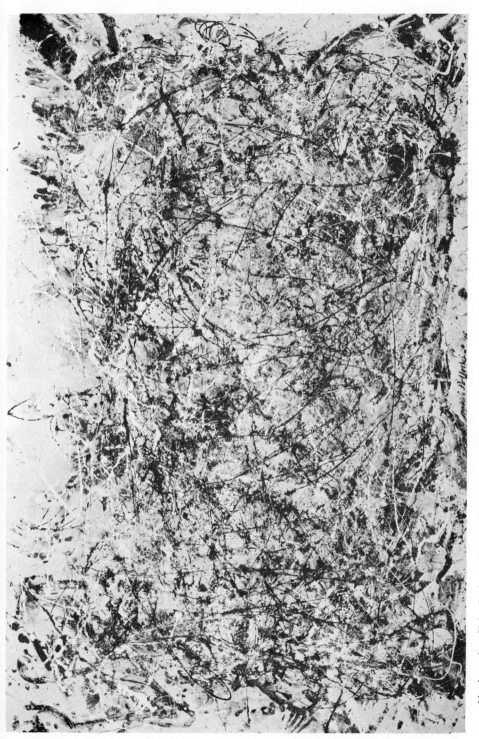

15   *Number 1* (1948) by Jackson Pollock (Collection, the Museum of Modern Art, New York)

Currently, artists in many different fields are showing interest in the 'happy accident'. The random procedures they adopt to produce their works often bridge the apparent gap between technology and creativity. Recently we have seen computer-generated graphics, computer verse, cybernetic environments, painting machines, computer composed and played music. Among this last category are works by Xenakis and Zinovieff (*Partita for Unattended Computer*). Schools possessing any equipment, mechanical or electronic, which could be employed for random selection processes, could perhaps follow-up this project in several ways other than the purely musical.

Look at reproductions of works by abstract expressionist artists such as Jackson Pollock and Mark Rothko. Discuss the possible reasons for random procedures in their work. Some useful information will be found in Albert Elsen's *Purposes of Art* (Holt, Reinhart and Winston, Inc., 1967). Compare the work of these painters with the philosophies of John Cage and the attitude to contemporary life expressed in a poem such as E. E. Cummings' *Pity this busy monster, manunkind* (*Faber Book of Modern American Verse*, W. H. Auden (ed.), Faber, 1956).

Project 25
Heterophony (1)

A

In the earlier projects on melody and rhythm we have seen how primitive music is closely associated with magic and ritual. The sounds made by percussion instruments—perhaps the beating of a hollow tree trunk or drum—seem to have magical powers because they can arouse great excitement and help to co-ordinate physical movement both in the dance and at work. Just as the rhythmic patterns of primitive ritual dance are usually short and repetitive, so primitive melody often consists of simple two- and three-note patterns repeated over and over again. The effect of this endless repetition soon becomes incantatory and hypnotic, and when several rhythmic patterns are played simultaneously (as happens in a great deal of African music) the effect is greatly intensified.

Primitive music is essentially monodic: however complex its rhythmic patterns may become, its melodies remain as single lines unsupported by harmony. This does not mean that the music is restricted to *solo* song. One of the oldest musical forms is that of alternating phrases between solo voice and chorus. It is most frequently heard in primitive work-songs, where the chorus repeats each phrase sung by the leader, and the combined singing of several voices can give rise to several versions of the tune being performed at the same time. This produces a crude, unintentional polyphony which, like the melody it elaborates, has no harmonic significance. The additional parts have happened by accident, and there is no attempt to control their shape: they are related to each other only in so much as they have arisen from the same rhythmic or melodic line. Such treatment is more properly called *heterophony*—literally 'other sounds'—and it constitutes the most primitive attempt to decorate a single rhythmic or melodic line by the addition of other parts.

In the music of primitive cultures—and this includes the music of children for they are also at a primitive stage of development—spontaneous heterophony occurs quite naturally in ensemble singing. Consider what happens when young children chant the rhymes and counting songs associated with play. Their chanting is half-way between speech and song, usually in a pattern of two notes roughly a minor third (three semitones) apart.

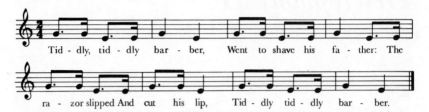

When a group of children chant this rhyme together, the two-note pattern is often maintained by some while others extend it to a pattern of three notes.

Thus the two versions are sung simultaneously, making simple heterophony. The three-note version is the heterophonic part, since it is derived from and elaborates the original.

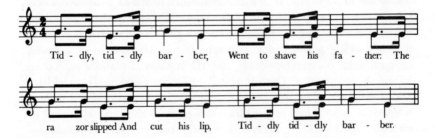

Frequently, the three-note pattern is further extended until the chanting has a four- or even five-note range.

It is probable that this process of extending simple note patterns led to the discovery of the five note, or pentatonic, scale which avoids the interval of a semitone. Certainly, versions of the pentatonic scale occur in musical cultures throughout the world, though the note pattern may have semitonal or even microtonal intensifications as frequently occurs in Indian music: but however we may elaborate the pattern by introducing other notes between the main steps of the scale, the music remains basically pentatonic. In the two following traditional Irish tunes, the additional 'decorative' notes are marked with a cross. In spite of their presence the music is clearly pentatonic.

Such melodic elaborations of the pentatonic scale are common: but the music could also be treated *heterophonically* without in any way destroying the pentatonic character of the note pattern. The additional parts might merely be an arbitrary ornamentation of the melody. Alternatively, it is possible to support the melodic line by adding drones and ostinati or by combining *different* melodies derived from the same pentatonic scale. In so doing, we shall be concerned with controlling the texture of the music as well as the melodic patterns, and this aspect of heterophony will be more thoroughly explored in the following project. For the moment we will concentrate on a less sophisticated use of the materials, starting with a heterophonic exploration of rhythm.

B

(i)   Choose four or five non-melodic percussion instruments of contrasted sound quality. Some could be high, dry sounds, others deeper and more resonant. You could use several drums of various sizes, including bongos and a tom-tom, but the contrast will be more striking if you can include some wooden instruments such as claves and temple blocks. Explore other sounds. What percussion effects can you make with your fingers or hands, either clapping or slapping different parts of your body?

When you have a selection of contrasted percussion sounds, invent a short rhythmic pattern which can be repeated over and over again on one of the larger drums. Don't make the pattern too complex because it's going to be used as a basis for elaboration by the other instruments. Such a pattern as ♩ ♩ ♩ ♫ or ♩ ♩ ♩ ♫ ♫ will be most suitable. Let the strongest accent fall on the first note of the group so that it's clear where the phrase begins. The rhythm can now be treated in a variety of ways:

(1) Working in pairs or groups of three, play the rhythmic pattern in unison. Decide which instrument is to maintain the rhythm without variation, and when the pattern has been established in unison, let the

other instruments elaborate the original by improvising more complex patterns against it. It is easiest if each instrument lets the strongest accent fall in the same place, but the music will be more interesting if the heterophonic parts occasionally have phrases which cross the original pattern;

(2) Working in larger groups, begin with a simple rhythmic pattern played repeatedly by one instrument while the others are added in turn. Let each new instrument introduce a variant of the original rhythm, maintaining their pattern throughout the improvisation. When all the instruments have entered, let them drop out in turn until you are again left with the instrument that began;

(3) Vary the above by letting each instrument take over the rhythmic pattern of the last while he proceeds to improvise variants of it;

(4) Explore the sound relationships between the instruments you are using, and group them in pairs by choosing instruments of similar quality or contrasting dry sounds with more resonant sounds. Make a more extensive composition by interpolating improvisations by each pair of instruments between repetitions of the 'refrain' played by the full ensemble. If you wish, the original pattern can be maintained by one instrument throughout;

(5) Make a heterophonic composition for three groups of percussion instruments set off by the idea of Earth, Fire and Water. Which instruments will be most suitable for each? When you have selected the instruments you want to use, decide on a basic rhythmic pattern which can be used by each group who can now work independently. Play your pieces to each other. Could they now be combined into one composition? You might begin with the Earth music, introducing Water and Fire in turn against it. Explore the spatial resources of the room. The effect will be greater if the three groups are separated from each other in different corners of the room.

(ii) Treat the following rhyme as you did *There was a man of double deed* in the first project on Exploring Melody. Read it together aloud, chanting the words rhythmically. Notice how your chanting soon begins to hover between speech and song. If you respond to the natural inflections and rhythms of the words, the chanting will quickly shape itself into simple patterns of two or three notes repeated over and over again. Allow these to develop until the chanting has become song and you have arranged the complete rhyme in a melodic pattern using only two or three notes. Work over your setting several times until you are completely satisfied with its rhythmic and melodic shape.

This is the key of the kingdom:
In that kingdom is a city,
In that city is a town,
In that town there is a street,
In that street there winds a lane,
In that lane there is a yard,
In that yard there is a house,
In that house there waits a room,
In that room there is a bed,
On that bed there is a basket,
   A basket of flowers.

Flowers in the basket,
Basket on the bed,
Bed in the chamber,
Chamber in the house,
House in the weedy yard,
Yard in the winding lane,
Lane in the broad street,
Street in the high town,
Town in the city,
City in the kingdom:
This is the key of the kingdom.

Now divide into two groups. Let the first sing the original version of
the music while the others elaborate the melodic line by adding other
notes around those of the tune. Don't try to be too adventurous at first:
much of the time you will be singing in unison with the other group, but
now and again you will feel able to decorate the melody with new
patterns that spring naturally from it and then return to join the main
tune. Notice how the added (heterophonic) parts tend to use the notes
of the pentatonic scale. Can you suggest why? You might also try
elaborating the melody on instruments. Xylophones and glockenspiels
could well be used.

(iii)   Sing this traditional Scottish lullaby. Notice that it is basically
pentatonic, with incidental melodic elaborations which pass between
the main degrees of the scale.

In our heterophonic setting of *This is the key of the kingdom* we noticed
how the melodies followed the pattern of the pentatonic scale. There
we were elaborating a two-note monody, and the additional parts arose
naturally from the original melodic shape. We could, however, use the

O Can Ye Sew Cushions?

Gently rocking

O can ye sew cush - ions, and can ye sew sheets? And can ye___ sing___ bal - lu - low___ when the bairn greets? And hee and baw, bird - ie, and hee and baw, lamb, And hee and baw, bird - ie, my bon - nie wee lamb. Hee - o, wee - o, what - 'll I do wi' ye? Black's the life that I lead wi' ye. Mo - ny o' ye, lit - tle for to gie ye, Hee - o, wee - o, what'll I do wi' ye?

principle of heterophony to *support* a melodic line rather than elaborate it. It would certainly seem more appropriate to treat this lullaby in such a way because the character of the melody might easily be lost if we decorate it too closely.

We have already discovered how several versions of the same melody can be played at the same time. The incidental dissonances which occur are not disturbing because we are not attempting to control them according to the conventions of harmonic progression. In the same way, melodies derived from the same pentatonic scale can be played simultaneously. Since there are no semitones in the pentatonic scale, the harsher dissonances (the minor second, major seventh and augmented fourth) do not arise, and the dissonances that do occur have no harmonic significance. We do not feel they have to be resolved. More important is the fact that the pentatonic scale has no clear tonic or 'home note'. A pentatonic melody can end equally well on *any* note, and the music will not sound unfinished. Because of this, no degree of the scale has a particular function. They are all equally important.

How shall we treat this lullaby? We don't want to disturb the serene, lilting nature of the melody by introducing too much movement in the other parts. Perhaps we could help to bring out the gentle rocking rhythm by adding a simple ostinato figure (possibly on C and D) and support this with a drone. If we use instruments, the drone could be played on a violin or cello which could be doubled by a metallophone, and the ostinato could be played on a xylophone using soft sticks. Perhaps we could echo the end of each phrase of the melody on a glockenspiel. Alternatively, we could use voices to support the melody. The accompaniment should again be simple with little rhythmic movement. It might be effective to add parts above as well as below the tune.

(iv)   Make a heterophonic setting of this poem by Kathleen Raine. Although written in the mid-twentieth century, the poem reminds us of an older (folk) tradition: the subject is one which has fired the imagination of poets for centuries, and much the same incantatory rhythms and associative chain of ideas are present in countless poems of folk origin. The poem is about incarnation and the mystery of growth, and we must try to reflect this in the music. Our setting could be for voices only, but we might well introduce some pitchless percussion instruments to elaborate the verbal rhythm. Perhaps we could find musical sounds to represent some of the verbal images. They might be linked in a chain just as the ideas are linked in the poem. How shall we make the music suggest growth? We could begin with a solo voice, gradually adding other voices

and instruments. Perhaps the rhythmic or melodic patterns could become more elaborate as the music progresses. Whatever we do, we
must not impose on the poem anything which destroys its essential
qualities or obscures its meaning.

Spell of Creation

Within the flower there lies a seed,
Within the seed there springs a tree,
Within the tree there spreads a wood.

In the wood there burns a fire,
And in the fire there melts a stone,
Within the stone a ring of iron.

Within the ring there lies an O
Within the O there looks an eye,
In the eye there swims a sea,

And in the sea reflected sky,
And in the sky there shines the sun,
Within the sun a bird of gold.

Within the bird there beats a heart,
And from the heart there flows a song,
And in the song there sings a word.

And in the word there speaks a world,
A word of joy, a world of grief,
From joy and grief there springs my love.

O love, my love, there springs a world,
And on the world there shines a sun
And in the sun there burns a fire,

Within the fire consumes my heart
And in my heart there beats a bird,
And in the bird there wakes an eye,

Within the eye, earth, sea and sky,
Earth, sky and sea within an O
Lie like the seed within the flower.

KATHLEEN RAINE, from *The Year One*

C

(i)   These two short pieces for percussion were made by a group of thirteen-year-old boys. The only available instruments were three hand drums, maracas, a tambourine and an assortment of triangles. At first, all the instruments were used; but the maracas, tambourine and all but one of the triangles were eventually discarded. The group decided to include some wood sounds to contrast with the triangle and drums, and a pair of claves were made out of suitable wood in the woodwork room.

The first piece, for two hand drums and claves, began as a unison rhythm. It was decided to maintain the regular crotchet pattern in the first hand drum while the other instrument improvised new rhythms growing from it. At first, there was a strong tendency for the music to get faster, and the heterophonic parts were so complex that all three players quickly lost the pulse. Eventually, the group began to realise the value of silence and of listening and reacting to each other, and the heterophonic parts settled into a repetitive two-bar pattern, the movement broken up by rests.

The second piece, involving five instruments, was built on the same rhythmic pattern. This time, hand drum I introduced the rhythm alone and the other instruments were added at two bar intervals. The players first decided on the order in which the instruments should appear, and agreed that each should play a two-bar pattern which would be repeated without variation. The decision to end the piece by dropping out each instrument in reverse order came later. The $\frac{3/6}{4/8}$ cross rhythm in hand drum 3 evolved from a group of six quavers accented normally in triple time as ♩♩ ♩♩ ♩♩. Over repeated improvisations, the natural accents were gradually displaced and became ♩♩♩ ♩♩♩. This $\frac{6}{8}$ rhythm was soon taken up by the claves, which had previously played three crotchets in the first bar of the group.

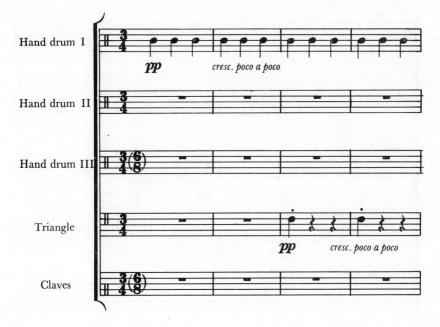

(ii)   *Earth, Water and Fire:* this was a classroom composition made by a group of dance students in a College of Education. The music was later used as a stimulus for movement by the rest of the class.

The players were divided into three groups and suitable instruments were chosen for each part of the composition. Those making the Earth music used voices (making grunting sounds) and hand drums, while others in their group beat the floor with their bare hands and feet. Those making the Water music used metal percussion (triangles, sleigh bells and small cymbal), claves, xylophones and glockenspiels. The group making the Fire music used a tam-tam, a large suspended cymbal played with soft sticks, a second cymbal which was swept in circular motions across the (wooden) floor, a wood block, and sheets of paper which were crumpled in the hand and rubbed together. Each piece was composed independently but over the same rhythmic ostinato. This was played on a large tom-tom in the middle of the room with the three groups arranged at the sides in a triangle.

FIRE

EARTH

Tom-tom

WATER

The tom-tom provided a continuous ostinato accompaniment to and link between the three pieces which were first played in sequence and then simultaneously. Later, when movement was introduced, the dancers moved within the triangle, approaching each group of players in turn and weaving around the tom-tom in the centre.

(iii)   *O Can Ye Sew Cushions?:* this arrangement was made by a mixed class of eleven-year-olds, some of whom had used the Orff *Schulwerk* at their previous school.

The melody was first sung unaccompanied in unison. When it was suggested that instruments might be added, several of the children assumed that these would play in unison with the tune. Some of the singers took glockenspiels and attempted to play the tune as they sang, finding the notes on the instruments by ear. To help them, the E bars were removed. The playing was at first not very accurate: there were several mistakes in pitch, especially where wide intervals were involved, and this led to considerable hesitation in the rhythmic flow.

The players were now encouraged to keep in time, ignoring any mistakes. As a result, the glockenspiels began to provide heterophonic parts which gave an arbitary ornamentation of the melodic line.

After working at this over several improvisations, the group decided to introduce other instruments, adding xylophones and a metallophone which also attempted to play in unison with the voices. The extreme resonance of the metallophone was soon considered unsuitable to 'double' the melody, and the player began to restrict the melodic range and rhythmic movement of his part. This was eventually limited to one note which was used as a drone.

The success of this was quickly acknowledged by the others, who immediately wanted to discipline their own parts by imposing some restriction on the melodic or rhythmic pattern. This led the xylophone players to devise a simple ostinato figure using only three notes, while the glockenspiel players limited their parts to echoing the end of each phrase of the tune. The result is an effective arrangement of the melody, and, like Orff's children's music, its beauty arises from its complete simplicity.

O Can Ye Sew Cushions?

Hee - o, wee - o, What'll I do wi ye?

D

Examples of primitive heterophony can be heard in *Ancient and Oriental Music*, which is vol. I in the HMV series 'The History of Music in Sound', and, significantly, twentieth-century composers who have taken inspiration from the music of primitive cultures have frequently used heterophonic techniques. In particular, the children's music of Carl Orff makes considerable use of heterophony, and vol. I of *Music for Children* (edited by Margaret Murray and published in five volumes by Schott) is devoted to exercises based on the pentatonic scale.

Examples of heterophony are also to be found in the work of Bartók, Kodály and Britten who, like Orff, have all written extensively for children. Listen to the opening section of the second 'Dance in Bulgarian Rhythm' from vol. VI of Bartók's *Mikrokosmos* (Boosey and Hawkes), and study the heterophonic treatment of the plainsong hymn in Britten's *Curlew River* (published by Faber).

Morton Feldman's *Piece for Four Pianos* explores a similar heterophonic technique. The four pianists each play the same music. They start together by sounding the first chord simultaneously, but thereafter

237

each proceeds independently from the others. The music is not technically difficult, and, if four pianos could be brought together, a performance could be given by pianists of modest ability.

Charles Ives' *General Putnam's Camp*, in which two brass bands playing different music converge on one another, would make an interesting follow-up to the fifth part of Assignment (i) above.

Project 26
Heterophony (2)

A

Heterophony in which a single melodic line is elaborated in another voice or instrument frequently occurs in primitive music which has no concept of harmony or harmonic progression. In its simplest form it is no more than a crude attempt at decorating monody, and the accidental dissonances which occur between the parts have no significance in harmonic terms. The music we made in Project 25 arose from the idea of combining different versions of the same melody. Our concern was with the rhythmic and melodic development of individual lines, but this didn't mean we accepted any random selection of notes put together without thought for the wholeness of the piece. The heterophonic parts grew out of the original melody, whether this was a three-note monody, a pentatonic scale, or one using a full diatonic range.

We can control our material in another way. Instead of beginning with a single melodic line from which everything else is derived we might take our melodic ideas from the shapes and patterns suggested by a *vertical* combination of sounds. An interesting chord discovered at the keyboard can provide the basis for a heterophonic composition. The notes can be arranged in any melodic order, rhythm or combination, and the sounds taken together will still be satisfying for they always form part or the whole of the chord from which they were derived.

B

(i)   Imagine a peal of bells. Some churches have only one or two bells, but the ever-changing pattern of a set of five or more bells expertly rung has a magic of its own. The sounds mingle with each other, and the reverberations go on indefinitely because there is no damper to stop the vibrations. We can imitate this effect on the piano by playing single notes one after another while the sustaining pedal is held down. Compared with bells the sound is thin, because a large, well-made bell is rich in upper partials which sound in sympathy with the most prominent note, called the 'strike' note. Several bells rung together or in quick succession produce an enormous number of notes all audible at the same time. It doesn't disturb us that these notes are not all consonant with each other or that the vertical pattern of sound remains the same whatever the order in which the bells are rung. Like the heterophonic music we explored in the previous project, the sounds come together without harmonic significance.

Let's make a piece of music about bells, or rather about the *idea* of bells because this composition will use only voices. If you like, we can use words to heighten the effect and to help set off our musical ideas. Bells immediately suggest verbal sounds like 'ding-dong-dell', but we could be more sophisticated and set a short phrase such as 'Hosanna in excelsis Deo' or 'Alleluia' repeated several times.

Begin at the keyboard by exploring the effect of different combinations of notes played simultaneously. Experiment with a variety of chords until you find one which suggests interesting patterns and shapes. If you use both hands the chord could be in ten parts, but you'll probably find five or six notes enough. Try using adjacent notes as well as wider intervals. The chord could consist of a cluster of tones and semitones, but this will restrict the range of the parts. Don't space the notes too widely because the melodic material will eventually be selected from the *complete* chord. Keep the notes within the compass of the voices in your group.

When you are satisfied with the shape, colour and spacing of your chord, play it several times at every dynamic level from the faintest whisper to the strongest fortissimo. Listen carefully to different parts of the chord. Play the lower half on its own, then the top part. Try the notes in every combination. Is it still satisfying when some are omitted?

Your group can experiment individually with melodic phrases derived from the chord. It might be helpful to use a short text. Here are two possible suggestions taken from songs in plays by Shakespeare:

> Full fathom five thy father lies.
> Sea-nymphs hourly ring his knell:
> Hark, now I hear them,—ding-dong bell.
>
> from *The Tempest*

> Let us all ring fancy's knell:
> I'll begin it,—ding-dong bell.
>
> from *The Merchant of Venice*

If you use a text, let the words suggest the shape and rhythm of the phrase. You might eventually decide on one particular melodic idea and treat it in various ways by altering the rhythm or note order or singing it in canon. Alternatively, you might devise several short melodic patterns, each beginning on a different note of the chord. Listen to each one separately and decide how they might be fitted together. You could begin with a solo voice repeating one phrase several times in different rhythms while you build up the texture with the other voices entering one by one. How will you continue? You could end there with an exciting dynamic climax; or reverse the procedure until you are again left with a single voice; or you could extend the piece, developing the material by varying the rhythms and texture. Perhaps you could group the voices in various ways and explore relationships between them. There are many possibilities.

(ii)   Voice grouping could in itself provide the inspiration for a hetero-phonic composition. The idea of spatial separation between groups of performers can lead to vivid contrasts of texture, and it has been used to great effect by many composers since the early sixteenth century. Let's make a piece of music for voices which explores the possibilities of *concerto*. We shall not impose any restrictions on the pitch of the sounds we use, but organise our material by controlling the texture and pattern of sonorities while rejecting anything which seems out of place.

The range of sounds we can produce with our voices is enormous. Experiment with sustained and short sounds, percussive noises of no definite pitch (a string of consonants such as TKTK could provide an exciting rhythmic figure) and explore the extremes as well as the middle of your vocal compass. You might also explore less usual effects like whispers, sighs and shrieks, but don't try to include in the piece every vocal sound you can produce.

The sounds you eventually select and the style and structure of the music will depend on the physical resources of the room you are working in. If it's a large room of irregular shape with a platform, recesses and even a balcony you could exploit the space in the way sixteenth-century Venetian composers made use of the special resources of St Mark's. If it's a small room, you could put a group of voices in each corner but on different levels by using boxes or chairs. The level of sound can play an important part in the structure of the music. Experiment with the size and composition of the various groups. You might put low voices in one, high voices in another, have some groups of two or three and others of twenty or more. Involve as many voices as you can. The greater the number, the more variety of texture is possible. You might decide that each group should make only one kind of musical sound (sustained chords, percussive noises) or that they react to the ideas of other groups by taking up and developing each other's material. Perhaps each group or pair of groups could have a separate conductor, or alternatively one conductor could control and shape the entire composition.

C

(i)   The short Alleluia on p. 243 combines the idea of concerto with a heterophonic canon derived from a note-cluster between E and C.

Spread horizontally, the chord forms a six-note scale consisting of two tones, semitone, tone and semitone:

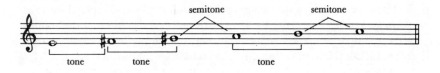

The melodic line closely follows the shape of the chord, with the notes heard in both descending and ascending order.

The piece is intended for performance by two three-part choirs of equal voices, spatially separated in the manner of Cantoris and Decani.* The music could, however, be adapted to involve any number of voices.

The phrases should be sung in free speech rhythm. Arrows indicate the approximate points of entry of each voice in relation to the other parts. The notation is otherwise self-explanatory.

The canon is here treated only at the interval of one note, but since the music is heterophonic it would work equally well at any point. The composition could be extended by delaying the interval of imitation at first, and gradually bringing it closer to the leading voice. This might

* In the Anglican church, the choir is normally divided into two groups called Cantoris and Decani. The Cantoris is positioned on the 'north' side, the Decani facing them on the 'south'. The 'north' and 'south' are ecclesiastical directions assuming that the altar is at the 'east' end.

242

make the music too repetitious, but the heterophonic passages could be balanced by linking monodic episodes, perhaps alternating between the antiphonal choirs.

(ii)   *Concerto for Voices:* this piece was a classroom composition involving about twenty-five children. They used a solo voice and divided the others into two groups of different size who responded, under the direction of a conductor, to the improvisations of the solo voice. The large group sustained chords by holding different notes pitched at random until a change was indicated by the conductor; the second group punctuated these chords with short, explosive rhythmic figures using a variety of hard and soft consonants; and the solo voice sang a mostly sustained melodic line in free rhythm which was evolved over repeated improvisations by interaction of tempi, texture and dynamics between the groups.

Movement was an important feature of the composition. The two groups were spaced apart and remained stationary while the solo voice took up various positions moving towards each group in turn and using the whole space of the room which was explored at a variety of levels by the use of boxes.

D

The spatial separation of groups of voices and instruments is an important feature of much sixteenth-century Venetian music, and the textural contrasts brought about by the principle of voice grouping was much used in the madrigal during the second half of the century. An excellent recording of Venetian polychoral music by Giovanni Gabrieli and other composers associated with St Mark's is listed in the discography, and it would be instructive to compare sixteenth-century concerto techniques with those of the late baroque and the virtuoso concerti of the nineteenth century.

Less conventional uses of the voice have been explored by a number of twentieth-century composers. Messiaen uses voices percussively in the first and fifth movements of *Cinq Rechants*, and there is a similar passage in the first of Alexander Goehr's *Two Choruses Op. 14*. A fuller range of vocal techniques is used in Penderecki's *St Luke Passion* and in Berio's *Visage*, where the vocal inflections, which range from inarticulated speech to song, are related to electronically produced sounds.

Improvisation on given chords and note-clusters is used in John Paynter's *Exultet coelum laudibus* for mixed voices and optional tuned percussion (O.U.P.). The work alternates freely notated heterophonic passages with monody and simple two-part writing.

16   Children singing with guitar

Project 27
Discovering harmony

A

To most of us a harmonic sense is instinctive. It does not depend on a formal academic training, but on aural experience of the harmonic conventions of western music. Most of the music we have heard and sung during our lives has a harmonic basis, for harmony has been a fundamental part of our music since the early renaissance. Consider the music we made in the projects on heterophony. There we were combining melodies without reference to the harmonic implications, and although we were aware of the vertical combination of sounds we did not try to control their progression. Our experience of western music makes this no longer seem completely natural. We want to control the progression of sounds according to the conventions of other music we hear.

Harmony—the ordered progression of consonance and dissonance—has traditionally been regarded as a specialist study beyond the ability of all but the musically gifted. Despite our common experience of music which is fundamentally harmonic, we delay introducing any creative work in harmony until the Secondary School, where we select the most gifted children and subject them to a text-book harmony course which is often unrelated to practical music-making. If it is to have any value, a harmony course must arise from practical experience. We must be allowed to discover harmonic principles for ourselves rather than learn a text-book formula or a set of 'rules' devised, often on somewhat dubious grounds, by someone else.

The most natural way to do this is with the voice. We can begin to develop our harmonic awareness through vocal improvisation: later on we can examine the implications of what we have done, deciding which intervals were pleasing, which best avoided in a particular context; discovering why a harmonic progression was satisfying; and finding where dissonance arose and how it was treated.

Like the folk-singer, our *first* authority is the ear. We don't need a *theoretical* knowledge of harmony before we can improvise in parts, as is shown by the spontaneous improvised part-singing prevalent in areas of Wales and in many non-conformist churches in the English industrial Midlands and the North. Few of these singers have had any formal training in harmony and many cannot read music, yet they respond intuitively to the harmonic implications of a single melodic line.

B

(i)   Before we begin to explore harmony creatively we must widen our experience of singing in parts. The best way to do this is by singing rounds and simple canons which have a harmonic basis. Here are three to add to your repertoire.

With easy movement

RAVENSCROFT from *Pammelia* (1609)

Quickly and rhythmically

RAVENSCROFT from *Pammelia* (1609)

TALLIS

248

Sing them first in unison, then in canon. Don't just concentrate on your own part, but listen to the others as you sing. Notice how your line contributes to the harmony, completing the chords and, in the canon by Tallis, adding colour by setting up moments of harmonic tension (dissonances) which are resolved on the next beat of the bar. Notice the *rhythm* of the harmony: how it flows on, where it repeats the same pattern of chords, how the interest is held by the changing texture as the voices continually cross each other. Is this music which would appeal to an audience, or is it only of interest to the performers?

Experiment with different ways of performing the music. Vary the dynamics, perhaps starting softly, building a crescendo in the middle and then dying away at the end. Try humming quietly instead of singing the words. Play your part on an instrument (glockenspiels and xylophones will do very well) or sing and play at the same time. Always try to be aware of what the other parts are doing. With practice you should be able to sing one part while you play another. Perhaps some pitchless percussion instruments could be added. They would certainly be effective in *Hey, ho, nobody at home*.

(ii)   Here's a song to sing without instrumental accompaniment. Don't learn it with the piano (this will impose someone else's idea of the harmony on you) but join in as soon as you can when you hear it. Don't worry if, after a time, your version of the words or music differs from the one you first heard. This is the essence of folk music.

Michael, Row the Boat Ashore

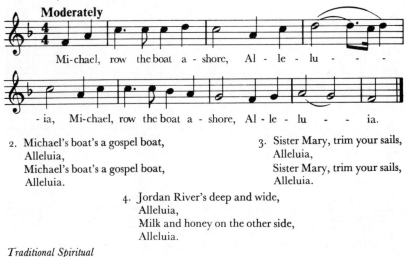

Mi-chael, row the boat a - shore, Al - le - lu - - -
- ia, Mi-chael, row the boat a - shore, Al - le - lu - - ia.

2. Michael's boat's a gospel boat,
Alleluia,
Michael's boat's a gospel boat,
Alleluia.

3. Sister Mary, trim your sails,
Alleluia,
Sister Mary, trim your sails,
Alleluia.

4. Jordan River's deep and wide,
Alleluia,
Milk and honey on the other side,
Alleluia.

Traditional Spiritual

249

When you know the song well, try to make up other tunes which will harmonise with it. You'll find it helpful to divide into two groups. Let the smaller group sing the melody while the others improvise harmony to it. At first, do this only in the *Alleluias*, singing the other phrases in unison. Later you will be able to add parts throughout the song. Don't worry if your first attempts produce too many discords: discords can be controlled by the way we continue the individual lines. Remember to listen to what the other parts are doing. Don't try to be too elaborate; the simplest way is often the best. You will soon find you can produce satisfying harmony which will enrich the melodic line.

As the added parts begin to take shape and form satisfying harmony, notice how they have dropped in number to two or three. This is because, in the compass of your voices, there are a limited number of notes which will form consonant harmony with each other.

A great deal of the music we hear every day has the tune in the highest part supported by harmony underneath. Most of the hymns we sing in church or assembly are arranged like this, but such treatment can become very dull. Try adding parts above as well as below the tune. If your new part closely follows the shape of the original melody you will probably have been singing the same tune three or six notes above or below it. Consecutive thirds and sixths are always pleasing. Can you suggest why?

Now improvise harmony to this song, another version of which appears in Junior Book I of the *Oxford School Music*.

The Old Grey Goose

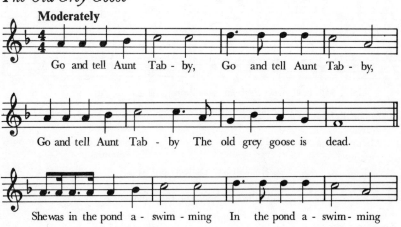

Moderately

Go and tell Aunt Tab - by,   Go and tell Aunt Tab - by,

Go and tell Aunt Tab - by   The old grey goose is   dead.

She was in the pond a - swim - ming   In   the pond a - swim - ming

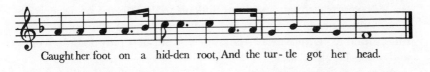

Caught her foot on a hid-den root, And the tur-tle got her head.

2. The gander is mourning,
   The gander is mourning,
   The gander is mourning,
   For now she is dead.
   She was in the pond etc.

3. The goslings are weeping,
   The goslings are weeping,
   The goslings are weeping,
   For the old grey goose is dead.
   She was in the pond etc.

English Traditional

Treat other songs you know in the same way and begin to build up a repertoire of unaccompanied folk-songs. *The Penguin Book of English Folk Songs*, edited by R. Vaughan Williams and A. L. Lloyd, will provide some excellent material.

C

(i)   Not every song will be suitable for improvised part-singing, of course, especially if the harmonic implications are too complex. We began with *Michael, Row the Boat Ashore* and *The Old Grey Goose* because both these songs are based entirely on three chords. These three chords, built on the first (tonic), fourth (subdominant) and fifth (dominant) degrees of the scale, are the basis of all diatonic harmony, and most of us find little difficulty in improvising vocally within this simple chord structure. Movement in parallel thirds should arise quite naturally in the *Alleluia* phrases of *Michael, Row the Boat Ashore* and, if necessary, help can be given by accompanying the singing with chords played on guitar or chordal dulcimer. The piano should not be used, however, as it will always suggest *melodic* shape even when playing block chords.

Al - le - lu - - - ia,

Even at this stage, work need not be limited to songs in major keys using only the primary triads. We have a natural harmonic sense and can improvise in parts without a technical understanding of the harmonic structure. We don't need a *theoretical* knowledge of harmony any more than we need a knowledge of linguistics before we can talk.

(ii) Nevertheless, it's sometimes difficult to do this at first, especially if our experience of singing in parts has been limited. We cling to the tune, afraid to venture away from it in case our new part doesn't 'work' and others laugh at us.

In such a situation assistance must be given in discovering independent part movement by adding vocal drones, perhaps doubled by instruments, beneath the melody. Although drones are non-harmonic (there is no *progression* of harmony) this will give practice in holding a part against the tune. The drones can later be developed into simple ostinato figures which will eventually lead to independent part-singing.

Here's a song which suggests effective use of drones.

The Cutty Wren Song

2. 'O what will you do there?' says Milder to Molder,
   'O what will you do there?' says Fessel to Fo.
   'We'll hunt the cutty wren,' says John the Red Nose,
   'We'll hunt the cutty wren,' says John the Red Nose.

3. 'O how will you shoot her?' says **Milder to Molder**,
'O how will you shoot her?' says **Fessel to Fo**.
'With bows and with arrows,' says John the Red Nose,
'With bows and with arrows,' says John the Red Nose.

4. 'O how will you bring her?' says **Milder to Molder**,
'O how will you bring her?' says **Fessel to Fo**.
'On four strong men's shoulders,' says John the Red Nose,
'On four strong men's shoulders,' says John the Red Nose.

English Traditional

Sing it first in unison while a drone is played on a violin bowing across the open D and A strings. Now let a group of four or five sing the tune while the others sing the drone. If we played the drone on an organ or bagpipe it could be sustained continuously, but voices need to breathe. Exploit this in shaping the phrasing. Make the parts more interesting by using both notes.

Experiment with the rhythm, perhaps taking ideas from some rhythmic figure in the melody. A possible treatment might be:

and this could be contined throughout the song or the figuration could be varied. The voices might be strengthened by instrumental doubling and some pitchless percussion—perhaps a single hand drum playing variants of ♩♫♩—might effectively be included.

Drones could also be added to this traditional Northumbrian song.

Sair Fyeld, Hinny

Sair fyeld, hinny, Sair fyeld now, Sair fyeld, hin-ny, Sin' I ken-ned thou. I was young and lust-y,— I was fair and clear, I was young and lus-ty— Man-ya long— year. Sair fyeld, hinny, Sair fyeld now, Sair fyeld, hinny, Sin' I ken-ned thou.

2. When I was five and twenty I was brave and bold;
But now I'm five and sixty I'm both stiff and cold.

3. Thus spoke the old man to the oak tree:
Sair fyeld is I sin' I kenned thee.

Northumberland Traditional

The open fifth A and E will make a good support for the refrain, but although it could be continued throughout the song it is less successful as an accompaniment to the verse. Using the same interval of a fifth, we might experiment at the keyboard to find more suitable harmonic support for these sections by alternating C and G with G and D and returning to A and E at the end of the verse. The drone is thus developed towards real harmonic movement in a simple pattern of alternating tonic and dominant chords.

etc.

This principle can be used to explore more complex harmonic movement involving three or more chords, as is illustrated by the following song which is first supported by a continuous drone on A and E. A simple rhythm seems appropriate to reflect the lilting nature of the tune.

Fair Maid is a Lily-o

in - ju - ry, Gent - ly, John - ny, my jing - le - o.'

La, la, la.

2. I said, 'You know I love you, dear,'
   Fair maid is a lily-o,
   She whispered softly in my ear,
   'Come to me' *etc.*

3. I'll take her to the church some day,
   Fair maid is a lily-o,
   The birds will sing, and she will say,
   'Come to me' *etc.*

English Traditional

Notice how the end of each phrase suggests harmonic movement which is ignored by the drone. We could alter our arrangement of the music at these points by allowing the under parts to respond to the harmonic implications of the melodic line.

Voice 1
I put my hand all in her own, Fair maid is a

Voice 2
Voice 3
La, la, La, la,

li - ly - o, She said, 'Do you love me a - lone?

la, la, La, la,

Add to this arrangement. Keep the under parts as they are, while those singing the tune improvise other phrases which will harmonise with it.

Project 28
Building a chord

A

While improvised part-singing can be a valuable approach to harmony, we will soon feel the need to refine our material and enlarge our harmonic resource. If we work by intuition alone, we are merely reproducing the harmonic conventions of music with which we are most familiar. This, of course, has a value, for we are made aware by practical experience of vertical sound combinations which are seen in relation to their temporal progression. Unlike monody and heterophony, harmony is two-dimensional. We must control both the horizontal and vertical pattern.

How do we do this? If we are working from practical group improvisation we can control only our own part. What we do is dependent on the way others respond to the harmonic implications of the melody. We need to get outside the music, to see it as a whole. If we are to shape and control the entire structure we must be able to consider the vertical sounds both in isolation and within the context of their harmonic progression.

This is easier said than done. We can hardly halt the improvisation mid-flow, discuss possible improvements, and put the new version back into its context. The circumstances which led to it will probably not arise on the next occasion. Neither can we take each sound in isolation and consider it without reference to the part it plays in the general harmonic structure: as Stravinsky has remarked, an isolated sound is as meaningless as a still photograph taken from a cinematograph film.

We must therefore find some way of defining and relating these two fundamental aspects of harmony. The vertical patterns, which we call chords, can consist of any number of notes sounded simultaneously: but the basis of traditional harmony is a chord of three notes (a triad) made by adding intervals of a third and fifth above the root note. The triad can be formed on any degree of the scale and can appear in any position by inverting the chord so that the third or fifth replaces the root as the lowest note. The *sequence* of chords and the position in which they appear is responsible for the harmonic flow of the music, which is managed according to certain conventions. These we will begin to consider in Project 29. For the moment let us concentrate on the vertical aspect of harmony by building a triad and exploring its inversions.

B

(i) We'll start by making a major triad—that is a chord of three notes with a major third and perfect fifth above the root note. Listen to the chord as it builds up and tune your part carefully to the others. If you're used to tonic sol-fa, sing the sol-fa names of the notes.

Divide into three equal groups and choose a conductor. Group I sing and hold the root note (*doh*); group II add to this the major third above (*me*); finally group III add the fifth ·(*soh*).

This is a familiar sound which we hear many times each day in every sort of music. It's called a *common* major chord, but its familiarity doesn't detract from its beauty. Build the chord again and vary the dynamics. Experiment with different qualities of attack, using a variety of open vowels and initial consonants. Now build the chord downwards starting with the fifth, or begin with the third and add the outer notes together.

We could invent a tune using these three notes and accompany it with the chord sung or played in an interesting rhythm. Not all the notes need be sounded together. Using this accompaniment, improvise a melody on *doh*, *me* and *soh*.

(ii) Build the chord again. This time hold your note until a change is indicated by the conductor. Group I now move up to the third, group II to the fifth and group III down to the root. At the next indication move on again. Does the chord sound the same on each occasion? Composers have often made use of contrasts in vocal timbre to colour the music by crossing parts in this way. Listen to a recording of Monteverdi's madrigal *O come é gran martire* from Book III (1592), and, if possible, perform the opening section, which is scored for three sopranos. The madrigal is published separately by Universal.

260

(iii)   Choose a new note for the root of the chord. This time, instead of building up the triad, sing all three notes together. Imagine what the *complete* chord will sound like before you sing. You will need to think of your note in relation to the other parts before you produce it.

(iv)   Build a major triad on a conveniently low note (say C or D♭). This time we'll move the root of the chord to the highest part, leaving the third as the bass.

Group I sing and hold the root (low *doh*). When the third and fifth have been added by the other groups, change to top *doh*.

Now build the chord again starting with the third. Hold it and listen carefully, comparing it with the original chord which had the root as the bass. We call that a triad in *root position*. Logically enough, this arrangement of the notes is a *first inversion*. What would a second inversion be? Make one.

(v)   Sing this round by Ravenscroft. Notice that the melody is based on a major triad. The additional notes are not important for they merely pass between notes of the triad on weak beats of the bar. Make an arrangement of the music for two groups of voices, one singing the melody in canon, the other providing an accompaniment using various positions of a major triad on F.

Quickly, with a bounce

for 3 voices

Der - ry ding ding Das-son,   I am John Ches-ton, we weed-on, we

wod-den, we weed-on, we wod-den, Bim, bom, bim, bom, bim, bom, bim, bom.

RAVENSCROFT, from *Melismata* (1611)

(vi)   Make a piece in free rhythm for wordless voices (singing to *Ah*) using various positions of a major chord. The music could again be in three parts, but we may want to strengthen the root position of the chord by having both low and high *doh* in addition to the third and fifth. This could be done by dividing one of the parts when a fuller effect is sought. Alternatively, we could compose the music in four parts throughout. This means that one note of the triad will always be doubled. What is the effect of this? Explore the various colours arising from octave and unison doublings of each note of the triad. The music will be more interesting if the parts cross each other to avoid consecutive octaves and unisons.

(vii)   Make a bitonal composition on the same lines by dividing into two groups, each working with a major triad on a different note. Triads on notes a minor third (three semitones) apart will yield some interesting tonal colours.

C

(i)   The following arrangement of *Derry ding ding Dasson* was made by a class of eleven-year-old boys. They had been exploring major triads by chord building for about four weeks and had nearly three terms' experience in non-harmonic group creative work, mainly with instruments. The round was already well known and a popular favourite.

   They began with a sustained triad of F major sung to *Ah* and held throughout the round. This was soon rejected in favour of a rhythmic treatment when it was suggested that the accompanying parts might also use words. A version of the introduction was earlier used as an accompaniment to the round itself, but this was generally felt to make the music sound 'too cluttered'. The melodic shape of the parts arose from a suggestion that 'dong derry ding dong' should sound like bells, but it's doubtful whether anyone realised that the melodic shape of the lowest part brought about alternating root positions and second inversions until this was pointed out. The idea of building up the texture with imitative entries came with the suggestion that there should be an introduction, and may (subconsciously?) have arisen from earlier work in chord building. The result was a convincing piece of music, and no-one minded the consecutive unisons in the last four bars! Indeed, they help to strengthen the bass at the cadence and suggest a richer sonority.

(ii)   This short composition for voices in four parts uses different positions of a C major triad. It was the result of a classroom improvisation by the same boys the week following their arrangement of *Derry ding ding Dasson*.

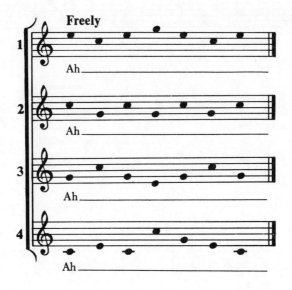

(iii)   This arrangement of *Crux Fidelis* is more sophisticated since it uses both major and minor triads. It was written by a fourteen-year-old G.C.E. pupil who does not disguise his admiration for Vaughan Williams and Holst. He began at the keyboard by exploring the effect of parallel triads moving mainly by step above the plainsong and matching the rhythm of the melody. The unrelieved triadic movement was soon considered monotonous and some independent part movement was introduced. The composition is included as an example of what might be done at a later stage by a gifted pupil who is beginning to develop a formal technique. A non-specialist class of mixed voices might like to sing it and compare it with their own treatment of the plainsong.

Crux Fidelis

Andante

Faith - ful cross a - bove all o - ther,_____

Faith - ful cross_____ a - bove all o - ther,_____

One_____ and_____ on - ly_____ no - ble_____ tree. None

One_____ and_____ on - ly_____ no - ble_____ tree. None

in - fo - liage, none in blos - som, None in

in_____ fo - liage,_____none in_____ blos - som,_____ None in_____

fruit_____ thy peer may be: Sweet - est

fruit_____ thy_____ peer_____ may be: Sweet - est_____

266

wood and   sweet - est   ir - - - on,

wood and___ sweet - est___   ir - - - on,___

Sweet - est   weight___ is   hung on   thee.

Sweet - est___   weight___ is___   hung___ on   thee.

D

Examples of passages based on a single triad are not difficult to find in the standard classical repertoire. The most frequently quoted is the opening of *Das Rheingold*, where Wagner has 136 bars based entirely on the chord of E♭. Extensive passages based on the tonic chord can be found in the closing sections of much late eighteenth- and nineteenth-century symphonic music, and a great deal of baroque music involving brass instruments contains long passages based on a single chord. A striking example is the magnificent 'Deus in Adiutorum' which opens the Monteverdi *Vespers* (1610).

Examples of a single triad used over several bars and of parallel root position triads can also be found in works by twentieth-century composers. Study the passages listed below, and try to hear performances of the music:

KODÁLY

Missa Brevis (Boosey and Hawkes). Compare the passage beginning at fig. 2 in the *Kyrie* (p. 6 in the vocal score) with the opening eight bars of the 'Allegro mosso' section in the *Credo* (p. 21). Both make extensive use of the chord of D major: in the former, five consecutive phrases grow from a repeated second inversion D major triad, sung by three solo

267

sopranos and echoed by the chorus, while in the latter the passage is based entirely on various positions of the D major chord. Here, the notes of the triad are decorated by others which are not an essential part of the harmony (see Projects 31 and 32).

BARTÓK

Mikrokosmos vol. III (Boosey and Hawkes). 'Chord Study' (p. 10) uses a succession of parallel root position triads to support a single melodic line, which is heard first above the chords and later in the bass. The piece offers obvious comparisons with the arrangement of *Crux Fidelis* given in C (iii) above.

VAUGHAN WILLIAMS

Mass in G Minor (Curwen). A further, but quite different, example of the effect of parallel root position triads occurs on pp. 12 and 13 at the words 'miserere nobis'. Although, like the sixteenth-century models on which it is based, so much of the music in this Mass is linear (i.e. conceived in terms of the progression of each individual line) there are several homophonic (or chordal) passages based either on a single triad or, more usually, on two conflicting triads. These would make useful 'follow-up' material to Assignment (vii) above.

17   Chime bars in chord groups

Project 29
The primary triads

A

In the previous project we were concerned only with the vertical aspect of harmony. By using a single triad and exploring its inversions, the problem of controlling the harmonic progression did not arise. As soon as we introduce other triads and relate them harmonically, the *horizontal* pattern of the music becomes equally important.

We can, of course, learn to order the progression of harmony by memorising various accepted sequences of chords. Most text-book harmony courses begin in this way by setting out the chord patterns which constitute the conventional cadences. They then go on to consider ways in which the cadences can be approached, outlining rules which must be observed in the treatment of the parts. Such a method has little value if it is not related to aural experience. Only by discovering for ourselves the harmonic function of each chord can we begin to develop a feeling for harmonic progression.

The function of each of the primary triads can best be illustrated by some preliminary exercises in which a melodic line is sung or played by one group while its harmonic implications are realised by another. This is most conveniently done with guitars or chordal dulcimers, but failing these it is quite possible to play triads on glockenspiels or xylophones with two or three players at each instrument. Chime bars arranged in chord groups can also be used, and any of these instruments can be doubled or even replaced by voices singing root position triads under the direction of a conductor.

It's best to begin with melodies based entirely on the tonic chord. In the previous project we discovered how a single triad could support a simple melodic line, and in tunes such as *Derry ding ding Dasson* and *Oliver Cromwell* the function of the triad is to provide tonic harmony throughout. If we then proceed to melodies which introduce dominant harmony at various points, we shall soon discover that the tonic chord will not fit all the time. The group providing the harmony can now be sub-divided so that, at the appropriate places, half play or sing the tonic chord and the others the dominant. Eventually the harmony group can practice changing from chord to chord while the others improvise a new melody above the same harmonic sequence.

When a feeling for the tonic and dominant triads has been established, the subdominant chord can be introduced in the same way, first in conjunction with the tonic chord and then in exercises which combine all three. In this way it is possible to develop an *aural* recognition of the harmonic function of the three primary triads, which are the basis of all tonal harmony.

B

(i)   Build a major triad on C. If the keynote of the music is also C, the triad is a tonic chord. However, unless we define the tonality by adding a melody above the chord or by introducing other triads, we cannot know which degree of the scale it is built on. Now build a major triad on G. We could regard this as a tonic chord in G major, but if we relate it to the first triad it will have been built on the fifth degree of the scale, which is the dominant. Thus, we might refer to the tonic triad as chord I and the dominant triad as chord V.

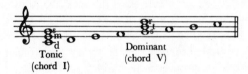

Tonic
(chord I)

Dominant
(chord V)

Choose a conductor, and move from chord I to chord V and back. If you're used to tonic sol-fa, sing the sol-fa names, but remember that the root of chord V is now *soh*. Devise sequences of the chords in various rhythms, repeating the same triad several times before you move to the other. Does it matter on which chord you end?

(ii)   We could make the music more interesting by introducing inversions of the tonic chord. It is usual to call a root position *a*, a first inversion *b* and a second inversion *c*. Devise sequences in which various positions of chord I lead to chord Va. Here are two to begin with:

(1) Ia Ib Ic Va
(2) Ib Ia Ib Ia Va

What is the effect of ending on the dominant chord? If we wanted the music to end at this point we would need to return to chord I after chord V. Which position of the tonic chord will make the music sound finished?

(iii)   Explore the inversions of chord V and devise sequences in which both chords appear in various positions. Here are two to begin with:

    (1) Ia Ib Va Ib Ic Va Ia

    (2) Vb Ia Vc Ib Ic Va Vb Ia

Notice that both of these end V to Ia. Which position of the dominant triad is strongest at the cadence?

(iv)   We have discovered the importance of the harmonic relationship between tonic and dominant triads, but without the addition of the subdominant chord the key centre is ambiguous. While G is the dominant of C, equally C is the subdominant of G. In order to confirm the tonality we must introduce the subdominant triad, which is formed on the fourth degree of the scale.

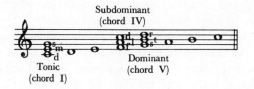

Under the direction of a conductor, build a tonic chord on C and move to chord IV on F. Practice changing from I to IV and from IV to V, and then incorporate all three triads in a sequence of root position chords beginning and ending on the tonic. With three chords a greater variety of harmonic movement is possible, but give careful consideration to the progression V to IV. What chord do we normally expect to follow the dominant?

(v)   Explore the inversions of chord IV and devise sequences in which various positions of the tonic and subdominant triads lead to chord Va. Here are two to begin with:

    (1) Ia Ib IVa IVb Ia Ib Va

    (2) Ia IVc Ia IVa Va

(vi)   Sing the following sequences in different keys and note the effect of the cadences which are bracketed and named. Follow the suggested rhythmic scheme.

Imperfect

(1) *In triple time:* Ia Ib IVa | Va — — ||

273

Imperfect

(2) *In quadruple time:* Va | Ia IVa Ib Ia | Va — — ‖

Plagal

(3) *In duple time:* Va | Ib Ia | IVa—|Ia ‖

Perfect

(4) *In triple time:* Ia IVb IVa | Va——|Ia — — ‖

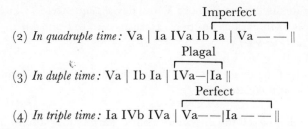

The first two, which end on the dominant, are 'half closes' (the musical equivalent of a comma) while (3) and (4), which return to the tonic, are 'full closes' (the musical equivalent of a full stop).

Within suitable rhythmic schemes, compose the following sequences:

(1) A two-bar phrase leading to an *imperfect* cadence IV–V answered by a two-bar phrase ending with a *perfect* cadence;

(2) A three-bar phrase leading to an *imperfect* cadence I–V answered by a three-bar phrase ending with a *plagal* cadence;

(3) Four short phrases, each ending with a different cadence.

Note that the chord patterns which make up cadences can occur at any point and not just at the end of a phrase. The following example is made up almost entirely of interlocking 'cadences', though not all appear in root position.

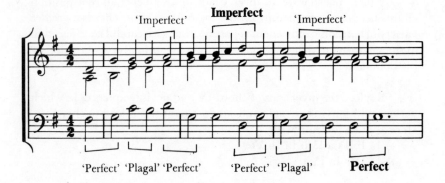

(vii) Working in groups, make homophonic settings for voices in three or four parts of the following texts. In the first two, suggestions for the musical rhythm and phrasing are given. Use all the primary triads and their inversions.

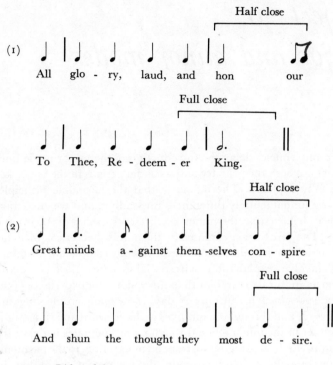

TATE, *Dido and Aeneas*

(3) These delights if thou canst give,
Mirth, with thee I mean to live.

MILTON, *L'Allegro*

Project 30
Major and minor modes

A

Most harmony courses delay the introduction of the minor mode until management of both the primary and secondary triads in the major key has been fully explored. The inference that the harmonic principles involved are fundamentally different is misleading, and we encourage our pupils to believe that the minor key presents special problems and difficulties. They are further confused by the purely theoretical 'melodic' and 'harmonic' minor scales; but however we may complicate the minor mode with involved explanations of its special structure, the fact remains that it is no less natural or familiar than the major. Our experience of the minor mode goes back to our nursery days (how many cradle songs are in major keys?) and throughout our lives we have heard and sung music which is either in the minor mode throughout or fluctuates between the two. In improvised part-singing we respond as naturally to the harmonic implications of melodies in either mode, and we are not aware that the minor key involves any particular problems until this is pointed out. It is therefore important that we explore the minor mode alongside the major, applying the harmonic principles we have already discovered.

B

(i)   In the key of C major, build tonic, subdominant and dominant triads in root position. As we have seen, the harmonic function of these chords depends on their relationship to each other and to the keynote. Taken out of their tonal context they are identical. Each is constructed in the same way, having intervals of a third between the two upper notes and between the two lower notes.

Build the tonic triad again. This time, pause before group III adds the fifth (*soh*). When all three notes are sounding, let group I release the root so only the upper two notes remain.

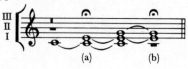

Listen to the two intervals at (a) and (b). Both are thirds, but they are not quite the same. Can you describe the difference in colour between them? The first is a *major* third and consists of four semitones, the second is *minor*, consisting of only three.

We could devise a simpler way of making major and minor thirds by dividing into two groups. Group II can now hold the middle note of the triad while group I moves between the root and the fifth.

We have now produced alternating major and minor thirds, but group II has a rather dull part. Make a more interesting piece based on major and minor thirds with movement in both parts.

(ii)   Build a minor third on A and add to this a perfect fifth above the root. Because the interval between the lower notes is a minor third, the chord is a *minor* triad. If we relate the chord to the key of C major it will have been formed on the submediant (the note midway between the subdominant and tonic); but we could regard it as the tonic chord of A minor. As a tonic chord, it will have its own subdominant and dominant, and its harmonic function will now depend on its relationship to the new key.

As we have seen, the three primary triads in the major key are all major chords. If we now build triads on the tonic, dominant and subdominant notes of the minor scale they will all be minor.

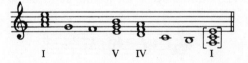

Choose a conductor and explore the relationship between these triads. Change from I to IV and back, and from I to V. Include all three chords in a sequence of five or six changes. What is the effect of chord V? Does it really establish itself as the dominant?

In the major key, we have discovered that chord V expects to be followed by chord I, and, if we do not end with the tonic chord, the music sounds unfinished. The three chords immediately establish a relationship, and together define the tonality. Is that the case here? No one chord seems more important than another, and however we end the sequence the music feels incomplete.

In order to emphasise A as the key-note we must make chord V *dominate* the others as it does in the major key. We can do that by making chord V a *major* triad.

Explore the relationship between the triads when chord V is major. Sing the following sequences, including inversions of the triads as well as root positions, and compose others of your own. Chord V is italicised to remind you it is a major triad.

(1) I IV I IV I IV *V* I

(2) I *V* I IV I *V* I

(iii)   Sing the progression IV *V* I in D minor, with each triad in root position. We have already discovered that chord V must normally be a major triad if it is to lead smoothly back to the tonic chord. The natural inclination of the part which has the leading note (the major third in chord V) is to rise to the tonic. Similarly, the voice which has the submediant (the minor third in chord IV) feels it should fall to the dominant in the next chord.

Now arrange the parts so that the voice which has the minor third in chord IV moves to the major third in chord V. Does the progression feel natural? We could avoid the awkward leap of an augmented second by making chord IV a *major* triad. Now the part which has the major third in chord IV feels it must move to the leading note and so to the tonic.

Arrange progressions of chords I, IV and V so that both major and minor forms of the subdominant triad are used. Here are three to begin with. The major chords are again italicised.

(1) I IV I *V* I *IV V* I

(2) *V* I IV I *IV V* I

(3) I *IV V* I IV *V* I

(iv) We have discovered that, in the major key, the dominant chord leads most naturally back to the tonic. While it is possible to follow the dominant chord by the subdominant, the progression is less satisfactory and we feel it must eventually return to chord V and so to chord I. The function of the dominant chord is exactly the same in the minor key, but the progression V to IV works much more smoothly. Sing the sequence I *V* IVb *V*.

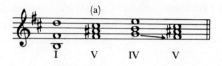

Since the subdominant chord is used in first inversion, the bass feels it must fall. If we substituted a first inversion of the dominant chord at (a) we would again have the awkward leap of an augmented second in the lowest part. Sing the progression I *V*b IVb *V*. Can you suggest how the augmented second might be avoided?

Arrange progressions of chords I, IV and V so that both major and minor forms of the subdominant and dominant chords are used. Here are two to begin with.

(1) I Vb IVb *V* Ib *IV V* I
(2) *IV*b *V*b I Vb IVb *V*

(v) Working in groups, make homophonic settings for voices in three or four parts of some of the following texts. The first three suggest the minor mode, but the last two might well be in the major. Take the musical rhythm from the natural verbal stresses, but don't try to be too elaborate. Balance the musical phrases by repeating words where this seems appropriate. Use all the primary triads and their inversions.

(1) O Absalom, my son, would I
      had died for thee.
(2) O pray for the peace of
      Jerusalem.
(3) Weep you no more, sad fountains:
      what need you flow so fast?
(4) Hosanna to the Son of David.
(5) His golden locks time hath to
      silver turned.

C

This setting of 'O pray for the peace of Jerusalem' was made by a second-year class in a Birmingham grammar school. The echo effects were inspired by the Schütz motet for double chorus *Lift up your heads, O ye gates* which the school choir had recently performed. It should be emphasised that the music was a group composition arising from improvisation and not dominated by individual children: indeed, the idea of balancing the phrases by using an echo chorus was suggested by a boy who had previously shown no particular musical talent but had obviously been impressed by the Schütz motet, which he was reminded of by the homophonic part-writing and harmonic movement of the primary triads.

Version (a) was the first attempt without refinements suggested by the teacher. It uses only tonic and dominant chords, mainly in root position. Version (b) includes the subdominant chord and both forms of the dominant. The inversions were suggested by the natural progression of individual parts, as was the omission of the third in the tonic chord.

O Pray for the Peace of Jerusalem

Version (b)

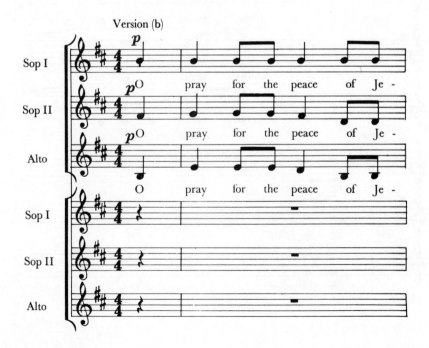

- lem, the peace of Je - ru - sa - lem.

- lem, the peace of Je - ru - sa - lem.

- lem, the peace of Je - ru - sa - lem.

the peace of Je - ru - sa - lem.

the peace of Je - ru - sa - lem.

the peace of Je - ru - sa - lem.

Project 31
Passing notes and auxiliary notes (1)

A

The melodies we made in Projects 28–30 use only the notes of the primary triads. As we have seen, it is possible to arrange these notes into interesting melodic patterns; but if we limit our melodies to *harmony* notes (the notes which make up each chord) we impose considerable restrictions on the melodic shape. Movement by step can only occur when there is a change of harmony: as long as we keep the same chord, the melody must either remain on one note or move to another note of that chord.

Some melodies are based entirely on harmony notes. It's not uncommon for hymn tunes to have several phrases composed of notes taken from the underlying chords. Harmony notes suggest firmness and strength. Even so, there are few hymn tunes which completely avoid introducing notes that are not an essential part of the harmony. Without these 'unessential' notes, the music would be dull and lacking in rhythmic subtlety. If we give equal emphasis to each note of the tune it will sound square and solid. Often we want to increase the rhythmic interest by varying the harmonic movement. We may decide to change the chord only on the strongest beat of the bar; occasionally we may want to keep the same chord over several bars. This does not mean the melody must use only the notes of that chord: we can make it more interesting by decorating these notes with others that are not an essential part of the harmony.

There are two kinds of unessential notes. The first (called *passing* notes) move by step between harmony notes a third apart; the second (*auxiliary* notes) move by step away from a harmony note and return to the same note. By using these unessential notes we can introduce a much greater variety into the character of our melodies. We might begin to explore the function of passing notes and auxiliary notes by decorating the harmony notes of a single triad.

B

(i)   Divide into three equal groups and build a major triad on F. While group I holds the root of the chord (*doh*) let groups II and III cross parts by changing between *soh* and *me*.

Build the chord again, but this time let groups II and III *pass through* the fourth degree of the scale (*fa*) as they change.

This new note does not belong to the chord, but in introducing it we don't need to change the harmony. We have merely decorated two of the harmony notes of the triad by passing by step between them. Because this happened on a weak beat of the bar, the note is an *unaccented* passing note: if it had occurred on a strong beat, it would have been an *accented* passing note.

(ii)   Build another major triad on F. While group III holds the fifth (*soh*) let groups I and II cross parts by changing between *doh* and *me*. Do the same again, this time introducing the second degree of the scale (*re*) as an unaccented passing note.

(iii)   Make a melody using the harmony notes of a major triad decorated with unaccented passing notes. Support the melody with the triad sustained by one group of voices while the others sing or play the tune. Experiment with various rhythms. The notes of the melody need not all be of the same length.

(iv)   Repeat each of the above using a *minor* triad.

(v)   Again, build a major triad on F. While groups I and II hold the root and third, let group III move from *soh* to the note above (*la*) and return to the fifth of the triad.

We have again introduced a note which is not part of the chord. Like a passing note, it moves by step away from the harmony note, but instead of continuing in the same direction it returns to the same note. Such notes are called *auxiliary*.

Build the triad again, and while groups I and II continue to hold the root and third, let group III introduce a *lower* auxiliary note by moving down to *fa* and returning to *soh*. Now incorporate both upper and lower auxiliary notes in a short melodic phrase. Vary the rhythm.

(vi)   Begin as above, but this time let group II introduce upper and lower auxiliary notes while groups I and III sustain the root and fifth. Repeat the process, with group I introducing auxiliary notes above and below the root of the triad.

(vii)   Make a melody using the harmony notes of a major triad decorated with unaccented passing notes and auxiliary notes. Accompany the melody with a group of voices sustaining the triad while the others sing or play the tune.

(viii)   Repeat the above, using a *minor* triad. Will the sixth degree of the scale (*la*) be sharp or flat?

(ix)   While one group of voices sustains a major triad let another sing or play a melody in $\frac{5}{4}$ time moving in even crotchets. Begin on the fifth (*soh*) and move by step down to *doh*. Now return to *soh* and end with an upper auxiliary note. Divide the rhythmic pattern into groups of 3 and 2.

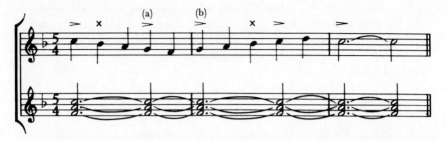

Since the accents fall on the first and fourth beats of the bar, the passing notes at (a) and (b) are accented. The other passing notes (marked with a cross) are unaccented. What is the effect of accented passing notes? Make melodies in duple and triple time incorporating both kinds of passing notes and include some auxiliary notes. Work with both major and minor triads.

(x)   Make a setting of this lullaby from Shakespeare's play *A Midsummer Night's Dream*:

Ye spotted snakes with double tongue,
Thorny hedge-hogs, be not seen:
Newts and blind worms do no wrong;
Come not near our fairy queen.

Philomel, with melody
Sing in our sweet lullaby;
Lulla, lulla, lullaby,
   Lulla, lulla, lullaby:
Never harm, nor spell nor charm,
Come our lovely lady nigh;
So, goodnight, with lullaby.

Weaving spiders, come not here;
Hence, you long-legg'd spinners, hence!
Beetles black, approach not near;
Worm nor snail do no offence.

Philomel, with melody
Sing in our sweet lullaby;
Lulla, lulla, lullaby,
   Lulla, lulla, lullaby:
Never harm, nor spell nor charm,
Come our lovely lady nigh;
So, goodnight, with lullaby.

The verses could be spoken or sung by a solo voice or small group of voices. Decide how you will bring out the spell-like quality of the words and how you will make the music reflect the contrast between the verses and refrain: one is addressed to evil, unpleasant creatures that haunt the woodland—snakes, blind worms, snails and black beetles; the other is a lullaby to charm Titania to sleep. Perhaps the verses could be chanted in a half-whisper and punctuated by percussion. Which instruments will be most suitable for this? We must try to evoke the mystery and magic of the spell and at the same time suggest the presence of the insects and other creatures. Claves will certainly be appropriate, and we might explore less usual sounds such as scratching the skin of a hand drum with the finger-nail.

In contrast, the lullaby refrain could be sung. We could again make a melody around the notes of a single triad (should it be major or minor?) and introduce passing notes and auxiliary notes to reflect the tenderness and smooth rhythmic flow of the words. Perhaps the melody could be accompanied by pitched instruments or a second group of voices simply sustaining the triad on which the melody is based.

C

Ye Spotted Snakes

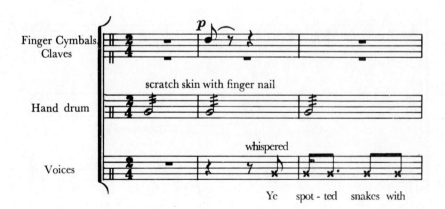

doub - le   tongue,   Thorn - y hedge-hogs, be not seen.

Newts   and blind worms   do no wrong: Come not near our

fai - ry   queen.

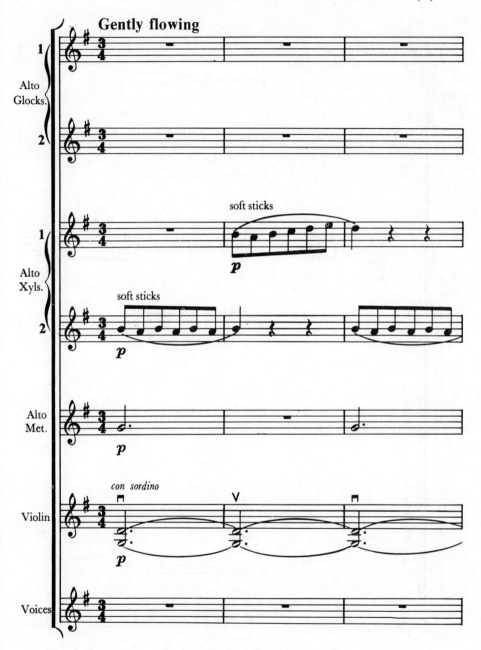

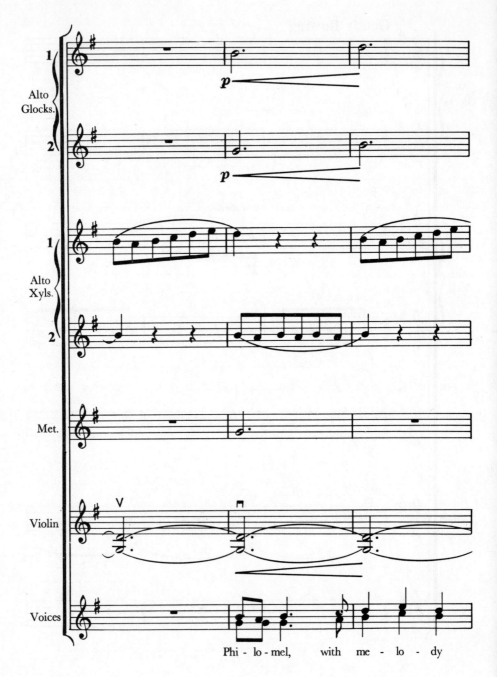

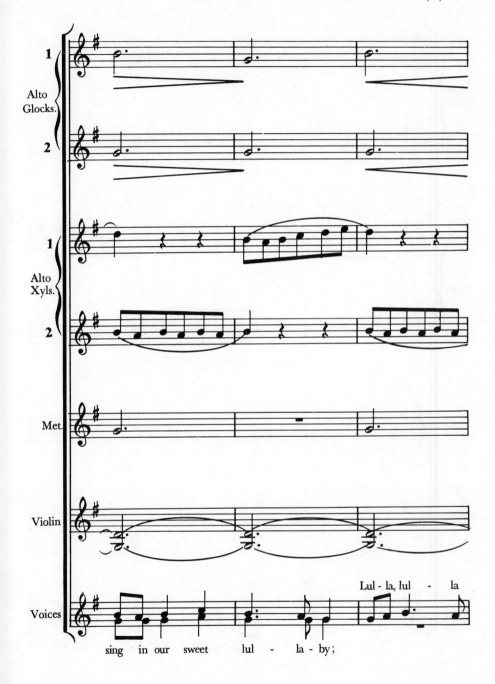

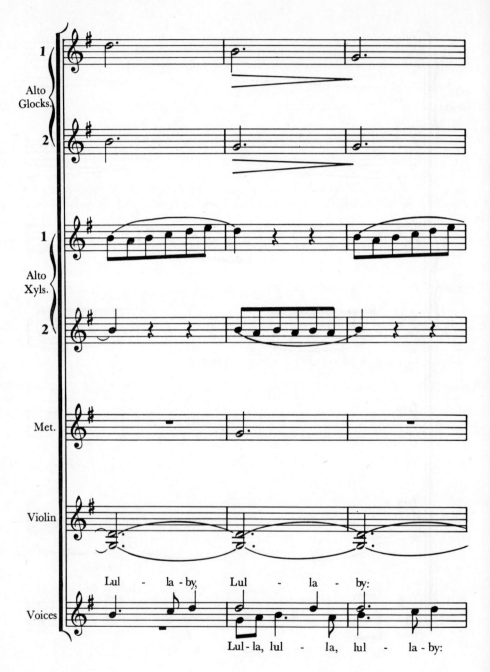

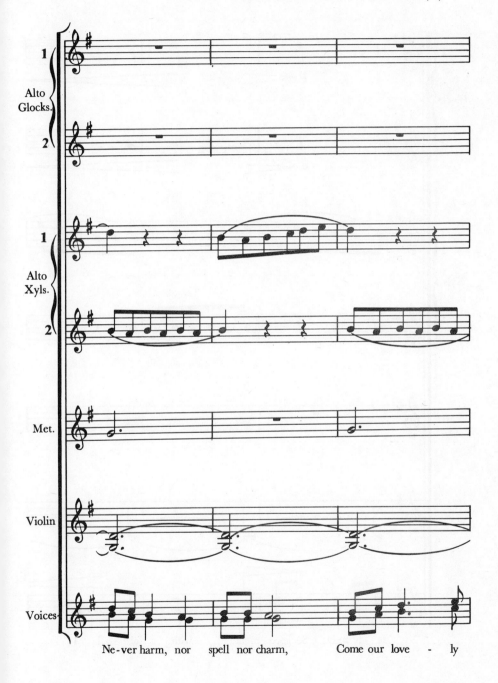

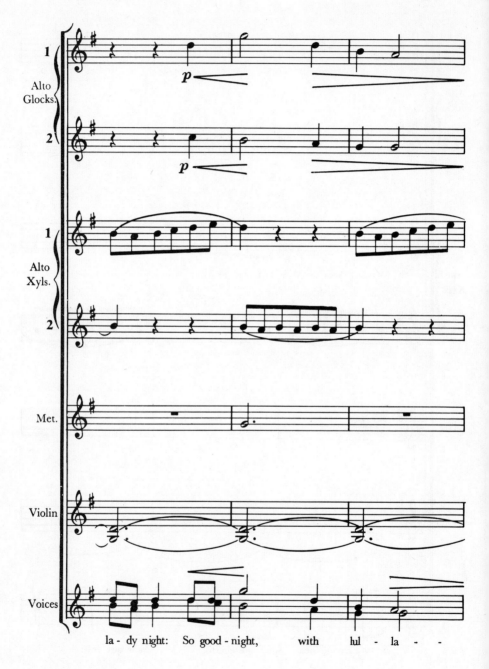

This setting of *Ye Spotted Snakes* was a group composition made by a class of thirteen-year-old boys. They began by reading the poem together aloud, and quickly decided that the verses should be spoken and the lullaby refrain sung.

During the first week they worked at the refrain only. While the class sang a sustained root position major triad, individual children improvised a melody incorporating passing notes and taking the rhythm from the words. At first, these melodies were extremely simple, consisting of even quaver movement in duple time running between *soh* and *doh*.

Phi - lo-mel, with me - lo - dy__ Sing in our sweet lu - la - by;__

The general shape of the melody was quickly established: each improvisation began in the same way with a descending figure starting on the dominant. For some time there was no attempt to break the even quaver movement, to introduce auxiliary notes, or to interrupt the stepwise movement by jumping from one harmony note to another. It seemed that the melodic and rhythmic pattern was firmly set until someone suggested that the line 'lulla, lulla, lullaby' would be more effective in triple time, taking the rhythm ♩. ♪♫ | ♩ ♩ ♩ |. He demonstrated this to the rest of the class, and the group next tried to fit the rest of the words into a triple rhythm. This brought about a fresh approach to the setting, and the next boy to improvise began, not on *soh* as before, but on *me*. The melody now began to centre around the mediant, incorporating auxiliary notes as well as passing notes.

Phi - lo - mel, with me - lo - dy Sing in our sweet lu - la - by;

From this evolved several variants, until the opening phrase was established in its final version.

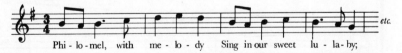

Phi - lo - mel, with me - lo - dy Sing in our sweet lu - la - by;

The rest of the melody grew naturally from this and was developed over several improvisations and finally written down. The following week instruments were added, replacing the voices sustaining the major triad, and work began on the verses. The composition occupied a large part of one of two weekly music periods for about one-third of the term.

Project 32
Passing notes and auxiliary notes (2)

A

In the previous project we began to extend our melodic resource by decorating the harmony notes of a triad. As we have seen, it is possible to introduce into the melody notes which are not an essential part of the harmony. These normally move by step between harmony notes, and so far we have limited the harmony to a single triad. We might next explore what happens when harmonic movement is introduced. Passing notes and auxiliary notes can still be used, but now they can be treated in two ways: they may move by step either to another note of the same triad or lead to a harmony note of another chord.

B

(i)   Make a short melody in duple time. Use only the harmony notes of a major triad on F, and begin and end on the fifth (*soh*). Let the rhythm be simple, perhaps moving in even crotchets: we shall later use this melody as a basis for a more elaborate composition.

When you have decided on a simple melodic pattern like the one suggested above, decorate the harmony notes by introducing unessential notes as we did in the previous project. You might begin with an upper auxiliary note, descend by step to the tonic (*doh*), and return by step to the dominant (*soh*), ending as you began with an upper auxiliary note.

Support the melody with a vocal or instrumental accompaniment derived from the tonic triad. It would be possible to sustain the triad throughout, but the music will be more interesting if you introduce some rhythmic movement. Experiment with various rhythmic patterns and explore other positions of the chord. Now make a more extensive composition by repeating the melody several times while you vary the accompaniment.

(ii)   The melody we have just made was derived from the chord of F major. We were therefore able to harmonise it throughout with that chord. Alternatively, we might decide to introduce harmonic movement. Sing the original version of the melody again. Notice that the notes marked with a cross belong both to the *tonic* chord and to one other primary triad.

We therefore have the choice of two triads at these points. Consequently, we can introduce harmonic movement by changing to another chord on each beat of the bar, but we must always bear in mind the *progression* of the harmony. Since the melody is in F major, the music should end with the tonic chord. Which chord will most effectively precede the tonic at the cadence? With which chord shall we begin?

When you have decided on a suitable sequence of chords, devise a vocal or instrumental accompaniment which will support the melody. Now sing the *decorated* version of the melody above the accompaniment. Notice that the passing notes and auxiliary notes are no longer moving to another harmony note of the same triad but to a harmony note of a different chord. Compare the result with the previous arrangement of the melody where only one triad was used. The original harmonisation and a version incorporating the three primary triads are given below.

Version(a):Tonic chord only   I   I   I   I   I   I   I
Version(b):Primary triads   I   V   I   IV   I   V   I

Notice how the character of the music is altered by the harmony. In the first version the interest is solely in the flowing melodic line, but in the second version the melody is supported by strong harmonic movement: there is a change of chord on each strong beat of the bar and passing notes occur only on weak beats. This has the effect of making the music sound square and solid. Sometimes we may deliberately organise the harmonic movement in this way, especially if we want the music to suggest majesty and strength. At other times we may want to avoid this squareness. This can be done by introducing *accented* passing notes so that harmony notes occasionally occur on weak beats of the bar.

(iii)   Sing or play the decorated version of the melody without harmonic support. Now divide into two groups and, while one sings the melody, let the other provide harmony using tonic and subdominant chords only. Begin with the tonic chord and change to chord IV (the subdominant) on the next strong beat. Repeat this pattern throughout. Notice the effect of the accented passing notes at the points indicated by a cross in the following example. Where do unaccented passing notes occur? Compare this harmonisation of the melody with those in (i) and (ii) above.

(iv)   Devise short sequences of the primary triads in both major and minor keys as we did in Projects 29 and 30. Here are three to begin with. The first two are in duple time, the third in triple. Introduce some first and second inversions as well as root positions of the chords.

(1) *Major:* V | I IV | I IV | V V | I ‖
(2) *Minor:* I IV | I IV | I V | I — ‖
(3) *Minor:* I IV V | I — IV | V — — | I — — ‖

Choose one of these sequences or one of your own. While it is sung or played by one group, make a melody derived from the chords. Introduce auxiliary notes as well as accented and unaccented passing notes.

(v)   *The Dominant Seventh:* build a root position major triad on the dominant of A major and add the root at the top so that the chord is in four parts. Since E is the fifth note of the scale of A major, the chord will be built on E. Now follow this by chord I, making a perfect cadence in A. Let the highest part, which had the root (E) in chord V, move to the third (C♯) in chord I.

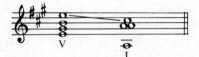

Since the top part has moved between harmony notes a third apart, it would again be possible to introduce a passing note.

This melodic decoration frequently occurs at cadences. It is so common that the passing note is often introduced *without being prepared by a harmony note*. Because the chord is built on the dominant and the additional note is seven notes above the root, the chord is called a DOMINANT SEVENTH, sometimes written V⁷. Notice that the seventh (in this case the note D) feels it must fall to the third in chord I. Can you suggest why?

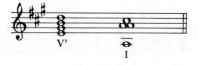

Working in groups of six or seven, make perfect cadences in various keys using the chord of the dominant seventh. Devise sequences of the primary triads to approach the cadence and perform your pieces to each other. Work with both voices and instruments, and use first and second inversions as well as root position chords. The dominant seventh can, of course, be used at other points besides the cadence.

C

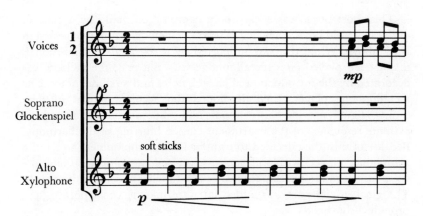

This short piece was a classroom composition made by a class of twelve-year-old boys. They began with the melodic outline suggested in B (i) above. While this was supported by a repeated root position F major triad played on a metallophone (two players), the melody was decorated by the introduction of passing notes and auxiliary notes. The metallophone players then developed the accompaniment into an ostinato figure, moving between tonic and subdominant chords, but the extreme resonance of the instrument caused blurring of the harmony. Because of this, they decided to transfer the accompaniment to an alto xylophone, played with soft sticks. Over several improvisations, the vocal line began to develop into two parts moving in consecutive thirds. The glockenspiel part was added later to link the vocal phrases and provide a short coda.

D

Examples of passing notes and auxiliary notes are so common that it would be difficult to find music with a harmonic basis in which they do not occur! However, we offer the following suggestions for follow-up material because in each case the melodic decoration is essential to the design of the passage. All are taken from vocal works by Britten. Scores and recordings are readily available, and the examples should be heard in the context of their particular movement or, if possible, of the complete work.

Cantata *St Nicolas* (Boosey and Hawkes): in sequence VII, 'Nicolas and the Pickled Boys', effective use is made of passing notes as the three boys who have been brought back to life enter singing 'Alleluia'. Listen to the 'Poco meno mosso' section (p. 63 of the vocal score) and compare the melodic pattern with the imitative passages in the following sequence at the words 'Let the legends that we tell' (fig. 58 on p. 72). The passing notes and auxiliary notes in this short canonic passage might also be compared with the 'Hallelujah' sections of the Festival Cantata *Rejoice the Lamb* (Boosey and Hawkes). These occur at fig. 9 on p. 11 and again at fig. 31 on p. 38.

Listen also to the soprano solo in the *Hymn to St Cecilia* (Boosey and Hawkes). The passage, which begins on p. 32, makes extensive use of both accented and unaccented passing notes and of appoggiaturas ('leaning' notes). Notice how the solo line is supported by the underlying harmony and by the continuous pedal note (A) sung first by the tenors and later at the lower octave by the basses.

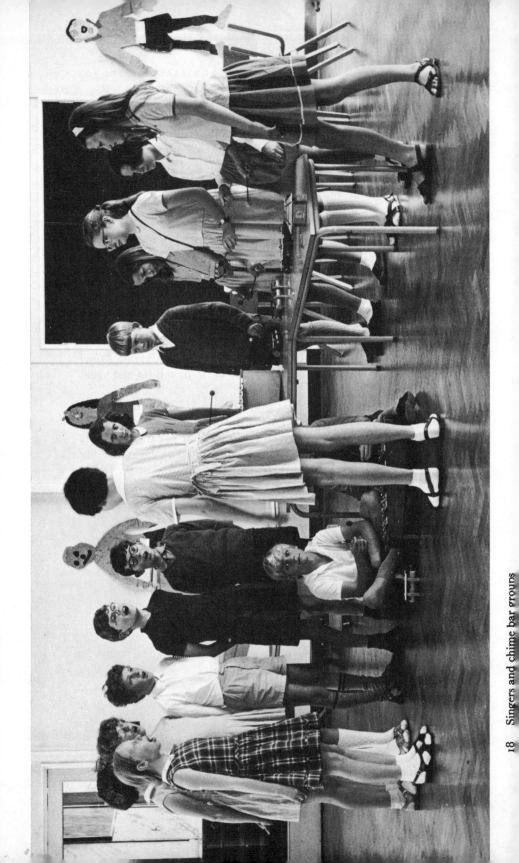

18   Singers and chime bar groups

Project 33
The secondary triads

A

We have already discovered the importance of the three primary triads, and in Projects 29–32 we have seen how harmonic interest can be sustained despite the limitations of using only chords built on the tonic, subdominant and dominant degrees of the major and minor scales. Even with three chords, a considerable variety of harmonic colour can be introduced. We can use the triads in root position, or in first or second inversion; we can vary the harmonic rhythm by changing the chord only occasionally, or by setting up a regular pattern of chord changes on each beat of the bar; we can suggest strong harmonic movement by deriving the melody entirely from harmony notes, or we can decorate the melody with unessential notes, introducing both accented and unaccented passing notes. In the minor key, we can vary the subdominant and dominant triads, using them in either their major or minor form; and we have discovered the chord of the dominant seventh, which can be used in both major and minor key.

Nevertheless, we can extend our harmonic resource still further by introducing the four *secondary* triads, so called because their harmonic importance is secondary to the tonic, subdominant and dominant chords. These secondary triads are built on the second, third, sixth and seventh degrees of the scale. In the key of C major, their roots are D, E, A and B:

Whereas, in the major key, the three primary triads are all major chords, the secondary triads are of two types. Chords II, III and VI are *minor*, and chord VII is *diminished*: that is, the interval between the root and third is a minor third (or three semitones) and that between the root and fifth is a diminished fifth (or six semitones). Thus, in using both primary and secondary triads we can add further colour and variety to the music by combining major, minor and diminished chords.

Similarly, the secondary triads in the minor key introduce major and diminished chords. In the key of C minor, the roots of the secondary triads are D, E♭, A♭ and B♮ (the leading note). Chords III and VI are therefore major, and chords II and VII diminished:

In this project we shall explore the harmonic function of the secondary triads by examining their relationship with the chords we have already used. For example, chord II can, in certain contexts, be substituted for chord IV. Compare the cadential progression IV V I with the progression II V I. The effect of chords II and IV here is similar because they have two notes in common:

If we add a seventh to chord II, the relationship is even closer:

Similarly, chords VII and V⁷ are closely related:

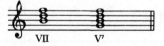

as are chords III and I:

Chord VI is related in this way both to chords IV and I:

It may occasionally be substituted for chord IV, as in the progression $\text{I}\{\substack{\text{VI}\\\text{IV}}\}\text{V}$, or it may be used to 'interrupt' an expected perfect cadence (see Assignment (iii) below). This is not to suggest that the secondary triads are interchangeable with the primary triads: each chord has its own individual colour and harmonic function which we must learn to feel and then use *for its own sake*.

B

(i)   Sing or play these two harmonisations of the hymn *Glory to thee, my God, this night* by Tallis. The first uses only the primary triads (including the dominant seventh) and their inversions; the second includes three of the secondary triads, chords II, III and VI.

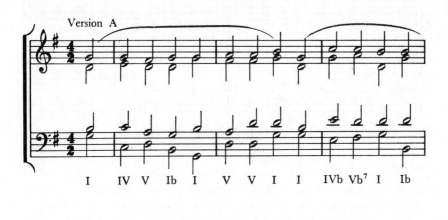

Notice that, in Version A, the harmonic pattern is constant through-out. The melody consists of four two-bar phrases, each of which ends with a perfect cadence. These four phrases are themselves subdivided into two one-bar phrases, and, because the harmony is limited to the three primary triads, each of these must also end with a perfect cadence. Thus, we have a regular pattern of the progression I | IV V I I | V V I repeated four times. This is made more interesting by the use of inversions and by the inclusion of the dominant seventh; but the *finality* of the perfect cadence, which occurs eight times in as many bars, makes the music lack any real sense of onward progression.

How is this feeling of finality avoided in Version B? In bars 1 and 6 chord V is followed, not by the expected tonic chord, but by chord VI. This adds variety to the cadential patterns and leads smoothly into the following phrase. The cadence V–VI is sometimes referred to as a

SURPRISE cadence or, more usually, as an INTERRUPTED cadence. Which term do you think is the more appropriate?

Two other secondary triads are used in Version B. Chord II replaces chord IV in bars 1 and 5, and in bars 2, 4, 6 and 8 the same chord is used to precede chord V. Notice how chord III is used at the end of bar 4. Which chord in Version A does it replace?

Make arrangements of both versions for voices and instruments. Let the voices sing the melody in unison, and divide the lower parts between three groups of suitable instruments. The bass line must be played at pitch, but the inner parts could be transposed up an octave so that they appear above the tune.

(ii) In the key of C major, build a root position triad on the supertonic (the note D).

Build the chord again, this time adding the note C seven degrees above the root:

This is the chord of the SUPERTONIC SEVENTH, usually written II⁷. Build the chord in root position, and then in first and second inversion. Since there are four notes in the chord, a third inversion is possible. Transposed down an octave so that it is more comfortable to sing, the third inversion will be formed like this:

Now sing or play the sequence IV V I Ib IV V I. Repeat it several times in this rhythmic pattern:

Add variety to the music by substituting various positions of chord II⁷ at the point marked by a cross. Decide how many times you will repeat the phrase and how you will use the chord of the supertonic seventh. For example, you might perform the sequence four times, using the root position twice and the first inversion twice. Play the complete sequence several times while individuals improvise melodies above it.

(iii)   In the key of C major, build a root position triad on the submediant (the note A). Explore its inversions.

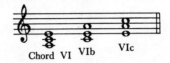

Chord VI   VIb   VIc

Now repeat the sequence of chords suggested in (ii) above, but this time introduce an interrupted cadence (V–VI) in place of the perfect cadence at the beginning of the second bar:

Interrupted cadence

V   VI

Use this sequence, repeated several times, to support improvised melodies as in (ii) above.

(iv)   Repeat (ii) and (iii) in the key of C minor. The dominant chord must appear in its *major* form because in each case the leading note rises to the tonic (see Project 30). Which form of the subdominant chord will you use? Could you include both?

(v)   In the key of C major, build a root position triad on the leading note (B). Explore its inversions.

Chord VII   VIIb   VIIc

Repeat the sequence suggested in (ii) above, substituting chord VIIb for chord V on the last beat of the first bar:

(vi)   In the same key, build a root position triad on the mediant (the note E). Explore its inversions. Now substitute chord III for chord Ib in the second bar of the sequence we have been using. You will need to modify the top part so that the fifth of chord III is included: otherwise, the chord will still be a first inversion tonic triad.

(vii)   Repeat (v) and (vi) above in the key of C minor.

(viii)   Make pieces for voices and/or instruments which use both primary and secondary triads. We give below some suggestions to set you off. Although you are now able to use all seven diatonic triads, don't try to include each one in every composition. They are there to draw on when you want a particular harmonic colour, just as the artist is able to select each *shade* of colour he will use.

  (1) A composition for three instruments (one high, one low, one middle register), or three groups of instruments, using the following sequence in a *major* key:

> Phrase 1: I II⁷ V VI IIb⁷ V
> Phrase 2: V⁷ I Ib IIb⁷ V I

Decide how you will use the sequence. Will you change the chord regularly on each beat, or will you vary the harmonic rhythm?;

  (2) As in (1) above, but in a *minor* key;

  (3) As in (1) and (2) above, but using your own harmonic sequence;

  (4) A composition for voices and/or instruments in three parts, consisting of four two-bar phrases, each ending with a different cadence as follows:

> Phrase 1: An *imperfect* cadence IV–V
> Phrase 2: A *perfect* cadence V–I
> Phrase 3: An *interrupted* cadence V–VI
> Phrase 4: A *plagal* cadence IV–I

Plan the complete harmonic scheme before you begin, and try to achieve a feeling of onward progression by avoiding too many root position tonic chords;

(5) A composition for a solo melody instrument or voice, supported by guitars or chime bars and glockenspiels in chord groups playing a short harmonic sequence repeated several times. Try to make the melody a *continuing* line, rather than a single phrase which is heard with each repetition of the chord sequence;

(6) A setting for voices in two or three parts of one of the following texts. The voices could be doubled or accompanied by instruments. The music need not necessarily be homophonic: such treatment would certainly not be suitable for the Devonshire folk-song.

> Jubal first made the wilder Notes agree,
> And Jubal tunéd Musick's Jubilee:
> He called the Ecchoes from their sullen Cell,
> And built the Organ's City where they dwell.
>
> ANDREW MARVELL, from *Musick's Empire*

> The trees they grow so high and the leaves
> they grow so green.
> The day is past and gone, my love, that
> you and I have seen.
> It's a cold winter's night, my love, when
> I must bide alone,
> For my bonny lad is young but a-growing.
>
> *Traditional Devonshire*

C

We give below examples of compositions arising from the suggestions made in (viii) (1) and (6). The first was one of a number of pieces by small groups of pupils who had been exploring the secondary triads on the lines of the assignments given above. The setting of 'The trees they grow so high' was a group composition involving the whole class. In addition to the primary triads it uses chords II, III, VI and chord VII built on the *flattened* leading note to give the music a modal flavour in keeping with the text. The melody grew out of vocal improvisations above a given chord pattern which was played on the piano by the teacher.

The Trees They Grow So High

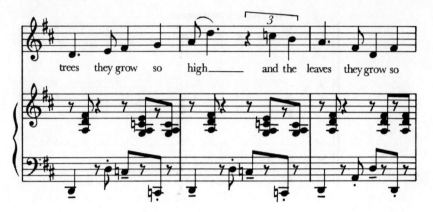

trees they grow so high _____ and the leaves they grow so

green. The day is past and gone, my love, that

you and I have seen. It's a cold win - ter's

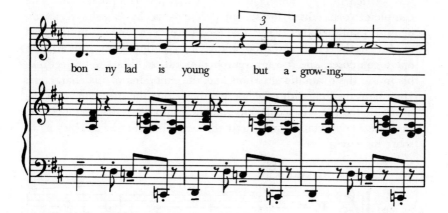

night, my love, when I must bide a - lone, For my

bon - ny lad is young but a - grow-ing,

———————— but a - grow-ing.

Project 34
Suspensions

A

Sing this extract from the beginning of Pergolesi's *Stabat Mater*, which was written in 1736 during the last year of the composer's life. The complete work, edited for school performance by Charles Kennedy Scott, is published by O.U.P. The long Latin poem reflects on the grief of Mary as she stands at the foot of the Cross. Pergolesi was primarily an opera composer, and it was an important part of his art to project into his music the dramatic situation and the emotions of his characters. Here he is dealing with a religious subject but the situation is no less dramatic than any in secular opera. The composer is deeply moved by the *humanity* of Mary's grief, and through his music he enables us to share his experience.

PERGOLESI from *Stabat Mater* (1736)

How does he do this in the passage quoted above? Unlike in opera, there is no visual aid to our understanding of the situation, yet the music vividly portrays the scene of the Crucifixion and the anguish of the Mother who stands at the feet of her dying Son. Moreover, the music conveys not only the grief of Mary, the Mother of Jesus, but that of all mothers who suffer the pain of personal loss. This is achieved first of all by the increasing tension of the rising melodic line which is not relaxed until the cadence. The voices cross each other, rising from the tonic (*doh*) to the submediant (*la*). The upper part then falls through a diminished fourth (C to G#), reaches again for the submediant, and finally descends by step to the supertonic (*re*). Combining the two parts by taking the higher note throughout, the overall melodic shape is this:

The effect of the rising melodic line is further emphasised by the rhythmic and harmonic structure of the passage. Above the regular throbbing quaver pattern in the bass there is an alternation of harmonic tension and relaxation: the soprano enters at the interval of a second above the alto, creating a dissonance which is resolved by the alto falling to the note below on the following beat. Throughout the first four bars this pattern is continued: a dissonance arises on each strong beat by the holding over of one of the notes of the previous chord. It is resolved on the following (weak) beat by the held note falling one degree to a note which forms a real part of the new chord.

This device is called a SUSPENSION. It is a three-fold process involving preparation of the dissonance, the dissonance itself, and its resolution. In this project we shall explore ways in which suspensions can be introduced to create harmonic tension.

B

(i)   Sing in unison a descending scale of C major to *Ah*, moving in slow, even minims ($\downarrow$=c. 44). Repeat this, but now begin by rising to the supertonic (*re'*) before descending by step to low *doh*. We'll call this Version A.

Now sing Version B which passes through low *doh* to *te₁*, returning immediately to the tonic.

Divide into two groups. Let group I sing Version A while group II sings Version B. Notice that the two parts begin and end on a unison, but move in parallel thirds throughout the rest of the phrase.

What is the effect of this part-writing? Although the intervals are not all the same (some are major thirds, others minor thirds) there is no feeling of rhythmic or harmonic tension in the passage. Regular stepwise

320

movement in consecutive thirds or consecutive sixths suggests tranquillity and repose. Sometimes we may deliberately seek this effect (consider the aria 'Slumber, beloved' in Part II of Bach's *Christmas Oratorio*), but without the introduction of some harmonic tension the music would soon begin to pall. Unrelieved consonance can quickly become tedious: when it is used to relax harmonic tension, the effect is much more satisfying.

We could introduce harmonic tension into this two-part passage by forming suspensions on the first beat of each bar. These will be resolved on the second beat, and can then prepare the way for another suspension at the beginning of the following bar. Suspensions must always be prepared by a consonant interval, and are resolved by the part which has been held over to create the dissonance falling by step to the note below.

Sing the passage again, but this time let the lower part hold the first note until the upper part has moved to the note above it. This will create a dissonance which can then be resolved by the lower part falling to the note below on the second beat of the bar. Repeat the process until you reach the cadence, when the lower part will rise to join the upper part on *doh*.

Notice the rhythm of the harmony: the voices begin and end on a unison, but throughout the rest of the phrase there is a regular alternation of tension and relaxation.

(ii)   We have already remarked that unrelieved movement in consecutive thirds or sixths can soon become dull. Equally, the regular pattern of tension and relaxation in the above example ceases to be interesting after a while. Once it is established, the progression from consonance to dissonance to consonance becomes so predictable that the element of surprise no longer exists. Rearrange the passage so that suspensions occur only occasionally. Limit yourself to two or three suspensions in the course of the phrase. Experiment with their placing. Decide at which points you want to increase the rhythmic movement and introduce harmonic tension.

(iii)   Sing the passage in triple time, forming suspensions on the first beat of each bar. The dissonances will now be prepared on the third beat and resolved on the second. Begin like this:

(iv)   If you have mixed voices in the class, invert the intervals so that the upper part in the above examples is sung an octave lower while the second part remains at its original pitch. Compare the result with the previous arrangement of the parts.

(v)   Repeat each of the above in the key of C minor. Remember that the leading-note, which will eventually rise to the tonic, is B♮ (see Project 30). When descending, it is best to retain the flattened forms of the seventh and sixth degrees of the minor scale.

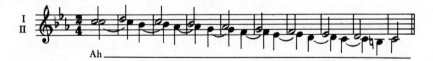

(vi)   Because of the pungency of the seconds and sevenths in the suspensions we have used in this project, these intervals are particularly suited to music which seeks to express grief or pain. Writing for voices in two parts, make settings of some of the following texts. Use suspensions sparingly, deciding beforehand which words or syllables to emphasise by the expressive use of dissonance. Compare your results with the pieces reproduced in Section C.

(1) I should for grief and
        anguish die recureless.

(2) Flow, my tears, fall from your
    springs!
    Exiled for ever let me mourn.

(3) Hence, Care, thou art too cruel,
    Come, music, sick man's jewel.

(4) Sound saddest notes with rueful
    moaning;
    Tune every strain with tears
    and weeping.

C

The three pieces given below were composed by children who had been working on the lines of the suggestions made in Section B. The first two were group compositions, originally notated in tonic sol-fa, by a non-specialist class of twelve-year-old boys. The third is an extract from a longer composition by a sixteen-year-old boy who was preparing for the G.C.E. examination.

19 City by night

Project 35
Night music

A

A great deal of the music we have made in the earlier projects has involved various aspects of Theatre. In the last two projects we return to Theatre, and we suggest assignments which can be approached in a variety of ways, perhaps drawing together some of the musical techniques explored in the earlier projects.

B

Make a list of ideas you associate with NIGHT. Some may be sounds, such as the hooting of an owl, rain lashing against the window pane, or the regular ticking of a clock; others may be abstract ideas, such as darkness, stillness, a colour, or an emotion. You will want to include in your list things seen at night such as the moon, stars and bright city lights, and this may lead you to think of some particular action, real or imaginary, or a series of events. Discuss your ideas with the rest of the class, and group the various suggestions so that any which are related appear together. For example, your complete list might include some of the following:

Sleep	City lights	Dreams
Peacefulness	Night clubs	Moon
Nightmare	Heat	Stars
Horror	Cold	Stillness
Fear	Crimson	Warmth
Darkness	Gold	Tenderness
Insects	Loneliness	A storm
Owls	Grief	The ticking of a clock

You might then decide to put *Sleep*, *Dreams*, *Peacefulness*, *Warmth*, *Tenderness* and *Stillness* together in one group, while *Darkness*, *Nightmare*, *Horror* and *Fear* seem to belong together in another. Try to find one word or phrase which conveys all the ideas in each group, and then choose from these four or five contrasted themes which suggest obvious dramatic or musical treatment. These will make up the individual movements of the composition.

How will you present the composition? It could, of course, be a purely musical work, but the nature of your ideas may well call for the inclusion of movement and the spoken word. If you decide to present the work as Theatre, perhaps in mime or as a dance-drama, the order of movements may already begin to suggest itself. Suppose you have decided your main themes or movements are to be *Sleep*, *Nightmare*, *Stars*, *Insects* and *City Lights*. You might begin with nightfall, suggested by the chimes of a clock, and progress from the natural world of insects to the artificial night-life of the city with its bright lights and blaring music, ending with more clock chimes or the crow of a cock to herald the coming of dawn. Where will sleep and the nightmare fit into this? Alternatively, you might decide to present several unconnected night-time activities. Could these be linked in some way? Perhaps the night sky, which is always overhead, could provide the necessary continuity. You might imagine that you begin by gazing at the stars and are drawn up into the sky so that you can look down in turn on the lights of the city, nocturnal insects in the country, a solitary sleeper gripped in some terrifying nightmare.

What instruments will you use for each movement? Stars suggest hard, bright, glittering sounds. When we gaze at the sky on a clear winter's night we are aware of the immensity of time and space: little clusters of light are gathered tightly together, making intricate shapes and patterns, and our eyes travel through the darkness to the next cluster and then on to one solitary star, brighter than all the rest. In terms of music, this seems to suggest long periods of silence with isolated notes on metal instruments such as triangles, glockenspiels and chime bars, followed by little bursts of activity as our attention is caught by a cluster of stars, some bright, others distant. The dynamic quality of each individual note will play an important part in the music, and the rhythms will be ametrical rather than fitted into a regular pulse.

Insects, on the other hand, suggest short, dry sounds. A variety of rapid rhythmic patterns played on claves, bongos or an assortment of high-pitched hand drums will help to evoke the atmosphere of a hot summer's night and will suggest a chorus of insect noises, while music for Sleep could grow out of the sounds we have discovered by stroking, tapping and plucking the strings of a piano. The music for City Lights could provide an opportunity to use some of the harmonic principles we have explored: here we may decide to include instruments associated with jazz, perhaps improvising melodic patterns above a harmonic sequence played on guitar or piano. Drums will play an important part in this music, and they could also be used in the Nightmare sequence together with cymbals, gongs and various vocal noises ranging from percussive sounds to moans and high-pitched yells and shrieks.

When you have selected the instruments you will use and have discussed how each movement will contribute to the whole piece, divide into groups of five or six and assign one movement to each. When the individual movements are complete, perform them to each other and decide how they could be fitted together.

C

We give here accounts of two very different compositions on the theme of NIGHT. The first was made during one afternoon by a class of ten-year-old children in the East Riding of Yorkshire. The second was a dance-drama composed over several weeks by a group of third-year students at a College of Education.

(i)   The teacher introduced the project by discussing with the children things they associated with night-time. He drew from them a variety of ideas: some were simple actions such as 'going to bed', and 'looking through a frosty window-pane at the stars', while others were more personal such as 'being alone in the dark'. A variety of sounds were suggested: 'owls hooting', 'voices outside in the street', 'the ticking of the clock in the hall'. This led to some excited discussion of the way things become distorted in the dark: quiet sounds not normally noticed in the daytime seem very loud, shapes such as the outline of a bedroom wardrobe or a coat hanging on the door take on a grotesque appearance and seem to come alive. Shafts of light from outside pick out various features in the room and seem to transform them into fantastic objects or creatures.

The music grew out of these ideas. The piece began with silence, broken only by the regular ticking of a distant clock played on claves. This simple rhythmic pattern continued throughout the composition, building up tension by getting gradually faster and louder until at the climax there was a long, falling scream together with a single fortissimo stroke on the gong which was allowed to die away into silence over several seconds. When the rhythmic ostinato had been established by the claves they were joined first by an alto xylophone, playing the tritone B to F, and later by a tambour. Against this other percussion instruments were added. These included a suspended cymbal, played with a hard stick and a wire brush drawn around the rim, various hand drums, temple blocks and a triangle. The piece became Theatre when, in the course of working at the composition, the children not playing instruments moved towards the front of the group to perform the long, falling scream. This idea was developed so that movement became an integral part of the composition: the 'actors' advanced menacingly and, forming a semi-circle to face the imaginary audience, thrust out their arms. As their scream fell in pitch and intensity, the arms were lowered and the 'actors' withdrew slowly to the back of the group.

(ii)   The dance-drama was presented in the form of three short sequences linked by lines from poems by Kathleen Raine, Edward Thomas, Rupert Brooke and C. Day Lewis. The drama was introduced by the chimes of a clock (played on a metallophone) ringing out the hour of ten, and this led into the first sequence, *Night in the City*. Some of the dancers, representing neon lights, were raised above floor level and made flickering circular motions with the arms while twisting the head sharply from side to side in a variety of regular patterns. Others at floor level enacted a night-club scene, dancing a slow blues played on piano, guitar and drums.

The music for the second sequence, *Stars*, was scored for voices, suspended cymbal, three triangles, water gong, and seven chime bars tuned in thirds to these notes:

Against a background of silence, isolated notes on chime bars and triangles gathered in periodic clusters with little bursts of (improvised) activity supported by a controlled roll on the suspended cymbal. After the third improvised section the voices, singing in consecutive major thirds, began a repeated two-note pattern which died away gradually from *mp* to a hushed *pp*:

When the voices were barely audible, the gong was struck once softly and then gently lowered into a trough of water until it was fully immersed.

As the gong reverberations died away in the water, the final sequence was introduced. In the lonely darkness of her room, a restless sleeper encountered the imaginary fears of a terrifying nightmare. Her dream fantasy was played out by masked dancers moving around her sleeping body and finally drawing her into the horrors of their dance. The music for this sequence was played on a tambour by one of the masked dancers. It consisted of regular pulse beats, starting slowly and quietly and then increasing in speed and rising in a terrifying crescendo until the sleeper awoke with a shattering scream, rejecting the images of her dream which melted away in the darkness.

D

The theme of NIGHT and its associative ideas has stimulated the imagination of composers in a variety of ways during the last three centuries, and several twentieth-century composers have written music around themes explored in this project. A great deal of Bartók's music is in some way associated with Night, and his preoccupation with insects is reflected in the intricate detail of his music. Listen to the second movement of *Music for Strings, Percussion and Celesta*, to the opening of the *Sonata for two Pianos and Percussion*, and to the third and fifth String Quartets. For a detailed discussion of Bartók's music, see Halsey Stevens' book *The Life and Music of Béla Bartók*, published by O.U.P.

Perform Harrison Birtwistle's *Music for Sleep* (Novello), and try to take part in a performance of Cornelius Cardew's *The Tiger's Mind* (Hinrichsen), which is scored for any number and any kind of instruments. In addition, it would be profitable to study the scores and try to hear performances of some of the following works:

BRITTEN
Notturno for piano (Boosey and Hawkes.)
Serenade for Tenor, Horn and Strings Op. 31 (Boosey and Hawkes.)
Nocturne for Tenor, seven Obbligato Instruments and Strings Op. 60 (Boosey and Hawkes.)

CAGE
She is asleep for voice, prepared piano and twelve tom-toms (Peters Edition.)

COPLAND
Quiet City for solo trumpet and strings (Boosey and Hawkes.)

331

DEBUSSY
Nocturnes for orchestra (Durand, Paris.)

HOLST
Orchestral suite: *The Planets* (Boosey and Hawkes.)

SCHÖNBERG
Verklärte Nacht Op. 4 for string sextet.

STRAVINSKY
In Memoriam Dylan Thomas: Dirge-Canons and Song (1954).

20   A scene from *Naboth's Vineyard* by Alexander Goehr

Project 36
Theatre piece

A

We have grown so accustomed to the idea of listening to performances by highly-skilled professional musicians that we sometimes forget concert music is a relatively recent notion. Primitive peoples were unable to conceive of music apart from words and actions. In growing from its primitive beginnings into a sophisticated art-form, music has become a highly specialised means of expression. While gaining from this special-ised process of refinement, it has lost its sense of ritual, of 'belonging' to the life of ordinary people. It has become the province of the gifted cognoscenti and has tended to remain so. For most people music is still 'something musicians do'. It is an art-form surrounded by mystique, partly because it cannot be *seen* to 'belong' or relate to life. It has lost its sense of Theatre.

In the mid-twentieth century, composers have looked back to primitive times for new inspiration. Many have tried to revive the relationship between music and ritual. They have associated their music with dance, with the spoken word, with stylised action, with mime and masked presentation. In this they have involved the players of instruments just as much as the actors and dancers, often in conscious imitation of the traditions of oriental theatre. Quite a lot of this music has been written for children, not only to satisfy a demand for works suitable for school production involving large numbers and having flexibility in their scor-ing, but also because composers have become conscious of the special qualities of children's imagination. The child-like sense of wonder can perhaps best be expressed in terms of magic and ritual. It demands action, and the music of its rituals is part of the action. It is Theatre.

As assignments for this final project we offer a variety of ideas which could be approached in many different ways. We hope they may be used to draw together a number of threads from previous projects, but above all we feel that they should be seen as bases for large-scale,

335

though perhaps flexible, presentations. They could involve instrumentalists, singers, speakers, dancers, masked actors.* The properties could
be elaborate or simple. The music could be defined throughout, or it
could leave room for improvisation. Any of these works could be
presented on a stage or on the floor of a school hall or in a church or even
in the open air.

In this final project we have departed from our previous practice of
including a section C, giving examples of ways in which the assignments
might be carried out. We have also omitted a D section, but suggest that
it would be profitable to examine the scores and try to see or hear performances of any of the following works. Those marked with a dagger are
intended for performance by children or include parts for child performers as well as adults.

PETER ASTON
Sacrapant, The Sorcerer† (Novello.)

RICHARD RODNEY BENNETT
The Midnight Thief† (Mills Music)

HARRISON BIRTWISTLE
The Visions of Francesca Petrarca† (Universal Edition.)

BRITTEN
Noye's Fludde†
The Little Sweep†   } (Boosey and Hawkes.)
Canticle II: *Abraham and Isaac*
Curlew River†
The Burning Fiery Furnace† } (Faber.)
The Prodigal Son†

COPLAND
The Second Hurricane† (Boosey and Hawkes.)

GORDON CROSSE
Ahmet, the Woodseller† (O.U.P.)

ALEXANDER GOEHR
Naboth's Vineyard

WILFRID MELLERS
Life Cycle† (C.U.P.)
The Happy Meadow† (Novello.)
Rose of May (Novello.)

---

* There are a number of books on the subject of mask-making: *Paper Faces* by Michael
Grater (Mills and Boon Ltd, 1967) is very good.

MENOTTI
Amahl and the Night Visitors† (Schirmer.)

STRAVINSKY
Oedipus Rex (Boosey and Hawkes.)
The Soldier's Tale (Chester.)
Renard (Chester.)

JOHN TAVENER
Dramatic cantata: *The Whale* (Chester.)

VAUGHAN WILLIAMS
Job: a masque for dancing (O.U.P.)

B

(i)   Make a *Theatre Piece* based in some way on the following account of a visit by a party of tourists to the city of York some time during the early eighteenth century. The text is taken from Daniel Defoe's *A Tour through the whole Island of Great Britain*. The words could be used as they stand, or they could become the basis of a libretto or scenario.

The Antiquity of York shewed itself so visibly at a distance that we could not but observe it before we came quite up to the City, I mean the Mount where the antient Castle stood.

The Cathedral, or Minster, as they call it, is a fine Building, but not so antient as some of the other Churches in the City seem to be: That Mount which, at a distance was a Mark of Antiquity, was some ages ago fortified and made very strong; but Time has eaten through not the Timber and Plank only, but even the stones and Mortar; for not the least Footstep of it remains but the hill.

York is indeed a pleasant and beautiful City. It has always been a strong Place, so it has been much contended for, been the Seat of War, the Rendezvous of Armies, and of the greatest Generals several times.

It boasts of being the Seat of some of the Roman Emperors, and the station of their Forces for the North of Britain, being itself a Roman Colony, and the like, all of which I leave as I find it. However, this I must not omit, namely, that Severus and Constantinus Chlorus, Father to Constantine the Great, both kept their courts here, and both died here. Here Constantine the Great took upon him the Purple, and began the first Christian Empire in the World; and this is truly and really an Honour to the City of York.

But all we see now is modern; the Bridge is vastly strong, and has one Arch which, they tell me, was near 70 Foot in diameter; it is, without exception, the greatest in England, some say it's as large as the Rialto at Venice, though I think not.

There is abundance of good Company here, and abundance of good Families live here, for the sake of the good Company and cheap living; a Man converses here with all the World as effectually as at London.

No city in England is better furnished with Provisions of every kind, nor any

21   An engraving of York in the eighteenth century by Nathan Drake

so cheap, in proportion to the goodness of Things; the River being so navigable the Merchants here trade directly to what part of the World they will; they import their own Wines from France and Portugal, and likewise their own Deals and Timber from Norway; and indeed what they please almost from where they please. The Publick Buildings erected here are very considerable, such as Halls for their Merchants and Trades, a large Town-Hall or Guild-Hall, and the Prison, which is spacious.

The old Walls are standing, and the Gates and Posterns; but the old additional Works, which were cast up in the late Rebellion, are slighted, so that York is not now defensible as it was then.

York, as I have said, is a spacious City. It stands upon a great deal of ground. But as York is full of Gentry and Persons of Distinction, so they live at large, and have houses proportioned to their Quality; and this makes the City lie so far extended on both Sides of the River. It is also very magnificent and makes a good Figure every way in its appearance, even at a distance; for the Cathedral is so noble and so august a Pile, that 'tis a Glory to all the rest.

From York we took a View of the Suburb over the River, opposite to the City, and then entering the East Riding, took our Audience *de conge* in form, and so stood over that Division towards Hull.

Before you set to work you'll need to ask yourself one or two basic questions such as:

(1) What resources of instrumentalists, actors, dancers, singers etc. are available?;

(2) How will the text be used? Will some of it be spoken? Will the action be entirely mimed with the narrative delivered by a separate group, or will the actors also be the singers and speakers?;

(3) Will there be passages of purely instrumental music, perhaps descriptive of some of the buildings? Can dancers also be used to 'describe' buildings, bridges and walls which the travellers see?;

(4) What do the tourists see? How will they approach the city, and how will you convey their approach in music and action? Think of ways in which you can show their wonder and amazement at the things they see.

(ii)   Make a *Theatre Piece* on the subject of CREATION. You could use one of the two accounts in Genesis either as it stands, or expanded by bringing together poems and writings on creation and evolution from many sources, old and new. Your final 'libretto' could combine both the spiritual and imaginative with scientific and factual description (such as the *Encyclopaedia Britannica* article on the coelacanth or passages from Darwin's *Origin of Species*). The work could be so constructed that it evolves and grows from a tiny unit or cell, the musical material of this cell being the basis of everything else that happens. You might make the

339

whole piece one immense *continuing* crescendo. How will it end? Can you find ways of suggesting the continuance of life and its forces? Alternatively, you might consider beginning the piece with a musical picture of chaos and darkness which gradually becomes order and light.

(iii)   Make a *Theatre Piece* (perhaps for performance in a church) based on one of the following subjects:

    (1) Joseph and his Brothers
    (2) Abraham and Isaac
    (3) Job
    (4) Jonah
    (5) The Pharisee and the Publican
    (6) Mary in the Garden of Gethsemane
    (7) The Good Samaritan

Glossary

Aeolian mode: a seven-note scale, represented on the piano by the white notes starting on A.

appoggiatura: an unprepared dissonant ornamental note which is resolved by step onto a harmony note, the dissonance taking the stress.

arco: an abbreviation for *coll'arco*, meaning to play with the bow.

atonal: having no defined key centre.

audio-frequency wave generator: an instrument which generates electrical wave-forms of audible frequency. To hear these sounds ear-phones or a loudspeaker must be used.

bitonal: simultaneously combining two key centres.

cadenza: originally, an improvised elaboration of the final cadence in eighteenth-century operatic arias. The practice was later taken over by soloists in instrumental concerti who used the cadenza to display their virtuosity while drawing together the main thematic material of the movement. Since the early nineteenth century, composers have tended to write out their cadenzas which have become an integral part of the composition. Consequently, the practice of improvisation in the performance of concerti has now disappeared.

canon: strict or near strict imitation of a single theme in two or more parts.

chromatic: music which introduces notes not belonging to the key prevailing at the moment.

cluster: a group of notes, very close to each other in pitch, sounded simultaneously; thus forming a dense chord.

diatonic: music derived entirely from the notes of the major or minor scale of the key prevailing at the moment.

direct movement (in dance): an effort element derived from the space motion factor and indicating a movement leading into one direction only.

indirect movement (sometimes known as *flexible movement*) indicates a movement leading into more than one direction. See Rudolf Laban *Modern Educational Dance* (Macdonald and Evans).

dominant: the fifth degree of the major or minor scale.

Dorian mode: a seven-note scale, represented on the piano by the white notes starting on D.

drone: a continuous bass note which has no harmonic function.

episode: a musical passage of subsidiary importance which is usually in contrast to the principal theme or themes. Episodes are most frequently used to link appearances of the main musical ideas.

fundamental : the first or lowest note of the harmonic series.

gamelan : Balinese and Javanese bands of pitched and unpitched percussion instruments.

glissando : sliding upwards or downwards through a series of adjacent notes. On keyboard instruments only the fixed tones and semitones will sound, but *glissandi* performed by voices or on string instruments pass through an infinite number of pitches.

heterophony : the combination of two or more independent melodic lines which are put together without reference to their harmonic implications. Most commonly, heterophony consists of different versions of the same melody sung or played simultaneously.

homophony : music in which a single melodic line is supported by chords.

interval : the difference in pitch between two notes, expressed numerically. For example, the interval between D and A is a fifth, and that between D and C sharp is a major seventh.

inversion : reversing the relative position of two notes so that the lower note becomes the higher one. Thus the interval of a fifth (D to A) when inverted becomes a fourth (A to D), and a minor third (D to F) becomes a major sixth (F to D).

leading note : the seventh degree of the major or minor scale.

legato : sustained, as opposed to *staccato* (detached).

Lydian mode : a seven-note scale, represented on the piano by the white notes starting on F.

marimbaphone : a steel pitched percussion instrument, lower in range than the glockenspiel, which was introduced in the early twentieth century.

mediant : the third degree of the major or minor scale.

microtone : interval smaller than a semitone.

Mixolydian mode : a seven-note scale, represented on the piano by the white notes starting on G.

monody, monophony : music such as plainsong which consists of a single unsupported melodic line. The term *monody* is also applied to solo song with accompaniment such as the lute songs of the early seventeenth century.

motif : a short melodic or rhythmic idea which is used as a basis for development by repetition or elaboration.

note-cluster : originally, a group of notes on the piano played simultaneously with the forearm or fist. The technique was first introduced in 1912 by the American composer Henry Cowell. The term is now used to refer to any group of several adjacent notes.

342

note-row: a preordained series of notes which is used as the basis for a composition.

ostinato: a short melodic or rhythmic pattern repeated insistently.

pedal note: a note sustained throughout a developing harmonic passage. The pedal note usually occurs in the bass: when it appears in an upper part it is called an *inverted pedal*.

Phrygian mode: a seven-note scale, represented on the piano by the white notes starting on E.

pizzicato: plucked. The term is used, generally in the abbreviated form *pizz.*, to indicate that the string should be plucked with the finger rather than played with the bow.

polyphony: music in which a number of separate melodic lines are combined.

sequence: most commonly, a melodic or harmonic pattern repeated exactly at a different pitch. The term is also used to refer to a series of chords which develop harmonically.

sine-wave: a pure tone incapable of further simplification. It can be produced by an audio-frequency wave generator.

square-wave: a complex tone consisting ideally of an infinite number of sine-waves. It would include all the odd-numbered harmonics of the fundamental. Some audio-frequency generators can produce only sine-waves, while others are fitted with a switch so that sine-waves or square-waves can be produced as required.

staccato: detached, as opposed to *legato* (sustained).

subdominant: the fourth degree of the major or minor scale.

submediant: the sixth degree of the major or minor scale.

sul ponticello: an indication to a string player to play close to the bridge.

supertonic: the second degree of the major or minor scale.

timbre: quality of tone.

tone-row: see *note-row*.

tonic: the first degree of the major or minor scale.

transposition: sounds reproduced at another pitch from that at which they were originally written. Thus, the notes DEF when transposed up a fourth would become GAB♭.

triad: a chord of three notes made by adding the intervals of a third and fifth above the root note. When the chord appears with the root as the lowest note it is in *root position*; when the third of the chord is the lowest note it is in *first inversion*; and a *second inversion* occurs when the lowest note is the fifth.

Discography

Not all the music referred to in the projects is available on record. Happily, an increasing amount of twentieth-century music is being added to the catalogue, though there is a tendency for recordings of new music to be deleted after a short time. We include deletions in this discography in the hope that teachers may still find the recordings available in public libraries and other collections.

BACH, JOHANN SEBASTIAN
Christmas Oratorio   DGG 271004
St Matthew Passion   SAWT 9572–5

BADINGS, HENK
Electronic ballet music: *Cain and Abel*   ABE 10073 (del)

BARTÓK, BÉLA
Concerto for Violin and Orchestra No. 2 (1938)   ASD 2281
Dance Suite (1923)   SLMP 138875
String Quartet No. 3   SAX 5261
String Quartet No. 5   SAX 5262
Mikrokosmos   VBX 425
Out of Doors—Suite   VBX 426
Piano Sonata (1926)   VBX 426
Allegro barbaro (1911)   VBX 426
Sonata for two Pianos and Percussion (1937)   SLPX 1280
Sonata for Unaccompanied Violin (1944)   SXL 2240
Music for Strings, Percussion and Celesta (1936)   SXL 6111

BEATLES, THE
'Sergeant Pepper's Lonely Hearts' Club Band'   PCS 7027
I am the Walrus ('Magical Mystery Tour')   SMMT 1
Strawberry Fields Forever   R 5570
Tomorrow Never Knows ('Revolver')   PCS 7009

BERG, ALBAN
Concerto for Violin and Orchestra (1935)   SAL 3650
Lyric Suite for String Quartet (1926)   TV 34021 S

BERIO, LUCIANO
Visage   TV 34046

BERLIOZ, HECTOR
Symphonie Fantastique   SXL 6343

BOULEZ, PIERRE
Le Marteau sans Maître   ABL 3386 (del)

BRITTEN, BENJAMIN
A Midsummer Night's Dream   SET 338–40
The Little Sweep   LXT 5163
Noye's Fludde   ZNF I
Curlew River   SET 301
The Burning Fiery Furnace—Parable Op. 77 SET 356
The Prodigal Son
The Rape of Lucretia
St Nicolas—Cantata Op. 42   LXT 5060
Nocturne for Tenor, seven Obbligato Instruments and
 Strings Op. 60   SWL 8025
Serenade for Tenor, Horn and Strings Op. 31 SXL 6110
Notturno
Canticle II—*Abraham and Isaac Op. 51* ZRG 5277
Rejoice in the Lamb—Festival Cantata, Op. 30 LXT 5416
Hymn to St Cecilia   SOL 60037

BROWN, EARLE
Available Forms 1 (1961)   VICS 1239

CAGE, JOHN
Williams Mix (1952)
She is asleep (1943)   } 3-AVAKIAN JCS–I
The Wonderful Widow of Eighteen Springs (1942)
Fontana Mix (1958)   TV 4046
Amores for prepared piano and percussion TIME 8000
String Quartet (1950)   COL. ML 4495 (del)
Sonatas and Interludes   DIAL 19 (del)
Indeterminacy (John Cage reads 90 stories to elec-
 tronic music)   FOLKWAYS FT 3704

CHÁVEZ, CARLOS
Toccata for Percussion   CTL 7094

COPLAND, AARON
Quiet City   MER 50076

COWELL, HENRY
Lilt of the Reel
Tyger   } FOLKWAYS FM 3349
The Banshee

CROSSE, GORDON
Ahmet, the Woodseller   CLP 1893

DEBUSSY, CLAUDE
Chansons de Bilitis   SBRG 72412
Syrinx for flute   SAL 3643
Nocturnes (1900)   SUAST 50575
La Mer   SUAST 50575
'Jardins sous la Pluie' (*Estampes*)   SAX 5291
'La Cathédrale Engloutie' (*Preludes* Bk 1, No. 10)   SLPM 138831
'Feux d'artifice' (*Preludes* Bk 2, No. 24)   SLPM 138872
Children's Corner—Suite   SLPM 138663
DUKAS, PAUL
The Sorcerer's Apprentice   SXL 6065
DYLAN, BOB
The Mighty Quinn   FONTANA TF 892
ELECTRONIC MUSIC
See CAGE, BERIO, MIMAROGLU, STOCKHAUSEN, BADINGS
ESPLÁ, OSCAR
5 Canciones playeras espanolas   ASD 505
Psalm 129 (1966)   SAL 3641
FELDMAN, MORTON
Projection 4   ⎫
Piece for Four Pianos   ⎬   COL. ML 5403 (del)
                             ⎭
FOLK-SONG
'Frost and Fire: A Calendar of Ceremonial Folk-
songs' (The Watersons)   TOPIC 12T136
The Lyke-Wake Dirge (The Young Tradition)   TRA 142
GABRIELI, GIOVANNI
Venetian Motets and Canzonas   SAWT 9456-A
GERHARD, ROBERTO
Concerto for Orchestra   ZRG 553
GOEHR, ALEXANDER
Two Choruses Op. 14   ASD 640
HABA, ALOIS
Duo in the Sixth-Tone System for two violins   COL. 'HIST. OF MUSIC'
                                                                  DB 1791 (78 rpm
                                                                  del)

String Quartets   SUAST 50524
HINDEMITH, PAUL
Herodiade   SBRG 72412
'HISTORY OF MUSIC IN SOUND'
Ancient and Oriental Music   HLP I

HOLST, GUSTAV
Orchestral Suite—*The Planets*   ASD 2301
HONEGGER, ARTHUR
Pacific 231   SXL 6065
INDIAN MUSIC
Anthologie de la Musique de L'Inde   DUCRETET-THOMSON
                                                        320C 096–8
India's Master Musician   EALP 1283
Music of India   ALP 1893
Classical Music of India   FOLKWAYS FI 8366
The Ragas of India (Lecture demonstration)   FOLKWAYS FI 8368
IVES, CHARLES
Fourth of July   SBRG 72451
Three Places in New England   SBRG 72384
KODÁLY, ZOLTÁN
Missa Brevis (1945)   ALP 1687 (del)
MELLERS, WILFRID
Life Cycle   PHILIPS 6589 001
MESSIAEN, OLIVIER
Et Expecto Resurrectionem Mortuorum (1964)   SBRG 72471
Couleurs de la Cité Celeste   SBRG 72471
Chronochromie   ASD 639
Cinq Rechants (1949)   ZRG 523
MIMAROGLU, ILHAN
Agony   TV 34046
MONTEVERDI, CLAUDIO
Vespro della Beata Vergine (1610)   SAWT 9501–2 and
                                                        SBRG 72602–3
Madrigal—*O come é gran martire*   ARCHIV SAPM
                                                        198021
ORFF, CARL
Carmina Burana   SAN 162
Catulli Carmina   TV 340615
Music for Children   33CX 549/550
PARTCH, HARRY
The Bewitched   GATE 5, ISSUE E
Revelation in Courthouse Park   GATE 5, ISSUE F
Water! Water!   GATE 5, ISSUE G
Study in an ancient Phrygian Scale   GATE 5, ISSUE A
Study in the ancient Enharmonic Scale   GATE 5, ISSUE A

347

PENDERECKI, KRYSTOF
Threnody: To the Victims of Hiroshima   VICS 1239
St Luke Passion   SAL 3613–4
PERGOLESI, GIOVANNI
Stabat Mater (1736)   SAL 3590
RAVEL, MAURICE
Introduction and Allegro   SLPM 139304
ROLLING STONES, THE
Two Thousand Light Years from Home ('Their Satanic
    Majesties Request')   TXS 103
SCHÖNBERG, ARNOLD
Five Pieces for Orchestra Op. 16   ABL 3397
Variations for Orchestra Op. 31   SBRG 72268
Survivor from Warsaw   BRG 72119–20
Six Little Piano Pieces Op. 19   SBRG 72460
Verklärte Nacht Op. 4   SDBR 3170
SCHULLER, GUNTHER
Seven Studies after Paul Klee   SB 6677
STOCKHAUSEN, KARLHEINZ
Mikrophonie I   SBRG 72647
Kontakte   SLPM 138811
Gesange der Junglinge   SLPM 138811
STRAUSS, RICHARD
Till Eulenspiegel's Merry Pranks   SDBR 3023
STRAVINSKY, IGOR
Petrushka   VICS 1296
Oedipus Rex   SUAST 50678
Renard—A Burlesque   SXL 6171
The Soldier's Tale   SBRG 72007
Cantata on anonymous 15th and 16th century
    English Lyrics   SBRG 72604
In Memoriam Dylan Thomas: Dirge-Canons and Song   SBRG 72604
TCHAIKOWSKY, PETER
Romeo and Juliet—Fantasy Overture (1880)   SBRG 72561
TIPPETT, MICHAEL
Concerto for Double String Orchestra (1939)   MFP 2069
VARÈSE, EDGARD
Déserts (1954)   SBRG 72106 (del)
Poème électronique   ABL 3392
VAUGHAN WILLIAMS, RALPH
Symphony No. 2 ('London')   ASD 2360

348

Job—a masque for dancing   SDBR 3019
The Lark Ascending for violin and orchestra   ASD 2329
Mass in G Minor   TPLS 13019
WATERSONS, THE
See FOLK-SONG
WEBERN, ANTON
Six Bagatelles for String Quartet Op. 9   SUAST 50629
Five Pieces for Orchestra   ASD 2349
YOUNG TRADITION, THE
See FOLK-SONG

Index

Page references in bold type indicate the most important entries.

359

Wagner, Richard
  Das Rheingold, 267
War Requiem (Britten), 4
water gong, 331
Watersons, The
  'Frost and Fire' (folk-songs), 148, 346
Water! Water! (Partch), 76, 347
Webern, Anton, 65, 102, 201, 349
  Six Bagatelles for String Quartet Op. 9, 65, 102, 103, 186, 349
  Symphonie Op. 21, 65, 186
  texture in the music of, 61, 103
  Variations for Piano Op. 27, 65, 186
Whale, The (Tavener), 337
whole-tone scale, **165–7**, 175
Williams Mix (Cage), 141, 345
Within You, Without You (Beatles), 4
Wolff, Christian, 214
Wonderful Widow of Eighteen Springs, The (Cage), 124–5, 345
work-songs, 144–5, 217
Wright, Austin, 20

Ye spotted snakes (children's composition), 288–99
York Children's Theatre Workshop, 74
Young Tradition, The
  version of *Lyke-Wake Dirge*, 42, 349

Zyklus for Percussion (Stockhausen), 34, 119, 124, 127, **132**